The Ro...

COLLINS

IRISH DANCING

Tom Quinn

HarperCollins*Publishers*

HarperCollins Publishers
PO Box, Glasgow G4 0NB

First published 1997

Reprint 10 9 8 7 6 5 4 3 2 1 0

© Tom Quinn, 1997

ISBN 0 00 472069 5

A catalogue record for this book is available from the British Library

Printed and bound in Great Britain by
Caledonian International Book Manufacturing, Glasgow

Contents

Foreword

In this generation, Tom Quinn and Irish dancing (both ceili and sets) have become synonymous. His sheer love of and enthusiasm for Ireland's native dancing is infectious. He has inspired many people to take the plunge and discover the joy and merriment of this great social pastime.

Tom Quinn didn't get his love of dancing from the trees! Tom is of South Armagh stock and began dancing at the early age of three. He learned his first steps from his great-aunt Nan Quinn, a lady who was instrumental in the revival of many of the now famous Armagh Ceili Dances.

This well known dancing master is an accomplished Irish step dancer and teaches traditional step dancing, set dancing and ceili dancing. With the revival of set dancing in Ireland, Tom has become one of the foremost instructors and has a large repertoire of sets from all parts of Ireland. He has conducted workshops in many parts of Ireland and also throughout Europe and the U.S.A.

Tom is married and now lives in Dundalk. His wife, Aine, is fully involved in dance and demonstrated with him on his first instructional dance video, *Set Dancing Made Easy* (Apollo Video '94).

This book on Irish dancing by Tom Quinn is timely: it reflects the popularity of a social pastime which, though ancient, is refreshed and revitalised by each new generation. It is timeless and captivating. To have danced an Irish dance is an exhilarating experience – simple perhaps in its execution, but profound in its intensity – full of camaraderie and interaction: the heady stuff of which lasting memories are made. In *Irish Dancing* Tom Quinn has further enhanced the prospects for Irish dancing into the next millennium and for this he has earned our unstinted appreciation.

Failtim roimh an leabhar seo agus molaim Tomas de bharr a shaothair. Molann an saothar an saotharai.

Labhras O Murchu
Director General of Comhaltas Ceoltoiri Eireann
1997

This book is dedicated to the memory of my great aunt, Nan Quinn who passed on to me her love of Irish dancing, and also to my mother, Eileen, for whose encouragement (sometimes forceful) I will always be grateful

Formation Of
Set And Céilí Dances

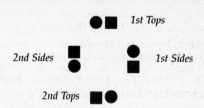

Positions in set and céilí dances

Above are the positions in a set, or a round or figure dance for eight people. (For a round dance for 16 people, see *The Sixteen-Hand Reel*.)
1st Tops (or leading couple) have their backs to the music;
2nd Top (or opposite Top couple) face 1st Top couple;
1st Sides (or leading Side couple) are to the left of 1st Top couple (but this changes in some sets, where 1st Sides are to the right of 1st Tops);
2nd Sides face 1st Side couple.
In a céilí dance, 1st Tops and 2nd Sides, and 2nd Tops and 1st Sides, are said to be contrary to each other.

Order and direction of a set dance

1st Tops are the first to perform the figure and are followed by 2nd Tops, 1st Sides and 2nd Sides. In some sets, the figure moves in a clockwise direction: 1st Tops, 1st Sides, 2nd Tops and 2nd Sides.
There are a few sets where 1st Sides are to the right of 1st Tops, and the figure moves in an anticlockwise direction. In a set where the figure is danced by Top couples, this is usually followed by Side couples, with Top couples and Sides Repeating the movement.

Types of set dances

A set comprises eight people; a half set comprises four people.
Set dances are danced time as follows:

Reels	4/4 time	Jigs	6/8 time
Polkas	2/4 time	Slides	12/8 & 6/8 time
Hornpipes	4/4 time	Flings	4/4 time

Dance Movements

These are some of the most frequently used calls for movements; they are listed in bold, and followed by local names of the movements.

Advance Balance Up.

Around The House Dance Around; House; House Around; Tops House; Top Couples House; Sides House; Side Couples House.

Chain All Chain; Chain All Around; Full Chain; Half Chain; Dance Around; Chain Behind; Women Chain; Men Chain; Double Quarter Chain; Chain Half-Way; Double Women Chain; Link Elbows.

Christmas Big Christmas; Little Christmas; Double Christmas; Basket; Bundle of Fun.

Circle All In; Circle In; Balance In; All Join Hands; Fáinne; Ring To The Right; Ring To The Left.

Dance At Home Dance Around At Home; Dance In Place; Dance Where You Are; Set In Place.

Lead Around Lead; Lead Back Again.

Slide In Half-Slide; Slide In And Out; Change Places; Slide In And Change Places.

Swing Swing Own; Swing Behind; Swing Opposite; Swing Lady On Left; Swing It Out; Swing With The Couple On Left; Three In A Swing; Swing All Around.

Wheel Hands Across; Star; Right-Hand Wheel; Left-Hand Wheel; Big Wheel.

When one couple dances around inside the set and the other three couples stand in place, the following terms can be used: Show The Woman; Dance Around; Figure In and House Around.

Glossary Of Dance Terms

Advance One or more dancers dance forward in a straight line or in a circle without turning. See also **Retire**.

Anticlockwise, Clockwise The turning movements of either an individual or couple as they dance around.

Arch Two dancers take each other's hands, raised for other dancers to pass under.

Big Christmas See **Christmas**.

Body/Polka In waltz hold, couples dance 1 bar of music to the centre and 1 bar back to place and move to the next position to their right, turning clockwise as they dance, repeating these movements until they come back to their starting position.

Céilí Swing A hold for the Swing. The man and woman place their right hands on each other's waists and join left hands under their right arms. They join right hands at chest level and grip their partner's right elbow with their left hands.

Chain Partners face each other, holding right hand in right hand. As they dance past each other, release hands and in take left hand the left hand of the person coming towards them, repeating these movements until partners return to starting position. In the chain men move in an anticlockwise direction and women clockwise. See also **1/2 Chain**, **3/4 Chain** and **Women Chain**.

1/2 Chain Repeat Chain until partners meet half-way around (opposite starting position).

3/4 Chain As in Chain, but meet three-quarters way around; usually danced in céilí dances.

Change Partners Any movement where dancers leave original partners.

Christmas *Big Christmas* and *Little Christmas* respectively are eight or four dancers forming a circle facing in to centre of set, arms behind each other's backs, swinging around clockwise or anticlockwise.

Circle Four or eight dancers joining hands and facing into the centre. Dancers either dance Advance And Retire or move clockwise or anticlockwise. This is also called *Women Circle* and *Men Circle*.

Crossover Dancing straight across to the opposite position.

Figure Each set is made up of different movements which are called figures. Set dances comprise three to seven figures. In céilí dancing the figure refers to the movement danced between the bodies.

First/1st Sides, Tops See **Formation Of Set And Céilí Dances**, p. 7.

Gallop Dancing across to the opposite position in a gallop rhythm.

Hands Around See **Wheel**.

Home The space on the dance floor around each individual couple.

House One or more couples dancing around anticlockwise around the set, turning clockwise around each other, back to home.

Lead Around A couple dance around the house in an anticlockwise direction without turning, as follows: firstly, hands crossed in front, right hand in right, left hand in left; then, with the man's right arm around the woman's waist, and the woman's left hand on the man's right shoulder; and finally, with the man's right hand holding the woman's right hand over her right shoulder, and left hands held in front.

Line Up A movement consisting of two lines, women in one and men in the other, facing out of the set.

Little Christmas See **Christmas**.

Men In The four men advance to the centre together.

Pass By Partners face each other and dance past right shoulder to right shoulder, and reverse when coming back to original position.

Pass Through A movement where two couples dance towards each other and pass, either with one couple dancing between the other or with men passing on the outside and women on the inside to the opposite position.

Retire As advance, except that dancers dance backwards to return to the position from where they advanced. (These movements are usually called together *Advance And Retire*).

Second/2nd Sides, Tops See **Formation Of Set And Céilí Dances**, p. 7.

Side-Step/Sevens A step used to dance sideways in either direction.

Square (In Céilí): Danced by two couples. Men dance side-step to the right and women dance side-step to their left, men passing behind women. Dance two threes, turn to face partner and dance side-step to opposite position. Continue these movements to own position.

Square (In Set) Opposite couples dance towards each other and pass with men on the outside to opposite position. Turn to face partner and dance past each other; turn and dance back to partner's place; turn and dance past partner, ending up in own position.

Square (With Sevens Or Diamond) Opposite couples dance seven towards couple on their right in the waltz hold. Reverse to opposite place dancing sevens. Dance forward to new couple on the right and reverse to own position, dancing Sevens.

1/2 Square (Dance To Home) In waltz hold or with man's right arm around woman's waist and her left hand on his right shoulder, slide towards couple on their right, turn slightly and reverse to opposite position. Dance to home anticlockwise, turning clockwise twice.

1/2 Square (With Sevens And 1/2 Square Dance To Home) These movements can be danced by one or more couples.

Slide In A movement danced by one or more couples from their home position to the centre and back again.

Standard Hold The man holds his partner's right hand in his left hand, the man's right hand is placed on the woman's waist and the woman's left hand is placed on the man's right shoulder. Also called the *Waltz Hold*.

Star See **Wheel**.

Swing A movement in which a couple turn rapidly clockwise while dancing at home. There are two holds for this movement: the Standard or Waltz Hold and the Céilí Swing

Turn The Woman A couple join right hands and the men dance in place while the women turn four times clockwise under the man's raised arm. Also called *Under The Finger*.

Waltz Hold See **Standard Hold**.

Wheel Two or more couples join right hands and dance around clockwise (or left hands and dance anticlockwise) for 4 or 8 bars of music. It is also called *Star* or *Hands Around*.

Big Wheel The four men hold left hands in the centre of the set, their right arm around the woman's waist, and the woman's left arm is on the man's right shoulder or around his waist. They dance 8 bars of music anticlockwise.

Women Chain Opposite women dance towards each other, taking right hand in right hand, passing right shoulder to right shoulder. Release rights and give left hand to opposite man. Dance around the man and return to own position, passing right shoulder to right shoulder with opposite woman. There are various ways of dancing around the opposite man: Under The Arm, Hook Left Arms, High And Low and Over The Head. In some dances the women may start the Chain with the left hands.

Women In The four women advance to the centre.

Acknowledgements

I would like to take this opportunity to thank all my dancers, the dancers who have attended my workshops and to my dance teachers.

My grateful thanks are owed to the following: Joe and Siobhán Donovan; Donncha O'Muíneacháin; Pat Murphy; Martin and Frances Bolger; Pat and Liz Moroney; Connie Ryan and Betty McCoy; Tony McNulty; Peter Joseph Quinn; Helen and Coleman Burns; Larry Lynch; Mary Fox; Margaret and Bill Wynnette; Jack Connolly; James Kane; Michael and Kathleen McGlynn; Marie Philbin; Brooks Academy; Timmy McCarthy; Brian O'Kane and the Fódhla Céilí Band; Siamba Céilí Band; J.J. Gardiner Branch, C.C.E.; Sean Walsh; Annette McArdle; Garland Graphics, Dundalk; Devenney Office Supplies, Dundalk; and to my employers Bus Eireann for their understanding and time off. Last but not least, a very special thank you goes to my family, Áine, Bronagh, Breanainn and Doireann – without your support and encouragement this could never have happened.

Aran Set
Seit Arainn

1ST FIGURE   *(Reels: 160 bars)*

Bars **A. Lead Around**

16   Lead around for 8 bars anticlockwise; turn without turning the
      woman. Lead back with woman on the outside all the time. On
      the last 2 bars men have their backs to the centre and women
      face their partners looking into the set as they dance on the spot.

      B. Swing

8   All swing céilí fashion for the full 8 bars.

      C. Grand Chain

16   Face partner and take right elbow. Instead of usual hand, dance
      one step back and chain all round, women going clockwise.
      Dance the last 2 bars facing partner.

      D. Swing

8   Repeat *B*.

      E. Chain

8   Top women chain, taking right elbows in centre. Left-hand turn
      with opposite man and pass back right shoulder to right, chain-
      ing, and give left hand to partner. The woman dances anti-
      clockwise around and behind her partner to her own side,
      holding his hand all the time, while he stays facing into the set,
      only turning, clockwise, to face her at the end.

      F. Swing

8   Top couples swing. As they do so, Side couples cross to oppo-
      site side (on right-hand side) with woman turning clockwise,
      first under man's two raised arms and then twice under right
      arm. Each couple dances the last 2 bars facing into the set.

G. Waves

16   Top couples advance and retire holding hands in front (waves) then cross on right-hand side to opposite position with woman turning twice, first under both arms, then under right arm clockwise. Repeat back to place.

H. Swing

8   Top couples swing, and Sides return to own side as at *F*.

I. Repeat

64   Repeat *C–H* with Side couples leading.

2ND FIGURE   *(Reels: 296 bars)*

A. Chain

16   Top couples chain as at *1st Figure, E* and Top couples swing.

B. Dance Around And Swing

16   Top man and opposite woman dance across, right shoulder to right shoulder, turn clockwise on 4th bar, dance back for 2 bars and turn anticlockwise to meet in the centre. They then swing for 8 bars, finishing with backs to their own position.

C. Arches

16   Swinging woman and man dance one step back *[1 bar]* while their partners dance one step forward to meet them; join hands in front. Both couples dance one step forward *[1 bar]* and two steps back, then cross to opposite positions on right-hand side, woman turning one turn clockwise under both arms and then under right arm. Top man, still holding his partner's right hand, dances forward alone so that he is in the centre with his back to the Side couple beside him. He and his partner form an arch. As he moves forward, opposite woman dances to the right, behind and around him to come back under the arch from the opposite side *[2 bars]*, while her partner dances forward to meet her and take her right hand as she comes through. Man and opposite couple reverse into position with partners without turning the woman, then dance back to their own side with the woman turning twice as before, first under both arms, then under right arm clockwise.

D. Christmas

24   Opposite Top couple swing 8 bars, moving to the centre. On the last 2 bars Top couple advance, the man's arm around his partner's waist. The opposite woman reverses back with them, on the left side of Top man with his arm around her waist, while her partner reverses on his own. All advance, reverse and advance again; swing in four in the centre. They swing for 7 bars and break back to place on the last bar. Side couples swing in place as Tops are swinging in the centre.

E. Repeat

216   Repeat *A–D*. 1st Sides, 2nd Tops and 2nd Sides lead in turn.

3RD FIGURE   *(Polkas: 88 bars)*

A. Circle

8   Circle, advance and retire twice. When retiring the second time men move slightly left and women move right, turning clockwise to face the man on their right.

B. Men Move To Left

8   All four couples now dance (not swing) two turns to their left to finish in women's position; all men are now in the position left of their own.

C. Repeat

64   Repeat *A* and *B* until back in place with own partner; circle and swing to finish.

Ardgroom Polka Set
Seit Ard Gruama

1ST FIGURE. *HOUSE AND SQUARE*   (Polkas: 164 bars)

Bars **A. *Advance And Retire***

8   Circle, advance and retire twice.
      (Step for circle: Women slide right, left, right, left forward.
      Reverse left, right 1-2-3; repeat. Men lead with the left foot.)

      B. *House*

8   1st Tops house.

      C. *Half Square And House*

8   Half square and house to home.

      D. *Polka*

16   Four couples dance 1 bar into centre, reverse woman 1 bar then
      dance 2 bars, turning clockwise into position to their right *[4
      bars]*. Repeat more three times until all end up in own position.

      E. *House*

8   Four couples house.

      F. *Repeat*

16   1st Sides repeat *B* and *C*.

      G. *Repeat*

24   Four couples repeat *D* and *E*.

      H. *Repeat*

16   2nd Tops repeat *B* and *C*.

I. Repeat

24   Four couples repeat **D** and **E**.

J. Repeat

16   2nd Sides repeat **B** and **C**.

I. Repeat

24   Four couples repeat **D** and **E**, and finish.

2ND FIGURE. *WOMEN'S CHAIN*   *(Polkas: 176 bars)*

A. Advance And Retire

8   Circle, advance and retire twice.

B. House

8   1st Tops house.

C. Chain

8   Top women chain.

D. Polka

4   (a) Four couples dance 1 bar to centre and 1 bar out; repeat.
12   (b) Dance half-way round. Repeat (a) and (b) back to home.

E. House

8   Four couples house.

F. Repeat

16   1st Sides dance **B** and **C**.

G. Repeat

24   Four couples repeat **D** and **E**.

H. Repeat

16 2nd Tops dance *B* and *C*.

I. Repeat

24 Four couples repeat *D* and *E*.

J. Repeat

16 2nd Sides dance *B* and *C*.

K. Repeat

24 Four couples repeat *D* and *E*, to finish

3RD FIGURE. *WALK POLKA*   *(Polkas: 176 bars)*

A. Advance And Retire

8 Circle, advance and retire twice.

B. House

8 1st Tops house.

C. Half Square And House

8 1st Tops half square and house to home.

D. Polka

8 *(a)* Walking to music, men reverse women 2 bars to men's left, 2 bars to men's right, 2 bars to men's left, turn 2 bars into opposite place.

8 *(b)* Still walking to music, repeat *(a)* returning to place.

E. House

8 Four couples house.

F. Repeat

16 1st Sides dance *B* and *C*.

G. Repeat

24 Four couples repeat *D* and *E*.

H. Repeat

16 2nd Tops dance *B* and *C*.

I. Repeat

24 Four couples repeat *D* and *E*.

J. Repeat

16 2nd Sides dance *B* and *C*.

K. Repeat

24 Four couples repeat *D* and *E*, to finish

4TH FIGURE   (Slides: 144 bars)

A. Advance And Retire

8 Circle, advance and retire twice.

B. House

8 Top couples house.

C. Slide And Change

32 Top couples slide in *[2 bars]*, slide out *[2 bars]*, dance half-way round *[4 bars]*. Slide in, slide out, dance to home. Repeat.

D. Polka

16 Polka as at *1st Figure, D*.

E. House

8   Four couples house.

F. Repeat

24   Side couples dance *B* and *C*.

G. Repeat

24   Four couples repeat *D* and *E* to finish.

5TH FIGURE. *SWING BEHIND*   *(Polkas: 208 bars)*

A. Advance And Retire

8   Circle, advance and retire twice.

B. House

8   1st Tops house.

C. Half Square And House

8   1st Tops half square and house to home.

D. Swing

8   All swing behind; men swing woman on left.

E. Polka

16   Men polka with new woman as at *1st Figure, D*.

F. House

8   Four couples house.

G. Repeat

16   1st Sides repeat *B* and C.

H. Swing

8   All swing behind.

I. Polka

16   Polka with new woman.

J. House

8   Four couples house.

K. Repeat

16   2nd Tops dance *B* and *C*.

L. Swing

8   All swing behind.

M. Polka

16   Polka with new woman.

N. House

8   Four couples house.

O. Repeat

16   2nd Sides dance *B* and **C**.

P. Swing

8   All swing behind.

Q. Polka

16   Polka with own woman.

R. House

8   All four couples house, to finish.

Armagh Quadrilles

1ST FIGURE   *(Single Reels or Polkas: 72 bars)*

Bars **A. Pass Through**

8   Top couples pass through, women on the inside, and change places with their partners *[4 bars]*; Top couples pass through; change places with their partners *[4 bars]*.

B. Swing

8   All swing.

C. Women Chain

8   Top women chain, right hands in the centre, turn twice around opposite man, hooking left arms *[4 bars]*; dance back to partner *[4 bars]*.

D. Swing

8   All swing.

E. Repeat

32   Sides repeat *A–D*.

2ND FIGURE   *(Single Reels or Polkas: 104 bars)*

A. Advance And Retire

8   Top couples advance and retire once *[4 bars]*; pass through to opposite position and change places with partners *[4 bars]*.

B. Advance And Retire

8   Repeat *A*.

C. Swing

8   All swing.

D. Repeat

24 Sides dance *A–C*.

E. Repeat

24 Tops repeat *A–C*.

F. Repeat

24 Sides repeat *A–C*.

3RD FIGURE   *(Jigs: 136 bars)*

A. Lead In The Centre

8 Top man and opposite woman hold left hands in the centre and
   dance around anticlockwise *[4 bars]*. Pick up partner, men with
   right arm around the woman's waist and woman's left arm on
   the man's right shoulder; lead around to opposite place *[4 bars]*.

B. Slide In And Out

8 In waltz hold, all slide in and out once *[4 bars]*, then slide across
   (4 steps to home) *[4 bars]*.

C. Women Chain

8 Top women chain as at *1st Figure, C*.

D. Swing

8 Four couples swing.

E. Repeat

32 Repeat *A–D*, 2nd Top man and opposite woman leading.

F. Repeat

32 Repeat *A–D*, 1st Side man and opposite woman leading.

G. Repeat

32   Repeat *A–D*, 2nd Side man and opposite woman leading.

4TH FIGURE   *(Single Reels or Polkas: 200 bars)*

A. Swing

8   Top couple swings across the set to the opposite couple.

B. Three And One

8   2nd Top man takes the hands of both women, 1st Top woman's left hand in his left; his own partner turns out and he holds her right hand in his right. Both Top women are facing 2nd Top man. 2nd Top man advances *[2 bars]* while the women retire *[2 bars]*. 1st Top man retires at the same time and dances in place for 6 bars. 2nd Top man advances and the women retire *[2 bars]*. 2nd Top man turns both women to face 1st top man *[2 bars]*.

C. Three And One

8   Repeat *B* with 1st Top man dancing with both women.

D. Basket

8   Basket of four.

E. Women Chain

8   Top women chain as at *1st Figure, C*.

F. Swing

8   Four couples swing.

G. Repeat

48   Repeat *A–F* with 2nd Tops leading.

H. Repeat

48   Repeat A–F with 1st Sides leading.

I. Repeat

48   Repeat A–F with 2nd Sides leading.

5TH FIGURE   (Single Reels or Polkas: 128 bars)

A. Circle

8   Circle, advance and retire twice.

B. Swing

8   All four couples swing.

C. Lead Around

8   Lead around, the man's right arm around the woman's waist and the woman's left arm on the man's right shoulder.

D. Circle

8   Circle, advance and retire twice.

E. Swing Behind

8   Swing behind; men turn to the left and women turn to the right; swing. During the swing the men take the women home to their position.

F. Lead Around

8   Lead around with new partner.

G. Repeat

72   Repeat A–C Three times until women return home.

Auban Set
Seit Abha Bán

Opening position, except where indicated: All four couples face anticlockwise around the circle, men on the inside, with arms behind each other's backs.

1ST FIGURE   (Jigs: 200 bars)

Bars **A. Body**

8   *(a) Lead around:* The dancers lead around until all couples reach their starting places.

16   *(b) Square:* Couples adopt the standard hold. Each couple dances straight over to the next position to their right. Women dance: R-L R-L LRL-RLR; men dance: L-R-L-R RLR-LRL. Each couple dances to the next position in 2 bars, then dances 2 bars in that position, turning slightly clockwise so they are ready to step off on the 'wrong' feet to reach the next position. Repeat the movement with opposite steps to bring each couple to the position opposite their own, then twice more to return to their own place.

8   *(c) House:* All four couples.

B. Figure

8   1st Tops and 1st Sides face each other, as do 2nd Tops and 2nd Sides. The facing women cross into each other's places, right shoulder to right *[2 bars]*; the facing men cross left shoulder to left *[2 bars]*. Women cross back; men cross back *[4 bars]*.

C. Body

32   All couples repeat *A*.

D. Figure

8   All couples repeat *B*.

E. Body

32   All couples repeat *A*.

F. Figure

8   All couples repeat **B**, facing the other direction this time.

G. Body

32   All couples repeat **A**.

H. Figure

8   All couples repeat **F**.

I. Body

32   All couples repeat **A**.

2ND FIGURE   *(Jigs: 264 bars)*

A. Body

8   *(a) Lead around:* The dancers lead around until all couples reach
    their starting places.
16 *(b) Square:* Couples adopt the standard hold. Each couple dances
    straight over to the next position to their right. Women dance:
    R-L-R-L LRL-RLR; men dance: L-R-L-R RLR-LRL. Each couple
    dances to the next position in 2 bars, then dances 2 bars in that
    position, turning slightly clockwise so they are ready to step off
    on the 'wrong' feet to reach the next position. Repeat the move-
    ment with opposite steps to bring each couple to the position
    opposite their own, then twice more to return to their own place.
8   *(c) House:* All four couples.

B. Figure

8   *(a) House:* Top couples.
16 *(b) Slide change:* Top couples slide into the centre and back out
    again *[4 bars]*, dance half-way around the house to opposite
    places *[4 bars]*, and finally repeat both these movements to
    bring them back to their own places again *[8 bars]*.

C. Body

32   All couples repeat A.

D. Figure

24   Side couples dance as at B.

E. Body

32   All couples repeat A.

F. Figure

24   Top couples dance as at B.

G. Body

32   All couples repeat A.

H. Figure

24   Side couples dance as at B.

I. Body

32   All couples repeat A.

3RD FIGURE   *(Jigs: 296 bars)*

A. Body

8   *(a) Lead around:* The dancers lead around until all couples reach their starting places.

16   *(b) Square:* Couples adopt the standard hold. Each couple dances straight over to the next position to their right. Women dance: R-L-R-L LRL-RLR; men dance: L-R-L-R RLR-LRL. Each couple dances to the next position in 2 bars, then dances 2 bars in that position, turning slightly clockwise so they are ready to step off on the 'wrong' feet to reach the next position. Repeat the move-

ment with opposite steps to bring each couple to the position opposite their own, then twice more to return to their own place.

8   *(c) House:* All four couples.

B. Figure

2   *(a) Set:* Top couples dance in place.

30   *(b) Swing all around:* Top men swing with each woman in turn, starting with the woman on their left for 6 bars, and the other women for 8 bars, finishing with their own partners.

C. Body

32   All couples repeat *A*.

D. Figure

32   Side couples dance as at *B*.

E. Body

32   All couples repeat *A*.

F. Figure

32   Top couples dance as at *B*.

G. Body

32   All couples repeat *A*.

H. Figure

32   Side couples dance as at *B*.

I. Body

32   All couples repeat *A*.

4TH FIGURE   (Slides: 200 bars)

Opening position: Couples adopt the standard position.

A. Figure

8   (a) *House:* Top couples.
16   (b) *Slide and change:* Top couples slide into the centre and back
     out again *[4 bars]*, dance half-way around the house to oppo-
     site places *[4 bars]*, and finally repeat both these movements to
     bring them back to their own places again *[8 bars]*.
8   (c) *House:* Top couples.
16   (d) *Slide and change:* Top couples repeat (b).

B. Figure

48   Side couples dance as at *A*.

C. Figure

48   Top couples repeat *A*.

D. Figure

48   Side couples repeat *A*.

5TH FIGURE   (Reels: 256 bars)

*Opening position: All four couples join hands in front and face anticlockwise
around the circle, men on the inside.*

A. Lead Around

8   All four couples dance anticlockwise around until back in orig-
     inal places.

B. Turn The Lady

8   As they reach own positions the men turn partners clockwise; all
     link left arms with partner and dance around them anticlockwise.

C. Swing

8   All four couples swing.

D. Figure

8   *(a) Square:* The two Top couples square all the way around.

8   *(b) House:* The two Top couples dance around the house inside.

8   *(c) Swing opposites:* The two Top men leave their partners and cross over to the opposite women and swing with them.

8   *(d) Link arms:* The two Top men return to the centre, link left arms and dance around each other, doubling the last 2 bars.

E. Repeat

24   Repeat *A–C*.

F. Figure

32   Side couples dance *D*.

G. Repeat

24   Repeat *A–C*.

H. Figure

32   Top couples repeat *D*.

I. Repeat

24   Repeat *A–C*.

J. Figure

32   Side couples repeat *D*.

K. Repeat

24   Repeat *A–C*.

Australian Half Set

Workshop notes by Margaret and Bill Winnett, 1996. This half set has been danced in Sydney, Australia for the past 40 years and was introduced by Peter McKenna, founder of the Sydney Irish Céilí Dancers. It is danced to jigs using a polka step (or 'Down jig') except for Around The House, when a normal jig step is used (as in the 5th figure of the plain set).

1ST FIGURE   (Jigs: 48 bars)

Bars **A. Change Places**

8   Right hand in right, each woman leads her partner to opposite position, turning once clockwise; repeat to return home.

B. Swing

8   Swing partner in céilí hold.

C. Women Chain And Swing

16   Women chain, right hand to opposite woman, left hand to opposite man. Turn and dance into a straight line, dancing on the spot for bars 7 and 8, then continue chain for another 2 bars and swing partner for the last 6 bars.

D. House Around

8   All dance around the house.

2ND FIGURE   (Jigs: 64 bars)

A. Advance And Retire

8   Right hand in right, advance and retire once; then women lead the men to opposite position, turning once clockwise.

B. Advance And Retire

8   Repeat *A* to return home.

C. Swing

8   Swing partners.

D. Repeat

24   Repeat *A–C*.

E. House Around

8   All dance around the house.

3RD FIGURE   *(Jigs: 64 bars)*

A. Swing And Sevens

8   1st man swings opposite woman while their partners dance sevens and threes into their positions and back to place.

B. Lead Around

8   Right hand in right, the woman leads the man to opposite position, turning clockwise, and repeats to return home.

C. Swing

8   All swing partners.

D. Swing And Sevens

8   2nd man swings opposite woman while their partners dance sevens and threes into their positions and back to place.

E. Lead Around

8   Right hand in right, the woman leads the man to opposite position, and repeats to return home.

F. Swing

8   All swing partners.

G. House Around

8   All dance around the house.

4TH FIGURE   *(Jigs: 128 bars)*

A. Women Chain And Swing

16   Women chain and swing as *1st Figure, C*.

B. House And Sevens

8   1st couple dance around the house leaving the woman on the left-hand side of the opposite man; meanwhile 2nd couple, with hands joined in front, dances sevens and threes to the right and back.

C. Advance And Retire

8   The line of three opposite single man advance and retire twice, turning the women over to the opposite man during last 2 bars.

D. Advance And Retire

8   Repeat *C*, but using the last 2 bars to form a basket.

E. Basket

8   All swing in four.

F. Women Chain And Swing

16   Repeat *A*.

G. House And Sevens

8   2nd couple dance *B*.

H. Advance And Retire

8   Repeat *C*.

I. Advance And Retire

8   Repeat D.

J. Basket

8   All swing in four.

K. Women Chain And Swing

16   Repeat A.

l. House Around

8   All dance around the house.

5TH FIGURE   (Jigs: 96 bars)

A. House Around

8   All dance around the house.

B. Gallop

8   Couples gallop sideways towards each other [2 bars], back to place [2 bars] and house to opposite side [4 bars].

C. Gallop

8   Repeat B to return home.

D. Women Chain And Swing

16   Women chain and swing as at 1st Figure, C.

E. House Around

8   All dance around the house.

F. Gallop

8   Repeat B.

G. Gallop

8   Repeat C.

H. Women Chain And Swing

16   Repeat D.

I. House Around

8   All dance around the house.

6TH FIGURE   (Jigs)

A. Circle

8   All half sets join to form a large circle, the women on the men's right-hand side; all advance and retire twice.

B. Swing

8   All swing partner.

C. House Around

8   All dance around the house.

D. Advance And Retire

8   All advance and retire twice.

E. Swing Behind

8   Each man swings the woman on his left-hand side.

F. House Around

8   All dance around the house.

G. Repeat

Repeat D–F as often as required.

Baile Bhuirne Jig Set
Scil Bhaile Bhúirne (Cor)

Opening position for all figures: Couples adopt the standard position.

1ST FIGURE *(Slides: 88 bars)*

Bars **A. House**

8   Top couples dance in place *[2 bars]*; house around inside *[6 bars]*.

B. Square

8   Top couples dance over to the Side positions to their right *[2 bars]*, dancing forward without turning. Men dance: L-R-LRL; women: R-L-RLR. When in these places the couples should be facing out of the set. Then, using opposite steps, they dance backwards into the next position *[2 bars]* and are now in each other's places facing into the set. They then dance half-way around the house inside to reach their original positions *[4 bars]*.

C. Figure

8   Top couples swing in place.

D. Slide And Change

16   All four couples slide into the centre and back out *[4 bars]* and dance half-way around the house to their own places *[4 bars]*. Repeat these movements to return to their opposite places again.

E. Repeat

40   Side couples dance *A–D*.

2ND FIGURE *(Slides: 104 bars)*

A. House

8   Top couples dance in place *[2 bars]*; house around inside *[6 bars]*.

B. Square

8   Top couples slide over to Side positions, then to opposite Tops positions and then house half-way around back to their own places again, as at *1st Figure, B*.

C. Figure

8   (a) *Swing opposites:* Top couples swap partners and swing in the middle of the set.

8   (b) *Swing own:* Top couples reform and swing in place.

D. Slide And Change

16   All four couples slide into the centre and back out *[4 bars]* and dance half-way around the house to their own places *[4 bars]*. Repeat these movements to return to their opposite places again.

E. Repeat

48   Side couples dance *A–D*.

3RD FIGURE   (Slides: 104 bars)

A. House

8   Top couples dance in place *[2 bars]*; house around inside *[6 bars]*.

B. Square

8   Top couples slide over to Side positions, then to opposite Tops positions and then house half-way around back to their own places again, as at *1st Figure, B*.

C. Figure

16   Little Christmas: The two Top couples form a tight circle in the centre of the set, arms joined behind each other's backs and dance around clockwise, breaking in time to start the next movement.

D. Slide And Change

16 All four couples slide into the centre and back out *[4 bars]* and dance half-way around the house to their own places *[4 bars]*. Repeat these movements to return to their opposite places again.

E. Repeat

48 Side couples dance *A–D*.

4TH FIGURE   *(Slides: 136 bars)*

A. House

8 Top couples dance in place *[2 bars]*; house around inside *[6 bars]*.

B. Square

8 Top couples slide over to Side positions, then to opposite Tops positions, and then house half-way around back to their own places again, as at *1st Figure, B*.

C. Figure

32 Swing All Around: Starting with the women to their left, the two Top men swing for 8 bars with each woman in turn.

D. Slide And Change

16 All four couples slide into the centre and back out *[4 bars]* and dance half-way around the house to their own places *[4 bars]*. Repeat these movements to return to their opposite places again.

E. Repeat

64 Side couples dance *A–D*.

5TH FIGURE   *(Slides: 112 bars)*

A. House

8   Top couples dance in place *[2 bars]*; house around inside *[6 bars]*.

B. Square

8   Top couples slide over to Side positions, then to opposite Tops positions, and then house half-way around back to their own places again, as at *1st Figure, B*.

C. Figure

8   *(a) Chain:* Each couple joins right hands and dances half-way around each other. Then the women chain half-way around the set in an anticlockwise direction, and the men clockwise, each dancer meeting their partner in the position opposite their own.

8   *(b) Swing:* The four couples reform and swing.

D. Slide And Change

16   All four couples slide into the centre and back out *[4 bars]* and dance half-way around the house to their own places *[4 bars]*. Repeat these movements to return to their opposite places again.

E. Repeat

48   Top couples repeat *A–D*. Side couples only dance *A* and *D*.

F. House

8   All four couples dance house around.

Baile Bhuirne Reel Set
Scil Baile Bhúirne (Port)

Opening position for all figures: All four couples join hands in front and face anticlockwise around the circle, men on the inside.

1ST FIGURE. *WHEEL* (Polkas: 80 bars)

Bars **A. Lead Around**

8 All four couples dance anticlockwise around until back in original places.

B. Figure

8 Wheel: Each Top couple turns to face the Side couple to their left. Each group of four dancers, 1st Tops and 1st Sides, and 2nd Tops and 2nd Sides, join right hands in the centre and dance clockwise for 4 bars, then turn, join left hands in centre and dance anticlockwise for 4 bars.

C. Body

16 Couples adopt the standard position. All four couples dance together into the centre *[1 bar]* and back to their own positions *[1 bar]*. They then dance 2 bars around to the position of the couple to their right, turning clockwise as they go. The four couples repeat this movement three more times until they end up back in their starting positions.

D. House

8 All four couples dance house around.

E. Figure

8 Repeat *B*. On this occasion the Side couples turn to the Top couples to their left.

F. Body

16   Repeat *C*.

G. House

8   All four couples dance house around.

2ND FIGURE   *(Polkas: 96 bars)*

A. Lead Around

8   All four couples dance anticlockwise around until back in original places.

B. Women To The Centre

4   *(a) Women in:* Each man holds his partner's right hand in his right hand. While the men dance in place, their partners dance past in front of them, turning anticlockwise, until all the women are back-to-back in the centre, facing out *[2 bars]*. They then dance back out past their partners, still turning anticlockwise until they are back on the outside again *[2 bars]*. The men's right arms should now be around the women's shoulders, still holding the women's right hands in their right hands. Men take the women's left hands in their left hands.

4   *(b) Lead around:* All four couples lead half-way around to the opposite places.

4   *(c) Women in:* The four women dance into the centre and back out again, as at *(a)*. On this occasion they dance in, turning clockwise but dance back out turning anticlockwise, as before.

4   *(d) Lead around:* All four couples lead half-way around back to their own places again.

C. Body

16   All four couples repeat *1st Figure, C*.

D. House

8   All four couples dance house around.

E. Figure

16   Repeat *B*.

F. Body

16   Repeat *C*.

G. House

8   All four couples dance house around.

3RD FIGURE. *SWING BEHIND, SWING YOUR OWN*
(Polkas: 96 bars)

A. Lead Around

8   All four couples dance anticlockwise around until back in original places.

B. Figure

8   *(a) Swing behind:* The couples separate. Each dancer turns away from their own partner to the nearest woman or man and swings with them.

8   *(b) Swing own partner:* The original couples reform and swing in place.

C. Body

16   All four couples repeat *1st Figure, C*.

D. House

8   All four couples dance house around.

E. Figure

16   Repeat *B*.

F. Body

16   Repeat *C*.

G. House

8   All four couples dance house around.

4TH FIGURE. *SIDE-STEP*   *(Polkas: 80 bars)*

A. Lead Around

8   All four couples dance anticlockwise around until back in original places.

B. Figure

8   Side-step: All couples face to centre, standing side-by-side. Women side step to left, in front of their partners, who side-step to the right. Women and men end up in each others' places *[2 bars]*. All dance in place *[2 bars]*, then all side-step back to their own places *[2 bars]*, men in front, and dance in place *[2 bars]*.

C. Body

16   All four couples repeat *1st Figure, C*.

D. House

8   All four couples dance house around.

E. Figure

8   Repeat *B*.

F. Body

16   Repeat *C*.

G. House

8   All four couples dance house around.

5TH FIGURE. *CHAIN*   *(Polkas: 96 bars)*

A. Lead Around

8   All four couples dance anticlockwise around until back in original places.

B. Figure

8   *(a) Chain:* Each couple joins right hands and dances half-way around each other. Then the women chain half-way around the set anticlockwise and the men clockwise, each dancer meeting their partner in the opposite position to their own.

8   *(b) Swing:* The four couples, who are now at opposite sides of the circle from their starting positions, swing in place.

C. Body

16   All four couples repeat *1st Figure, C*.

D. House

8   All four couples dance house around.

E. Figure

16   Repeat *B*. Each couple ends up back in their original position and swings there.

F. Body

16   Repeat *C*.

G. House

8   All four couples dance house around.

6TH FIGURE. *LARGE WHEEL*   (Polkas: 112 bars)

A. Lead Around

8   All four couples dance anticlockwise around until back in original places.

B. Figure

6   (a) *Women's Circle:* The four women join hands to form a circle, and dance into the centre and out again, twice.

16   (b) *Wheel:* The four men join right hands in the centre and dance 4 bars around clockwise, then turn clockwise, join left hands in the centre and dance 4 bars anticlockwise, back to their own places. Men do not release hands or stop dancing but pick up their partners by placing their right arms around their waists, then wheel around with them until back in place *[8 bars]*.

C. Body

16   All four couples repeat *1st Figure, C.*

D. House

8   All four couples dance house around.

E. Figure

24   Repeat *B*.

F. Body

16   Repeat *C*.

G. House

8   All four couples dance house around.

Ballinascarty Half Set
Leathscil Bhéal Na Scairte

Ballinascarty is situated in west Cork about 10 miles from Bandon and 5 miles from Clonakilty on the main Cork–Skibbereen road. Years ago Ballinascarty was well known for its Sunday crossroads dancing.
Note: The standard waltz hold is used throughout except where stated.

1ST FIGURE   (Polkas: 128 bars)

Bars   **A. Lead Around**

8   Hands crossed in front, both couples lead around anticlockwise to place; turn the women with both hands during the last 2 bars.

B. Swing

8   Both couples swing.

C. Square The House

8   The women going backward and the men forward, both couples dance along one side of a square going quarter-way round, dancing 1-2, 1-2-3, the man dancing L-R, L-R-L and the woman dancing R-L, R-L-R, making a quarter turn on the last beat and then the men going backward and the women forward, the two couples dance along the second line of the square to the half-way position *[4 bars]*. Repeat to get back to place *[4 bars]*.

D. Round The House

8   Both couples house around.

E. Women Back-To-Back And Men Change Places

8   The two women dance forward and pass left shoulder to left *[2 bars]*. Still facing forward, the women dancing back-to-back, go to their left *[2 bars]*. Still facing forward, they retire *[2 bars]* and then turn clockwise to face the man *[2 bars]*. The men in the meantime dance anticlockwise to opposite place.

F. Swing

8   Swing with new partners.

G. Repeat

48   Repeat *A–F*, men returning to original place at *E*.

H. Repeat

16   Repeat *A* and *B*.

I. Round The House

8   Both couples house around and finish.

2ND FIGURE   *(Jigs: 176 bars)*

A. Lead Around

8   Repeat *1st Figure, A*.

B. Swing

8   Repeat *1st Figure, B*.

C. Square The House

8   The men release left hands and the women their right hands
     and face quarter way to the right. Then square the house as at
     1st Figure, C, going forward 1-2, 1-2-3, backward 1-2, 1-2-3,
     going forward 1-2, 1-2-3 and backward 1-2, 1-2-3 to place.

D. Round The House

8   Repeat *1st Figure, D*.

E. Slide And Change

8   Both couples going sideways to centre, dance in, 1-2, 1-kick and
     dance out, 1-2, 1-2-3; dance half-way round to opposite place.

F. Slide And Change

8   Repeat *E* and back to place.

G. Round The House

8   Repeat *D*.

H. Women Chain And Change

8   The men remain in place while the women cross over to the opposite man with a left-hand chain, both turn around each other with the hands at waist level, give right hand back to their partner, go round each other again and women over to opposite side.

I. Swing

8   Swing with new partners.

J. Repeat

72   Repeat *A–I*, women returning to partner at *H*.

K. Repeat

16   Repeat *A* and *B*.

L. Round The House.

8   Both couples dance house around and finish.

3RD FIGURE   *(Hornpipes: 128 bars)*

A. Lead Around

8   Repeat *1st Figure, A*, but with hornpipe steps: hop 1-2-3 kick, 1-2-3 kick, etc.

B. Swing

8   A slow, lazy swing.

C. Square The House

8   Going to the men's left and the women's right, couples dance hop 1-2-3-4-5-6-7, and making a quarter turn to the men's right and the women's left, hop 1-2-3-4-5-6-7 and repeat to get back to place.

D. Round The House

8   Hop 1-2-3, hop 1-2-3, etc.

E. Quarter Square And Quarter Round

8   Men release left hands, women right hands and face the right. Dance hop 1-2-3 kick and 1-2-3, then take the opposite place. Repeat quarter square and quarter round to get back to place.

F. Women Change And Men All Round

8   Women give right hands to each other in the centre and go one-and-a-half times round (hop 1-2-3 x 8) to the other woman's place. At the same time, the men dance (hop 1-2-3) anticlockwise all the way round to their own place.

G. Round The House

8   Repeat D.

H. Repeat

56   Repeat A–G, and women return to their own place at F.

I. Round The House

8   Dance double (hop 1, hop 2, hop 3, etc.) all round and finish.

Ballycommon Set
Seit Bhaile Choimín

Opening position for all figures: Couples adopt the standard position.

1ST FIGURE
(Polkas: 56 bars)

Bars **A. House**

8 All four couples dance house around.

B. Figure

8 Hook: Dancers turn from their partner to the nearest woman or man, hook arms with them and turn around them twice.

C. Swing

8 Original couples reform and swing in place.

D. Figure

8 All couples repeat *B*.

E. Swing

8 All couples repeat *C*.

F. House

8 All four couples dance house around.

2ND FIGURE
(Polkas: 88 bars)

A. House

8 All four couples dance house around.

B. Advance And Retire

8 All couples advance to the centre and retire twice in waltz hold.

C. Swing Behind

8   Each dancer turns from his or her own partner to the nearest woman or man and swings with them, in the men's position.

D. Advance And Retire

8   All four new couples advance to the centre and retire twice.

E. Swing Behind

8   Repeat **C** to bring the women around to their opposite men.

F. Advance And Retire

8   All four new couples advance to the centre and retire twice.

G. Swing Behind

8   Repeat **C** to bring the women around to the men on the left of their own places.

H. Advance And Retire

8   All four new couples advance to the centre and retire twice.

I. Swing

8   The women rejoin their own partners and swing in place.

J. House

8   All four couples dance house around.

3RD FIGURE   (Slides: 112 bars)

A. House

8   All four couples dance house around.

B. Figure

8   *(a) Hook:* Dancers turn from their partner to the nearest woman or man, hook arms with them and dance around them twice.

8   *(b) Circle:* Women give right hands to their partners and left hands to the men on their right-hand sides, forming a circle of eight, with the men facing inwards and women out. In this poisition they dance one full turn around.

C. Advance And Retire

8   Each couple joins hands in front and all couples advance to the centre and retire, twice.

D. Slide And Change

16   Couples adopt the waltz hold, slide into the centre and retire once *[4 bars]*; dance half-way around the house to opposite positions *[4 bars]*. Repeat these movements to bring all dancers back to their own places again.

E. House

8   All four couples dance house around.

F. Repeat

48   Repeat *B–E*.

4TH FIGURE   *(Slides: 96 bars)*

A. House

8   All four couples dance house around.

B. Hook

8   Each dancer turns from his or her partner to the nearest woman or man, hooks arms with them and dances around them twice.

C. Swing

8   All four couples swing in place.

D. Slide And Change

16   Top couples dance 2 bars towards each other and 2 bars back to their own places again *[4 bars]*; dance half-way around the house to each other's places *[4 bars]*. Repeat these movements to bring them back to their own places again *[8 bars]*.

E. House

8   All four couples dance house around.

F. Hook

8   Repeat *B*.

G. Swing

8   Repeat *C*.

H. Slide And Change

16   Side couples dance *D*.

I. House

8   All four couples dance house around.

5TH FIGURE   *(Slides: 64 bars)*

A. House

8   All four couples dance house around.

B. Slide And Change

16   All four couples dance 2 bars in towards the centre and 2 bars back to their own places *[4 bars]*; dance half-way around the

house to opposite places *[4 bars]*. Repeat these movements to bring them back to their own places again.

C. House

8 All four couples dance house around.

D. Slide And Change

16 Repeat *B*.

E. House

8 All four couples dance house around.

Ballyhahill Half Set
Leathseit Bhaile Uí Chathail

1ST FIGURE *(Jigs: 80 bars)*

Bars   *A. Advance And Retire*

8   With hands crossed in front, couples advance and retire twice.

B. Dance At Home

8   Couples dance around at home.

C. Women Chain

8   Women chain right hands in centre, left arm to opposite man and around, quick right hand in centre, and back home to partner in waltz position.

D. Swing

8   Couples swing in place.

E. House

8   Couples dance house around.

F. Repeat

40   Repeat *A–E* with Advance And Retire in waltz position.

2ND FIGURE *(Jigs: 80 bars)*

A. Advance And Retire

8   With hands crossed in front, couples advance and retire twice.

B. House

8   Couples dance house around.

C. Women Across And Swing

8   Women dance straight across slowly to opposite man *[4 bars]* and swing *[4 bars]*.

D. House

8   Couples dance house around.

E. Women Home And Swing

8   Women dance straight across and swing.

F. Repeat

40   Repeat *A–E* with Advance And Retire in waltz position *[40 bars]*.

3RD FIGURE   *(Jigs: 48 bars)*

A. Advance And Retire

8   With hands crossed in front, couples advance and retire twice.

B. Opposites Swing

8   Top man and opposite woman swing in centre while Top woman and opposite man dance slowly anticlockwise half-way around square to opposite position. Swinging man delivers woman to her partner.

C. Advance And Retire And Swing

8   Couples advance and retire one time with hands crossed in front *[4 bars]* and then swing in place *[4 bars]*.

D. Opposites Repeat

24   Couples repeat *A–C* with Top woman and opposite man swinging in centre while Top man and opposite woman dance half-way around.

4TH FIGURE

(Jigs: 96 bars)

A. Advance And Retire

8   With hands crossed in front, couples advance and retire twice.

B. Women Chain

8   Women chain, right hands in centre, left arm to opposite man and around, quick right hand in centre, and back home to partner in waltz position.

C. Swing

8   Couples swing in place.

D. Advance And Retire And Dance At Home

8   In waltz position, couples advance once and retire once *[4 bars]* and then dance at home *[4 bars]*.

E. Advance And Retire And Dance At Home

8   Repeat *D*.

F. House

8   Couples dance house around.

G. Repeat

40   Repeat *B–F* with Advance And Retire in waltz position.

Barndance

Music: Barndance. *Partners stand facing each other, with no touching.*

Bars *A. Hop 1-2-3*

4   *(a)* Hop 1, right foot crossing in front of left; hop 2, left foot crossing in front of right; hop 1-2-3, right foot crossing in front of left.

12   *(b)* Repeat *(a)* three more times.

B. House

8   With the man holding his partner's hand in his own, couples dance house around (hop 1-2-3, hop 1-2-3).

C. Repeat

Repeat *A* and *B* as often as desired.

Barney Set

1ST FIGURE   *(Jigs: 96 bars)*

Opening position: All four couples face to centre with hands held in front.

Bars A. Body

8 *(a) Figure of eight:* Top couples, with hands crossed in front, and keeping shoulders abreast while dancing, dance 2 bars to face the Side couple on their left; then reverse 2 bars to opposite positions *[4 bars]*. Top couples repeat this movement to bring them back to their original positions *[4 bars]*.

8 *(b) Figure of eight:* Side couples dance *(a)*.

8 *(c) Swing:* All four couples swing in place adopting the céilí hold.

B. Figure

8 *(a) Advance and retire:* Top couples advance to the centre and retire twice with hands crossed in front.

4 *(b) Change:* Top couples, keeping the same hold and keeping shoulders abreast while dancing, dance 2 bars to face the Side couple on their left, then reverse 2 bars to opposite positions.

8 *(c) Advance and retire:* Top couples repeat *(a)*.

4 *(d) Change:* Top couples repeat *(b)* to bring them back to their original positions.

8 *(e) Swing:* Top couples swing in place.

C. Repeat

32 Side couples dance **B**.

2ND FIGURE   *(Jigs: 120 bars)*

Opening position: All four couples face to centre.

A. Figure

8 *(a) Swing:* 1st Tops man and 2nd Tops woman dance to the cen-

tre and swing, breaking out of the swing to return to their original positions during the last 2 bars.

8   *(b) Advance and retire:* Top couples advance and retire twice with hands crossed in front.

4   *(c) Change:* Top couples, with hands crossed in front and keeping shoulders abreast while dancing, dance 2 bars to face the Side couple on their left, then reverse 2 bars to opposite positions.

4   *(d) Advance and retire:* Top couples advance and retire once.

8   *(e) Swing:* 2nd Tops man and 1st Tops woman dance *(a)*.

8   *(f) Advance and retire:* Top couples repeat *(b)*.

4   *(g) Change:* Top couples repeat *(c)*.

4   *(h) Advance and retire:* Top couples repeat *(d)*.

8   *(i) Swing:* Top couples swing in place.

B. Repeat

56   Side couples repeat *A* with 1st Sides man and 2nd Sides woman swinging as in *(a)*, and 2nd Sides man and 1st Sides woman swinging as in *(e)*.

3RD FIGURE   *(Jigs: 64 bars)*

Opening position: All four couples face to centre.

A. Figure

8   *(a) Women chain:* Top women chain with right hands in the centre, give left hands to opposite men who dance around with them, dance to the centre again, chain with right hands and pass each other to return to their own partners.

8   *(b) Swing:* Top couples swing in place.

8   *(c) Little Christmas:* Top couples form circle, arms behind each other's backs. They swing in a circle clockwise.

B. Repeat

24   Side couples dance *A*.

C. Swing

8   All four couples swing in place.

4TH FIGURE   *(Polkas: 136 bars)*

Opening position: All four couples adopt the standard hold.

A. Body

8   *(a) Advance and retire:* Top couples advance to the centre and retire twice.

8   *(b) Swing:* All four couples swing in place.

B. Figure

8   *(a) Advance and retire:* Top couples advance and retire twice.

8   *(b) House:* Top couples dance house around inside.

8   *(c) Chain:* Top women chain with right hands in the centre, give left hands to opposite men who dance around with them, dance to the centre again, chain with right hands, and pass each other to return to their own partners.

8   *(d) Swing:* Top couples swing in place.

C. Figure

32   Side couples dance *B.*

D. Advance And Retire

8   All four couples advance and retire twice, using standard hold.

E. House

8   Top couples dance house around.

F. House

8   Side couples dance house around.

G. Chain

8 Top women repeat *B (c)*.

H. Chain

8 Side women dance as at *B (c)*.

I. Swing

8 All four couples swing.

Blacktown Set

1ST FIGURE. *OPPOSITES DANCE AROUND* *(Jigs: 288 bars)*

Bars **A. Pass Through**

8 Top couples pass through and swap places *[4 bars]*, men dancing in front of the women; pass back, swapping places *[4 bars]*.

B. Swing

8 Top couples swing.

C. Women Chain

8 Tops women dance to the centre, right hand in right, left hand to left with opposite man; the men dance in place but do not turn to follow the women. The woman dances under the man's left arm, turning clockwise, and dances around the man anticlockwise; then take right hands in the centre and back to her original position.

D. Swing

8 Top couples swing.

E. Repeat

32 Sides repeat *A–D*.

F. Figure

4 *(a)* Top couples advance and retire, right hand in right over the woman's shoulder.
4 *(b)* Change places, dancing clockwise around woman leading.
8 *(c)* Repeat *(a)* and *(b)* back to home.

G. Swing

8 Top couples swing.

H. Repeat

24   Repeat *F* and *G* with Sides leading.

I. Dance Around Opposite

16   Top woman and opposite man dance, passing right shoulder to right *[4 bars]*; turn anticlockwise and dance, passing right shoulder to right *[4 bars]*, turn anticlockwise and swing for 6 bars in the centre of the set; reverse to home *[2 bars]*.

J. Repeat

24   Top couples repeat *F* and *G*.

K. Dance Around Opposite

16   Top man and opposite woman dance *I*.

L. Repeat

24   Top couples repeat *F* and *G*.

M. Repeat

80   Side couples repeat *I–L*; Top couples join in the last swing.

2ND FIGURE. *THREE AND ONE PLUS CHRISTMAS*
(Reels: 176 bars)

A. Women Chain

8   Top women chain as at *1st Figure, C*.

B. Swing

8   Top couples swing, swinging to the centre of the set on the last 2 bars where Top woman joins 2nd Top couple.

C. Figure

2   (a) 2nd Top man holds his own partner's right hand in his right and 1st Top woman's left hand in his left, in front of the women. The line of three reverse to 2nd Top position; at the same time 1st Top man reverses to home.

4   (b) The line of three and Top man advance to the centre; reverse.

2   (c) The line of three advance; this time 2nd Top man turns the women under his raised arms, turning 1st Top woman clockwise and 2nd Top woman anticlockwise, and passes the women to Top man.

8   (d) Tops repeat (a)–(c), with Top man dancing with both women. On the last 2 bars when the two women turn they form a Christmas.

D. Christmas

8   Top couples swing in four.

E. Repeat

40 Tops repeat A–D with 2nd Top woman joining 1st Tops.

F. Repeat

40 Sides repeat A–D with 1st Side woman joining 2nd Sides.

G. Repeat

40 Sides repeat A–D with 2nd Side woman joining 1st Sides.

H. Swing

8   Swing to finish.

3RD FIGURE. CHANGE WOMEN
(Marches or Hornpipes: 88 bars)

A. Circle

8   Advance and retire twice.

B. House

8   All four couples house.

C. Circle

8   Advance and retire twice. On second retire the men take the women from the left home.

D. House

8   All four couples house with new partners.

E. Repeat

48   Repeat C and D three more times, until original partners meet at home.

Blackvalley Square Jig Set

1ST FIGURE. *STAR*   *(Slides or Jigs: 88 bars)*

Bars **A. Lead Around**

8   All lead around, men's right arm around the women's waists and women's left hand on the men's right shoulders.

B. Square

8   Couples slide to the position on their right, men with backs to the centre *[1 bar]* and dance in place, turning clockwise and ending with the women's backs to the centre *[1 bar]*. Slide to the next position with women's backs to the centre *[1 bar]*; dance in place, turning clockwise, ending with men's backs to the centre *[1 bar]*. Repeat until the four couples are back home *[4 bars]*.

C. House

8   All four couples dance around the house.

D. Right-Hand Star

8   1st Tops and 1st Sides, and 2nd Tops and 2nd Sides dance right-hand star.

E. Swing

8   All four couples swing.

F. Repeat

16   Repeat *B* and *C*.

G. Right-Hand Star

8   1st Tops and 2nd Sides, and 1st Sides and 2nd Tops dance right-hand star.

H. Repeat

16   Repeat *B* and *C* to finish.

2ND FIGURE. *SWING OPPOSITE*   (Slides or Jigs: 112 bars)

A. Lead Around

8   Lead around, as at *1st Figure, A*.

B. Square

8   Square, as at *1st Figure, B*.

C. House

8   All four couples dance around the house.

D. Swing Opposite

8   Top men swing opposite women.

E. Slide In And Out And Dance At Home

8   All four couples slide in and out *[4 bars]*; dance at home *[4 bars]*.

F. Swing

8   Top men swing own partners.

G. Repeat

16   Repeat *B* and *C*.

H. Repeat

24   Sides repeat *D–F*.

I. Repeat

16   Repeat *B* and *C* to finish.

3RD FIGURE. *SLIDE AND SWING*   *(Slides or Jigs: 208 bars)*

A. Lead Around

8   Lead around, as at *1st Figure, A*.

B. Square

8   Square, as at *1st Figure, B*.

C. House

8   All four couples dance around the house.

D. Dance At Home

8   Top couples dance at home.

E. Slide In And Out And Dance At Home

8   Top couples slide in and out *[4 bars]*; dance at home *[4 bars]*.

F. Swing Opposite

8   Top men swing opposite women.

G. Slide In And Out And Dance At Home

8   Repeat *E* with new partner.

H. Swing

8   Top men swing the woman to their left.

I. Slide In And Out And Dance At Home

8   Repeat *E* with new partner.

J. Swing Opposite

8   Top men swing opposite women.

K. Slide In And Out And Dance At Home

8   Repeat *E* with new partner.

L. Swing

8   Top men swing their own partner.

M. Repeat

24   Repeat *B–D*.

N. Repeat

64   Sides repeat movements *E–L*.

O. Repeat

16   Repeat *B* and *C* to finish.

4TH FIGURE. *SLIDE AND CHANGE*   (Slides or Jigs: 120 bars)

A. Lead Around

8   Lead around, Top men's right arm around the women's waists and women's left hands on the men's right shoulders; Top men hold left hands in the centre. Sides stand.

B. House.

8   Tops house around.

C. Half Square And Dance To Home

8   Top couples slide to position on the right *[2 bars]*, then slide to the position opposite *[2 bars]*; house to home *[4 bars]*.

D. Half Square And Dance To Home

24   Repeat *C* three more times.

E. House

8   Top couples house.

F. Repeat

56   Sides *A–E* to finish.

5TH FIGURE   *(Reels: 160 bars)*

A. Lead Around

8   Lead around as at *1st Figure, A*.

B. Side-Step

8   Men side-step to the right out of the set, then two threes; women side-step to the left into the centre, and two threes; repeat these movements, back to place.

C. Swing

8   All swing.

D. Home

8   Top couples dance at home.

E. Slide In And Out And Dance At Home

8   Top couples slide in and out *[4 bars]*; dance at home *[4 bars]*.

F. Swing

8   Top men swing opposite women.

G. Hook

8   Top men hook left arms and dance around for 6 bars; double the last 2 bars.

H. Repeat

24   Repeat *A–C*.

I. Repeat

32   Side couples dance *D–G*.

J. Repeat

24   Repeat *A–C*.

H. Square

8   The four couples dance sevens to the position to their right, turn slightly and reverse to the next position, dancing sevens *[4 bars]*. Repeat until back at home *[4 bars]*.

I. House

8   All house to finish.

Borlin Jenny Set

1ST FIGURE. *THE STAR*   (Reels: 88 bars)

Bars *A. Lead Around*

8   All couples join hands, crossed in front, and dance around with a skip-type threes step, anticlockwise until back home.

B. Advance And Retire

8   All couples, with hands crossed, advance and retire to the centre twice.

C. Star

4   (a) Top couples make a right-hand star, give right hands in the centre with the couple on the left, and dance around clockwise.

4   (b) Turn, give left hands in centre and dance back to home.

D. Square

16   All couples adopt waltz hold and, with a skip-like threes step, dance to the next position on the right in diamond formation. Dance two threes in position, half-turn and repeat in each position until back home.

E. House

8   All couples dance house around with a skip-type style.

F. Star

8   Side couples give right hands in the centre, with Top couple on the left (opposite couples making a star to above); turn and give left hands in the centre and back home.

G. Square

16   Repeat *D*.

H. House

16 Repeat *E*.

2ND FIGURE. *ADVANCE AND RETIRE* (Reels: 128 bars)

A. Lead Around

8 All couples lead around as at *1st Figure, A*.

B. Part

8 *(a)* All couples, with hands crossed, advance and retire twice.
8 *(b)* All women raise right hands and hold the man's right hand over her shoulder and dance around to opposite position.
8 *(c)* Repeat *(a)*.
8 *(d)* Repeat *(b)*, dancing back to place.

C. Square

16 All couples dance Square as at *1st Figure, D*.

D. House

8 All couples dance house around.

E. Part

32 Repeat *B*.

F. Square

16 Repeat *C*.

G. House

8 All couples dance house around.

3RD FIGURE. *SWING*   *(Reels: 120 bars)*

A. Lead Around

8   All couples lead around as at *1st Figure, A*.

B. Advance And Retire

8   All couples advance and retire to the centre twice, with hands crossed in front.

C. Part

8   *(a)* All women turn to the man on their right and swing.
8   *(b)* All couples advance and retire with new partner twice.
8   *(c)* All women return to their own partner and swing.

D. Square

16   All couples dance Square as at *1st Figure, D*.

E. House

8   All couples dance house around.

F. Part

24   Repeat *C*.

G. Square

16   Repeat *D*.

H. House

8   All couples dance house around.

4TH FIGURE. *SIDE-STEP*   *(Reels: 80 bars)*

A. Lead Around

8   All couples lead around as at *1st Figure, A*.

B. Part

4   (a) All couples side-step with partner, women crossing to the left in front, dancing sevens and two threes.

4   (b) All couples dance back to place, women passing behind partner on return.

C. Square

16   All couples dance Square as at *1st Figure, D.*

D. House

8   All couples dance house around.

E. Part

8   Repeat *B.*

F. Square

16   Repeat *C.*

G. House

8   All couples dance house around.

5TH FIGURE. *CHAIN*   (Reels: 112 bars)

A. Lead Around

8   All couples lead around as at *1st Figure, A.*

B. Part

16   (a) All women face partner, give right hand, turn in place, give left hand to the man and dance anticlockwise, while the men dance clockwise, passing their partner and back to home.

8   (b) All couples swing in place.

C. Square

16   All couples dance Square as at *1st Figure, D*.

D. House

8   All couples dance house around.

E. Part

24   Repeat *B*.

F. Square

16   Repeat *C*.

G. House

8   All couples dance house around.

6TH FIGURE. WHEEL   *(Reels: 112 bars)*

A. Lead Around

8   All couples lead around as at *1st Figure, A*.

B. Part

8   *(a)* All women give right hands in the centre and dance clock-wise; turn, give left hands in the centre and dance back to place.

8   *(b)* All men give right hands in the centre and dance clockwise; turn, give left hands in the centre and dance back to place.

8   *(c)* Men continue to hold left hands, place right hands on their partners' shoulders and dance around anticlockwise to home.

C. Square

16   All couples dance Square as at *1st Figure, D*.

D. House

8   All couples dance house around.

E. Part

24   Repeat *B*.

F. Square

16   Repeat *C*.

G. House

8   All couples dance house around.

Borlin Set
Seit Borlin

Opening position, except where indicated: All four couples join hands in front and face anti-clockwise around the circle, men on the inide.

1ST FIGURE *(Polkas: 152 bars)*

Bars **A. Lead Around**

8   All four couples dance anticlockwise around until back in original places. During the last 2 bars each man turns his partner clockwise under both arms and them adopts the standard hold.

B. Body

16   *(a) Polka:* All four couples dance 2 bars in place then dance around to the position to their right, turning clockwise *[4 bars]*. The four couples repeat these movements three more times to bring them back to their starting positions. (A commonly danced variation is where all four couples dance 2 bars in place as follows: men stamp on both feet and kick with right foot slightly lifted then dance 1 bar in place, while the women dance 2 bars in place. All couples then dance 2 bars around to the position to their right, turning clockwise. A combination of both variations is often seen and the 'stamp' is not always exclusive to the man.)

8   *(b) House:* All four couples dance house around.

C. Figure

8   *(a) House:* Top couples dance house around inside.

8   *(b) Square the house:* Top couples dance forward without turning, to the Side positions to their right; men dance, skip, Left-Right-L-R-L, and women skip, Right-Left-R-L-R *[2 bars]*. Using opposite steps men dance backwards and women forwards, the dancers in each couple dancing side-by-side to bring them to each other's original positions *[2 bars]*. The two couples dance halfway around the house inside to reach original positions *[4 bars]*.

8   *(c) Women chain:* Top women dance to the centre, chain with

right hands, then hook with left arms to opposite men who dance around with them, dance to the centre again, chain with right hands then return to their partners.

8   *(d) Swing:* Top couples swing in place using the céilí hold.

D. Body

24   All four couples repeat *B*.

E. Figure

32   Side couples dance *C*.

F. Body

24   All four couples repeat *B*.

2ND FIGURE   *(Polkas: 136 bars)*

A. Lead Around

8   All four couples dance anticlockwise around until back in original places. During the last 2 bars each man turns his partner clockwise under both arms and them adopts the standard hold.

B. Body

16   *(a) Polka:* All four couples dance 2 bars in place then dance around to the position to their right, turning clockwise *[4 bars]*. The four couples repeat these movements three more times to bring them back to their starting positions.

8   *(b) House:* All four couples dance house around.

C. Figure

8   *(a) House:* Top couples dance house around inside.

8   *(b) Square the house:* Top couples dance forward without turning, to the Side positions to their right; men dance, skip, Left-Right-L-R-L, and women skip, Right-Left-R-L-R *[2 bars]*. Using oppo-

site steps men dance backwards and women forwards, the dancers in each couple dancing side-by-side to bring them to each other's original positions *[2 bars]*. The two couples dance halfway around the house inside to reach original positions *[4 bars]*.

8   *(c) Square the house:* Repeat *(b)*

D. Body

24   All four couples repeat *B*.

E. Figure

24   Side couples dance *C*.

F. Body

24   All four couples repeat *B*.

3RD FIGURE   (Polkas: 168 bars)

A. Lead Around

8   All four couples dance anticlockwise around until back in original places. During the last 2 bars each man turns his partner clockwise under both arms and them adopts the standard hold.

B. Body

16   *(a) Polka:* All four couples dance 2 bars in place then dance around in 2 bars to the position to their right, turning clockwise *[4 bars]*. The four couples repeat these movements three more times to bring them back to their starting positions.

8   *(b) House:* All four couples dance house around.

C. Figure

8   *(a) House:* Top couples dance house around inside.

8   *(b) Square the house:* Top couples dance forward without turning, to the Side positions to their right; men dance, skip, Left-Right-

L-R-L, and women skip, Right-Left-R-L-R *[2 bars]*. Using opposite steps men dance backwards and women forwards, the dancers in each couple dancing side-by-side to bring them to each other's original positions *[2 bars]*. The two couples dance halfway around the house inside to reach original positions *[4 bars]*.

6 (c) *Advance and retire:* Top men take their partner's right hands in their right hands and advance to the centre and retire once. When they retire the women dance across into the men's left-hand sides, keeping the same hold.

2 (d) *Pass through:* Top couples release hands and advance to the centre again, this time passing through each other, men on the inside passing right shoulder to right shoulder, and women on the outside. Top couples turn in place in opposite positions.

6 (e) *Advance and retire:* Top couples repeat (c).

2 (f) *Pass through:* Top couples repeat (d).

8 (g) *Swing:* Top couples swing in place.

D. Body

24 All four couples repeat *B*.

E. Figure

40 Side couples dance *C*.

F. Body

24 All four couples repeat *B*.

4TH FIGURE   (Polkas: 184 bars)

Opening position: Top couples face anticlockwise around the circle, men on the inside with left hands held and right arms around the women's waists, and women with left arms on the men's shoulders.

A. Figure

8 (a) *Lead around:* Top couples dance anticlockwise until back in

their original places. During the last 2 bars each man turns his partner clockwise under both arms and then adopts the standard hold.

16   *(b) Polka:* Top couples dance 2 bars in place then dance around to the position to their right, turning clockwise *[4 bars]*. The Top couples repeat these movements three more times to bring them back to their starting positions.

8   *(c) House:* Top couples dance house around.

8   *(b) Square the house:* Top couples dance forward without turning, to the Side positions to their right; men dance, skip, Left-Right-L-R-L, and women skip, Right-Left-R-L-R *[2 bars]*. Using opposite steps men dance backwards and women forwards, the dancers in each couple dancing side-by-side to bring them to each other's original positions *[2 bars]*. The two couples dance halfway around the house inside to reach original positions *[4 bars]*.

24   *(e)* Repeat *(d)* three more times.

16   *(f) Polka:* Top couples dance 2 bars in place then dance around to the position to their right, turning clockwise *[4 bars]*. The Top couples repeat these movements three more times to bring them back to their starting positions

8   *(g) House:* Top couples dance house around.

B. Repeat

92   Side couples dance *A*.

5TH FIGURE   (Hornpipes: 160 bars)

Opening position: All four couples face anticlockwise around the circle, hands behind each other's backs, and men on the inside.

A. Body

16   All four couples dance anticlockwise for 2 bars, then use the double step for the next 2 bars to bring them into opposite positions. *[4 bars]*. This movement is repeated three more times with the couples finishing in original positions. (In practice, the

'opposite' and 'original' positions do move somewhat anti-clockwise as the *Body* progresses. When doubling the step, the women face the men with arms on the men's shoulders and the men place both hands around the women's waists, thus giving a balanced hold.)

B. House

8   All four couples dance house around using the doubled step.

C. Change Partners

8   The four women walk on to the next man on their right.

D. Repeat

32   Repeat *A*, *B* and *C* to bring the women around to the men opposite their original partners.

E. Repeat

32   Repeat *A*, *B* and *C* to bring the women around to the men to the left of their original partners.

F. Repeat

32   Repeat *A*, *B* and *C* to bring the women back to their original partners.

G. Repeat

24   Repeat *A* and *B*.

Caledonian Set
Seit Alban

Opening position, except where stated: All face centre, joining hands in a circle.

1ST FIGURE
(Reels: 128 bars)

Bars *A. Start*

8   *(a) Circle:* Advance and retire twice.
8   *(b) Home:* All four couples dance around at home.

B. Figure

16   *(a) Slide and change:* Top couples advance to centre and retire *[4 bars]*; dance half-way around the house to each other's places *[4 bars]*. Repeat movement to return to their own positions.
8   *(b) Home:* Top couples dance around at home.
16   *(c) Slide and change:* Top couples repeat *(a)*.

C. Middle

4   *(a) Slide:* All four couples advance to centre and retire once.
4   *(b) Home:* Side couples dance around at home.

D. Figure

40   Side couples dance *B*.

E. Finish

4   *(a) Slide:* All four couples advance to centre and retire once.
4   *(b) Home:* All four couples dance around at home.
8   *(c) House:* All four couples dance house around.

2ND FIGURE
(Reels: 96 bars)

A. Start

8   *(a) Circle:* Advance and retire twice.
8   *(b) Home:* All four couples dance around at home.

B. Figure

8 (a) *House:* Top couples dance around the house inside.
8 (b) *Home:* Top couples dance around at home.
8 (c) *House:* Top couples dance around the house inside.

C. Middle

4 (a) *Slide:* All four couples advance to centre and retire once.
4 (b) *Home:* Side couples dance around at home.

D. Figure

24 Side couples dance *B*.

E. Finish

16 Repeat Finish as at *1st Figure, E*.

3RD FIGURE   *(Reels: 192 bars)*

A. Start

8 (a) *Circle:* Advance and retire twice.
8 (b) *Home:* All four couples dance around at home.

B. Figure

8 (a) *Slide and home:* Top couples advance to centre and retire once
  [4 bars], and then dance around at home *[4 bars]*.
8 (b) *Slide and change:* Top couples advance to centre and retire *[4 bars]*; dance half-way around house to each other's place *[4 bars]*.
8 (c) *Slide and home:* Top couples repeat (a).
8 (d) *Slide and change:* Top couples repeat (b) to bring them back to their original positions.
8 (e) *Home:* Top couples dance around at home.
8 (f) *Slide and home:* Top couples repeat (a).
8 (g) *Slide and change:* Top couples repeat (b).
8 (h) *Slide and home:* Top couples repeat (c).
8 (i) *Slide and change:* Top couples repeat (d).

C. Middle

4   *(a) Slide:* All four couples advance to centre and retire once.

4   *(b) Home:* Side couples dance around at home.

D. Figure

72   Side couples dance *B*.

E. Finish

16   Repeat Finish as at *1st Figure, E*.

4TH FIGURE   *(Jigs: 224 bars)*

A. Circle

8   All four couples circle, advance and retire twice.

B. Dance In Place

8   All four couples dance in place.

C. House

8   Top couples house around each other.

D. Advance And Retire And Change Partners

8   Top couples advance and retire once *[4 bars]*; then men cross on right-hand side, turning twice, while women turn once *[4 bars]*.

E. House

8   Top couples house with their new partners.

F. Advance And Retire And Back To Partners

8   Top couples advance and retire, and men return to own partners.

G. House

8   Top couples house with their own partners again.

H. Dance In Place

8   Top couples dance in place, turning twice.

I. Repeat

40   Top couples repeat *C–G*.

J. Advance And Retire And Dance In Place

8   All couples advance, retire *[4 bars]* and dance in place *[4 bars]*.

K. Repeat

96   Repeat *C–J* with Side couples leading.

L. House

8   All couples house around.

5TH FIGURE   (Reels: 192 bars)

A. Start

8   *(a) Circle:* Advance and retire twice.
8   *(b) Home.* All four couples dance around at home.

B. Figure

8   *(a) House:* Top couples dance around the house inside.
8   *(b) Slide and change partners:* Top couples advance and retire *[4 bars]*; the couples separate and the men dance anticlockwise around each other to pick up the Side women to their left *[4 bars]*. The Side women dance on the spot for the last 4 bars.
8   *(c) House:* Top men and new partners dance around the house inside, starting and finishing at their new partner's position.
8   *(d) Slide and change partners:* Top men and new partners repeat *(b)*. Men move one place around to pick up opposite Top women.
8   *(e) House:* Top men and their new partners repeat *(c)*.
8   *(f) Slide and change partners:* Top men and new partners repeat

(b). Men move one place around again to pick up Side women.

8   (g) *House:* Top men and their new partners repeat (c).

8   (h) *Slide and change partners:* Top men and new partners repeat (b). Men move one place around again to pick up original partners.

8   (i) *House:* Top couples repeat (a).

C. Middle

4   (a) *Slide:* All four couples advance to centre and retire once.

4   (b) *Home:* Side couples dance around at home.

D. Figure

72   Side couples dance *B*.

E. Finish

16   Repeat Finish as at *1st Figure, E*.

6TH FIGURE   *(Hornpipes: 40 bars)*

Opening position: Couples adopt waltz hold.

A. Body

16   Couples advance to centre, retire back to starting place *[2 bars]*, then dance around to position of couple on their right *[2 bars]*. Repeat three more times, to end up back in original positions.

B. Slide

4   All four couples advance to the centre and retire once.

C. Home

4   All four couples dance around at home.

D. House

8   All four couples dance house around.

Caragh Lake Jig Set
Seit Loch Charra Port

1ST FIGURE   *(Jigs: 136 bars)*

Bars   **A. Lead Around**

8   *(a) Lead around:* All couples lead around in polka step holding
        crossed hands.

16   *(b) Square:* All couples square: slide 1-2, 1-2-3 to the corner *[2
        bars]*, turn slightly clockwise, the man reversing as they dance
        1-2, 1-2-3 to the position on the right *[2 bars]*. Dance 1-2-3, 1-2-
        3 through this position *[2 bars]*, turning clockwise, so that the
        man is facing the opposite poistion and dance 1-2-3, 1-2-3 with
        the man going forward to there *[2 bars]*. Repeat back to home.

8   *(c) Diamond* All couples dance the diamond: dance 1-2, 1-2-3 to
        each position, turning slightly there to continue around the set.

        B. Home

8   Top couples right hands in with couples on left, clockwise to
        home.

        C. Swing

8   All swing.

        D. Lead Around

32   Repeat *A*.

        E. Home

8   Side couples dance *B*.

        F. Swing

8   All swing.

        G. Lead Around

32   Repeat *A*.

2ND FIGURE   *(Jigs: 152 bars)*

A. Lead Around

32   Dance Lead Around, Square and Diamond as at *1st Figure, A*.

B. Body

8   *(a)* Top men cross over *[2 bars]* and swing opposite woman.
8   *(b)* Top men slide in and out; dance in place with opposite woman.
8   *(c)* Top men cross to home *[2 bars]* and swing own partner.

C. Lead Around

32   Repeat *A*.

D. Body

24   Side couples dance *B*.

E. Lead Around

32   Repeat *A*.

3RD FIGURE   *(Jigs: 248 bars)*

A. Lead Around

32   Dance Lead Around, Square and Diamond as at *1st Figure, A*.

B. Body

8   *(a)* Top men swing own partner.
8   *(b)* Top couples slide in and out and dance at home.
48   *(c)* Top men dance *(a)* and *(b)* with the three other women, moving into the women's place each time.
8   *(d)* Top men swing own partner.

C. Lead Around

32   Repeat *A*.

D. Body

32   Side men dance **B**.

E. Lead Around

32   Repeat **A**.

4TH FIGURE. *FACE THE HOB*   *(Jigs: 328 bars)*

A. Lead Around

32   Dance Lead Around, Square and Diamond as at *1st Figure, A*.

B. Home

8   Tops dance at home.

C. Slide In And Out

8   Tops slide in and out and dance at home. Both Tops stand in place, 1st Tops facing out, opposite Tops facing in.

D. Dance In Place

8   Side couples dance in place.

E. Slide And Line Up

8   Side couples slide in and out and dance into line behind 1st Tops (1st Sides go second).

F. Circle

8   All circle off, men left, women right; pick up partners in 2nd Top position and lead into place; 2nd Tops turn anticlockwise into their own place.

G. Lead Around

32   Dance Lead Around, Square and Diamond as at *1st Figure, A*.

H. Dance At Home

8 Sides dance at home.

I. Side In And Out

8 Slide in and out and dance in place, Sides dance in place with 1st Sides facing out.

J. Dance At Home

32 Tops dance at home.

K. Slide And Line Up

8 Slide in and out and dance in behind 1st Sides. Tops dance into line (2nd Tops go second).

L. Circle

8 Repeat F.

M. Repeat

144 Tops and Sides repeat A–J.

N. Lead Around

32 Repeat A.

5TH FIGURE   (Slides: 176 bars)

A. Lead Around

8 All lead around.

B. Home

32 (a) Top couples square inside four times (slide across, slide along opposite side and dance to home).

8 (b) Top couples dance around each other for four turns.

C. Repeat

40   Side couples dance *B*.

D. Repeat

40   Tops repeat *B*.

E. Repeat

40   Sides repeat *B*.

6TH FIGURE   *(Reels: 144 bars)*

A. Lead Around

8   All lead around, hands in front, to half-way. Man turns woman twice under right arm to home.

B. Advance And Retire

8   1st Tops advance, retire and dance in place.

C. Swing

8   Top men cross over and swing opposite woman.

D. Home

8   Top men hook left arms and dance around each other two-and-a-half times to home.

E. Lead Around

8   Repeat *A*.

F. Advance And Retire

24   1st Sides advance, retire and dance in place. Sides dance *C* and *D*.

G. Lead Around

8 Repeat *A*.

H. Advance

24 2nd Tops advance then dance in place. Tops repeat *C* and *D*.

I. Lead Around

8 Repeat *A*.

J. Advance And Retire

24 2nd Sides advance, retire and dance in place. Sides repeat *C* and *D*.

K. Lead Around

8 Repeat *A*.

7TH FIGURE   (Hornpipes: 160 bars)

A. Body

24 All couples body and house.

B. Circle And Women Move On

4 *(a)* All circle, advance, hop 1-2-3, stamp. Retire 1-2-3; dance in place, hop 1-2-3, hop 1-2-3.

4 *(b)* Women form a circle, advancing hop 1-2-3, stamp, and as they retire 1-2-3, the circle moves to the right; finish beside the man to the right.

C. Repeat

96 Repeat *A* and *B* three times.

D. Body

24 Repeat *A* with own partner.

Castle Set
Seit Chaiseal Muinhan

Opening position, except where stated: Couples adopt the standard position.

1ST FIGURE (Slides: 200 bars)

Bars *A. House*

8 Top couples dance around the house inside.

B. Pass Through

8 1st Tops and 2nd Tops advance towards each other and pass through, women in the centre, left shoulder to left *[4 bars]*. When they reach the opposite side each dancer turns clockwise on the spot. The two couples advance and pass back through to their own places, women in the centre, right shoulder to right, and turn clockwise to face in again *[4 bars]*.

C. Advance And Retire

8 Top couples join right hands in front. They advance to the centre and retire twice.

D. Swing

8 All four women turn to the men on their right and swing with them. At the end of the swing the women should end up to the right of their new partners.

E. Advance And Retire

8 All dancers join hands in a circle and advance to the centre and retire twice.

F. Swing

8 The women return to their original partners and all four couples swing in place.

G. Repeat

48   Top couples repeat *A–F*.

H. Repeat

48   Side couples dance *A–F*. When Sides dance the movement the women go to men on their left at *D*.

I. Repeat

48   Side couples repeat *A–F*. Women go to men on their left at *D*.

2ND FIGURE   (Polkas: 136 bars)

A. House

8   Top couples dance around the house inside.

B. Advance And Retire

4   Top couples join right hands in front. They advance to the centre and retire once.

C. Change

4   Top women dance straight across to the opposite man *[2 bars]* and swing once with him *[2 bars]*.

D. Wheel

8   Top men keep their hold on their new partners with their right arms and release their partners' right hands. Top women join right hands in the centre and Top couples form a straight line, each couple facing clockwise around the circle. They wheel around in a clockwise direction until back in men's place.

E. Swing

8   Top couples swing in place (men in their own place and women in the opposite places).

F. Repeat

32   Top couples repeat *A–E*. During the repeat the Top women return to their original partners.

G. Repeat

32   Side couples dance *A–E*. During their first time through the movement the Side women change partners.

H. Repeat

32   Side couples repeat *A–E*. During the repeat the Side women return to their original partners.

3RD FIGURE   *(Polkas: 200 bars)*

A. House

8   Top couples dance around the house inside.

B. Women Chain

8   Top women dance to centre, chain with right hands and pass each other; give left hands to opposite men and dance around them, the men turning with the women; dance straight back to own partners, give right hands to them and dance around them.

C. Swing

8   1st Tops man and 2nd Tops woman come out of chain to face each other in the centre, each with their back to the couple on their left. They swing in the centre. At the end of the swing they separate and dance back between the Side couples they had their backs to. Each group of three dancers links arms behind each others' backs.

D. Advance And Retire

16   1st Tops woman and 2nd Tops man advance to centre and retire

twice. While they are advancing and retiring the Side threes dance in place *[8 bars]*. Then the Side threes advance to the centre and retire twice while the Tops dance in place *[8 bars]*.

E. Swing

8   The four original couples reform and swing in place. The dancers should take 2 bars to dance into place and then join up and swing.

F. Repeat

48   Top couples repeat *A–E*. 1st Tops woman and 2nd Tops man dance the Figure at *C*, leading into the swing from the same direction as their partners did, and dancing in threes with the same couples as their partners.

G. Repeat

48   Side couples repeat *A–E*. 1st Sides man and 2nd Sides woman dance the movement at *C*.

H. Repeat

48   Side couples repeat *A–E*. 1st Sides woman and 2nd Sides man dance the movement at *C*.

4TH FIGURE   *(Hornpipes: 152 bars)*

Opening position: All dancers face to centre, joining hands in a circle.

A. House

4   1st Tops and 2nd Tops dance around to each other's place in 2 bars, using the normal hornpipe step (hop 1-2-3, hop 1-2-3) and then dance on around, back to their own places in 2 bars using the doubled hornpipe step (hop 1, hop 2, hop 3, hop 4).

B. Change

2   Top men dance straight across to the opposite women.

C. Clap And Stamp

2   Tops clap hands three times *[1 bar]*; dance on the spot *[1 bar]*.

D. House

4   Top men with their new partners repeat *A*.

E. Change

2   Top men dance straight across back to own partners.

F. Clap And Stamp

2   Top couples repeat *C*.

G. Repeat

16   Top couples repeat *A–F*.

H. House

4   Top couples repeat *A*.

I. Repeat

36   Side couples dance *A–H*.

J. Repeat

36   Top couples repeat *A–H*.

K. Repeat

36   Side couples repeat *A–H*.

5TH FIGURE   (Polkas: 264 bars)

Opening position: All dancers face to centre, joining hands in a circle.

A. Circle

8   Advance and retire twice.

B. House

8   Top couples dance around the house inside.

C. Slide And Change

4   *(a) Slide:* Top couples dance sideways to the centre. Men
     dance L-R-LRL and women, R-L-RLR *[2 bars].* They then dance
     back to their original places using the opposite steps *[2 bars].*

4   *(b) Change:* Top couples dance half-way around the house to
     each other's places.

8   *(c) Repeat:* Top couples repeat *(a)* and *(b)* to bring them back to
     their original places again.

D. House

8   Top couples dance around the house inside.

E. Women Chain

8   Top women dance to centre, chain with right elbows and pass
     each other; give left hands to opposite men and dance around
     them, the men turning with the women. Dance to centre again,
     chain with right hands and pass each other to join left hands
     with their partners' left hands; dance around them, ending up
     the outside the circle facing anticlockwise around, holding their
     partners' left hands in front and right hands behind. During the
     last 2 bars the other two couples dance into the same position.

F. Lead Around

16   All four couples dance around anticlockwise to the next posi-

tion *[2 bars]* and dance in place *[2 bars]*. This movement is repeated three more times until all couples are back in their original positions.

G. Repeat

64   Repeat *B–F*, with Side couples dancing the movements.

H. Repeat

64   Repeat *B–F*, with Top couples dancing the movements.

I. Repeat

64   Repeat *B–F*, with Side couples dancing the movements.

6TH FIGURE   *(Slides: 168 bars)*

Opening position: All dancers face to centre, joining hands in a circle.

A. Circle

8   Advance and retire twice.

B. Swing

8   All four couples swing in place.

C. Change Partners

8   All couples separate. Men dance 1 bar into the centre and then dance 1 bar on the spot while turning clockwise to face around the set in an anticlockwise direction. During the same 2 bars the women dance around anticlockwise to the next position to their right, level with the man at that position with whom they link up, arms around each other's backs. The four new couples lead around anticlockwise in 6 bars until they return to the men's original places.

D. Circle

8   All dancers face to the centre, joining hands in a circle, and advance to the centre and retire, twice.

E. Swing

8   All four couples swing in place, men in their original places and with new partners.

F. Repeat

40   Repeat A–E. The four women move on one place again.

G. Repeat

40   Repeat A–E. The four women move on one place again.

H. Repeat

40   Repeat A–E. The four women return to their original partners.

Cavan Reel Set
Seit Chabháin (Cor)

1ST FIGURE   *(Reels: 232 bars)*

Bars *A. Advance And Retire*

16   Top couples advance and retire, hands crossed in front *[4 bars]*;
      Side couples advance and retire *[4 bars]*; Top couples advance
      and retire *[4 bars]*; Side couples advance and retire *[4 bars]*.

      B. Swing

8   Four couples swing.

      C. Arch

4   *(a)* Top couples, right hand in right hand, advance and retire.
4   *(b)* Top couple make an arch under which opposite couple pass.
8   *(c)* Repeat *(a)* and *(b)* with the Top couple passing under.
8   *(d)* Top couples swing.

      D. Repeat

24   Side couples dance *C*.

      E. Women Chain

8   *(a) Top women chain:* Right hands in centre, give left hand to
      opposite man and dance around him (man does not turn); right
      hands in centre in waltz hold with partner.
8   *(b)* Top couples house.

      F. Repeat

16   Side couples dance *E*.

      G. Three In One

4   *(a)* Top couples hold right hands over women's right shoulder,
      advance and retire.

4   *(b)* They advance again. Top man takes opposite woman and retires in line of three. Single man also retires.

4   *(c)* They advance again, three and one. Opposite man takes women and all retire.

4   *(d)* They advance again. Man turns women out, men take hands around women's waists and women place hands on men's shoulders.

8   *(e)* Basket of four.

24   *(f)* Sides dance *(a)–(e)* with 1st Side couple leading.

24   *(g)* Tops repeat *(a)–(e)* with 2nd Top couple leading.

24   *(h)* Sides repeat *(a)–(e)* with 2nd Side couple leading.

H. Repeat

24   Repeat *A* and *B*.

2ND FIGURE   *(Reels: 168 bars)*

A. Advance And Retire

8   Circle, advance and retire twice.

B. Swing

8   Four couples swing.

C. Train

4   *(a)* Top couples advance and retire, right hand in right over women's shoulders.

4   *(b)* Change places, women leading and men following.

8   *(c)* Tops repeat back to place.

8   *(d)* Top couples swing.

D. Repeat

24   Side couples dance *C*.

E. Singles

8   *(a)* Top man and opposite woman dance to centre, passing right to right and dancing around each other *[6 bars]*; reverse to place *[2 bars]*.

8   *(b)* Top woman and opposite man repeat *(a)*.

8   *(c)* Top couples house.

24   *(d)* Side couples dance *(a)–(c)*.

F. Doubles

4   *(a)* Top couples pass through, right shoulder to right.

4   *(b)* Pass back, right shoulder to right.

8   *(c)* Side couples repeat.

4   *(d)* Men turn left, women turn right, and dance in the corner.

4   *(e)* All face own partner and dance in place.

G. Swing

8   Four couples swing.

H. Repeat

16   Repeat *A* and *B*.

Clare Lancers
Lannsuidhthe Co An Clár

Opening positions for all figures: All four couples join hands in front and face anticlockwise around the circle, men on the inside.

1ST FIGURE   *(Reels: 160 bars)*

Bars **A. Lead Around**

8   All couples dance anticlockwise around until back in original places. During the last 2 bars each couple changes to standard position by man turning woman clockwise under both arms.

    B. Swing

8   All four couples swing in place.

    C. Figure

8   *(a) Advance and swing:* 1st Tops man and 2nd Tops woman dance to centre, arriving left shoulder to left *[2 bars]*; turn clockwise to face each other *[2 bars]*. They join up and swing in place.

8   *(b) Square:* 1st Tops and 2nd Tops women and men dance around the side of a square inside, the women going anticlockwise and the men clockwise, taking 2 bars to dance along each side of the square. (Because 1st Tops man and Tops woman are starting from the mid-point of one side of the square, the steps they dance to the first 2 bars must be shortened.)

8   *(c) Swing:* At the end of *(b)* each dancer from Top couples goes to nearest dancer from the Side couples and swings with them.

8   *(d) Swing:* The four original couples reform and swing in place.

    D. Figure

32   Repeat *C*, with 2nd Tops man and 1st Tops woman leading.

    E. Figure

32   Repeat *C*, with 1st Sides man and 2nd Side woman leading.

F. Figure

32   Repeat *C*, with 2nd Sides man and 1st Sides woman leading.

G. House

8   All four couples dance house around, doubling the last 2 bars.

2ND FIGURE
(Reels: 192 bars)

A. Lead Around

8   All couples dance anticlockwise around until back in original places. During the last 2 bars each couple changes to standard position by man turning woman clockwise under both arms.

B. Swing

8   All four couples swing in place.

C. Figure

8   *(a) House:* 1st Tops dance around the house inside.

8   *(b) Turn the lady:* 1st Tops man turns his partner clockwise four times under his right arm, while dancing in place himself.

8   *(c) Pass by:* 1st Tops woman and man dance past each other to the Sides and turn. Man dances towards the Side couple to his right, woman towards Side couple to her left *[4 bars]*; then dance back to opposite sides and turn, Top woman taking man's hand and Top man taking Side woman's hand *[4 bars]*. During the last 2 bars 2nd Tops dance into place at other end of lines.

8   *(d) Advance and retire:* The two lines advance towards each other and retire twice; the second time retiring the end couples (here the Tops) do not retire but dance the 2 bars in place in centre.

8   *(e) Swing:* All four couples swing in place.

D. Figure

40   Repeat *C*, with 2nd Tops leading.

E. Figure

40   Repeat C, with 1st Sides leading.

F. Figure

40   Repeat C, with 2nd Sides leading.

G. House

8   All four couples dance house around, doubling the last 2 bars.

3RD FIGURE   (Reels: 144 bars)

A. Lead Around

8   All couples dance anticlockwise around until back in original places. During the last 2 bars each couple changes to standard position by man turning woman clockwise under both arms.

B. Swing

8   All four couples swing in place.

C. Figure

8   (a) *Women in:* The four women dance forwards to the centre and
8   back out twice. The second time dancing in they bow heads.
8   (b) *Men in:* The four men repeat (a).
     (c) *Wheel:* The four men link left hands in the centre and, with right arms around partners' waists, dance around anticlockwise.
8   (d) *Wheel back:* The four couples reverse direction, each dancer turning towards their partner to change direction. The men link right hands in centre and, with left arms around partners' waists, dance in a clockwise direction back around to original places.
16   (e) *Big Christmas:* All dancers link up together into a big circle, arms behind each others' backs and dance around clockwise *[8 bars]*. Then keeping the same position, they reverse direction and dance back around anticlockwise to their original places *[8*

bars]. When changing from the wheel position to the circle position at the beginning of this movement, dancers must again turn towards their partners on their way into the circle. When dancing anticlockwise the left foot should come down.

8   *(f) Swing:* All four couples swing in place.

D. Figure

56   Repeat *C*.

E. House

8   All four couples dance house around, doubling the last 2 bars.

4TH FIGURE   *(Reels: 192 bars)*

A. Lead Around

8   All couples dance anticlockwise around until back in original places. During the last 2 bars each couple changes to standard position by man turning woman clockwise under both arms.

B. Swing

8   All four couples swing in place.

C. Figure

8   *(a) House:* Tops dance around the house inside.
8   *(b) Lead Around:* 1st Tops and 2nd Tops lead around inside, dancing clockwise, women at the centre beside each other.
8   *(c) Wheel:* Each Top couple regains original place, passes it, and gives right hands to Side couple to their left. The two groups of four dancers, right hands joined, wheel clockwise *[4 bars]*, change direction, join left hands and wheel back anticlockwise *[4 bars]*.
8   *(d) Little Christmas:* Each group of dancers forms into a tight circle, arms around each others' backs, and dances around clockwise. Each man should have his right arm around his partner's back under her left arm so as to be able to move easily into the

swing. While dancing around in the Little Christmas each dancer's right foot should come down on the beat of the music.

8 *(e) Swing:* Circles break to original couples who swing in place.

D. Figure

40 Repeat *C*. 2nd Tops dance around the house at *(a)*. Dance anti-clockwise at *(b)*, the men at the centre beside each other. In *(c)*, Top couples join up with the Side couples to their right.

E. Figure

40 Repeat *C*. 1st Sides dance around the house at *(a)*.

F. Figure

40 Repeat *C*. 2nd Sides dance around the house at *(a)*. Dance anti-clockwise at *(b)*, the men at the centre beside each other. In *(c)* the Side couples join up with the Top couples to their right.

G. House

8 All four couples dance around, doubling the last 2 bars.

5TH FIGURE   *(Reels: 192 bars)*

A. Lead Around

8 All couples dance anticlockwise around until back in original places. During the last 2 bars each couple changes to standard position by man turning woman clockwise under both arms.

B. Swing

8 All four couples swing in place.

C. Figure

16 *(a) Chain and line up:* Starting with right hand to their own part-ners, women and men chain around clockwise and anticlock-

wise respectively. Half-way around, partners meet each other and swing once. The chain is then continued to bring all dancers back to their original places. They do not form couples again, but line up as follows:

On the first occasion the line forms up behind 1st Tops woman, facing out of the set in the direction of 1st Tops position. The order in the line should be: the leading couple, the couple to the left of the leading couple, the couple to the right of the leading couple, and the couple opposite the leading couple. As each couple gets into place in the line each woman should be in front of her partner.

8 (b) *Side-step:* The line splits. Men step sideways to the left and women sideways to the right *[4 bars]*; the lines then return in opposite directions, passing through each other to the opposite sides, and turn to face each other *[4 bars]*.

8 (c) *Advance and retire:* Lines join hands, advance and retire twice.

8 (d) *Dance to place and swing:* Each dancer dances back to their original place in 4 bars, then couples join up and swing in place for 4 bars (i.e. dancers at the end of the lines dance towards each other and meet in the centre. In the case of the other two couples, the woman and man that are in their correct places simply dance in place, and their partners dance across to them).

D. Figure

40 Repeat *C*, the line forming behind 2nd Tops.

E. Figure

40 Repeat *C*, the line forming behind 1st Sides.

F. Figure

40 Repeat *C*, the line forming behind 2nd Sides.

G. House

8 All four couples dance house around, doubling the last 2 bars.

Clare Orange And Green
Seit Co. An Chlair (Oraiste Agus Glas)

Opening position, except where indicated: All dancers face in to the centre.

1ST FIGURE   *(Reels: 168 bars)*

Bars   *A. Figure*

4   *(a) Advance and retire:* Top couples join hands in front and advance to the centre and retire, once.

4   *(b) Pass through:* Top couples release hands and advance to the centre again, this time passing through each other, women left shoulder to left and men on the outside. The couples having passed each other, each man dances to the right behind his partner, while she dances left (in order to reach the correct place) and they turn to face the centre again.

8   *(c) Repeat:* Top couples repeat *(a)* and *(b)* to bring them back to their own places.

8   *(d) Women chain:* Top women dance to the centre, chain with right hands and pass each other; give left hands to opposite men, turn clockwise under their left arms and dance around behind them, the men turning with the women. The women then chain again with right hands in the centre and dance back to their own partners.

B. Contrary

8   *(a) Circle and pass under:* Each of the couples that danced *A* turn to the left and form a circle of four with the couple there. Each group of four dancers dances around clockwise *[4 bars]*, then back anticlockwise *[4 bars]*. During the last 2 bars the women that danced *A* release their right hands and dance under their partners' left arms and the other women's right arms, followed by their partners. All couples dance into place.

8   *(b) House:* All couples adopt the standard hold and the couples that have danced in each circle now dance around each other and back into place.

C. Figure

24   Top couples repeat *A*.

D. Contrary

16   Repeat *B*.

E. Figure

24   Side couples dance *A*.

F. Contrary

16   Repeat *B*; Sides dance this movement on the opposite side.

G. Figure

24   Side couples repeat *A*.

H. Contrary

16   Repeat *F*.

2ND FIGURE. *BACK-TO-BACK*   (Single Jigs: 264 bars)

A. Back-To-Back

8   Each dancer and his or her partner dance around each other in an anticlockwise direction, turning clockwise as they go.

B. Swing

8   All four couples swing in place.

C. Figure

8   *(a) House:* 1st Tops dance around the house inside, ending up facing 2nd Tops.

8   *(b) Swing in three:* 1st Tops woman forms a tight circle with 2nd Tops and they swing in place while 1st Tops man dances around in his own place.

8   *(c) Advance and bow:* The three who swung at *(b)* form a straight
     line, man in the middle, and dance in place. The lone man ad-
     vances towards the woman on his left in the line *[2 bars]* and
     bows, then retires *[2 bars]*. He repeats this movement towards
     the woman on his right in the line, i.e. his own partner *[4 bars]*.

8   *(d) Swing in four:* The lone man joins the three dancers and they
     form a tight circle and swing in place, breaking away in time to
     be back in their respective positions by the eighth bar.

D. Contrary

16   All dancers dance this movement as at *1st Figure, B*.

E. Back-To-Back And Swing

16   Repeat *A* and *B*.

F. Figure

32   2nd Tops dance *C*.

G. Contrary

16   Repeat *D*.

H. Back-To-Back And Swing

16   Repeat *A* and *B*.

I. Figure

32   1st Sides dance *C*.

J. Contrary

16   Repeat *D*. Form a circle on the opposite side.

K. Back-To-Back And Swing

16   Repeat *A* and *B*.

L. Figure

32   2nd Sides dance *C*.

M. Contrary

16   Repeat *J*.

3RD FIGURE. *THE KNOT*   (Reels: 120 bars)

A. Figure

8   *(a) Pass through and return:* Top couples advance to the centre and pass through each other, women left shoulder to left, and men on the outside. Having passed each other, each couple dances into the position just vacated by the other couple, the woman passing in front of the man, and they turn again to face the centre *[4 bars]*. This movement is then repeated to bring them back to their own places *[4 bars]*.

8   *(b) Women chain:* Top women dance to the centre, chain with right hands and pass each other; give left hands to opposite men, turn clockwise under their left arms and dance around behind them, the men turning with the women. The women then chain again with right hands in the centre and dance back to their own partners.

8   *(c) Pass through and return to circle:* Top couples repeat *(a)* but with this difference: when returning to their original places the Top men dance into place and do not turn, but remain facing out of the set. Each Top man takes his partner's left hand in his left and the nearest other woman's right hand in his right. The Side men complete each group of four by taking their partner's left hand in their left, and the Top women's right hands in their right. Each Top couple forms a circle with the couple to their left, in which the women face in towards each other and the men are back-to-back, facing out.

8   *(d) Circle and turn in:* Each group of four dances around clockwise *[4 bars]* then back anticlockwise *[4 bars]*. During the last 2 bars the dancers raise their arms, hands still joined, the men

turn to face in and the joined hands are brought into the centre.

8 *(e) Dance on the spot:* The two groups dance on the spot in this position.

B. Contrary

16 All dance this movement as at *1st Figure, B*.

C. Figure

40 Side couples repeat *A*.

D. Contrary

16 Repeat *B*. Form a circle on the opposite side.

4TH FIGURE. *WOMEN WHEEL*   (Polkas: 120 bars)

Opening position: All four couples join hands in front and face anticlockwise around the circle, men on the inside.

A. Lead Around

8 All couples dance anticlockwise around until back in their original places.

B. Swing

8 All four couples swing in place.

C. Figure

8 *(a) Women wheel:* The four women join right hands in the centre and wheel around clockwise *[4 bars]*, then join left hands and wheel back anticlockwise to their starting positions *[4 bars]*. While the women dance the wheel each man dances on his own in an anticlockwise direction half-way around the outside to the opposite side of the set *[4 bars]*, then turns and dances back to meet his partner at home. As each man meets his partner he

takes her right hand in his right hand and the four men join left hands in the centre *[4 bars]*. The men now face anticlockwise on the inside and the women clockwise on the outside.

8 *(b) Dance in place:* Remaining in this position, each couple dances one step towards the centre and one back out again, and repeats this three more times.

8 *(c) Wheel and turn the lady:* The men wheel around anticlockwise and the women, moving with them, turn clockwise four times under their partners' raised arms as they dance around.

D. Contrary

16 All dance this movement as at *1st Figure, B.*

E. Lead Around

8 Repeat *A.*

F. Swing

8 All four couples swing in place.

G. Figure

24 Repeat *C.*

H. Contrary

16 Repeat *D.*

5TH FIGURE. *GALLOP* (Double Jigs: 144 bars)

Opening position: Couples adopt the standard position.

A. House

8 All four couples dance house around.

B. Swing

8   All four couples swing in place.

C. Figure

8   *(a) Gallop:* Top couples cross straight over to each other's place without turning, men on the inside *[2 bars]*; Side couples do likewise *[2 bars]*. Top couples cross back to their original places, women on the inside *[2 bars]*; Side couples do likewise *[2 bars]*.

8   *(b) Women chain:* Top women chain with right hands in the centre, dance over to opposite men and chain left hands with them *[2 bars]*; Side women do likewise *[2 bars]*. Top women chain again in the centre and return to their own partners *[2 bars]*; Side women do likewise *[2 bars]*.

16   *(c) Repeat:* Repeat *(a)* and *(b)*.

D. Contrary

16   All dance this movement as at *1st Figure, B*.

E. House

8   All four couples dance house around.

F. Swing

8   All four couples swing in place.

G. Figure

32   Repeat *C*; the Side couples perform each movement first.

H. Contrary

16   Repeat *D*.

I. House

8   All four couples dance house around.

6TH FIGURE. *CHANGE PARTNERS*   *(Reels: 120 bars)*

Opening position: All dancers face to centre, joining hands in a circle.

A. Circle

8   Advance and retire twice.

B. Swing

8   All four couples swing in place.

C. Figure

32   *(a) Dance in place and change partners:* Starting from the standard position, each couple dances 1 step towards the centre and 1 back to position again *[2 bars]*, and then repeats this movement once more *[2 bars]*. Then the couples separate: the four women, turning, dance in and out again alone as they did in the previous 4 bars with their partners, while each man dances in an anticlockwise direction around to the next woman, turning clockwise as he goes *[4 bars]*. The four women and their new partners join up and the same two movements are repeated three more times until the men return to their own partners again *[24 bars]*.

8   *(b) Swing:* All four couples swing in place.

32   *(c) Dance in place and change partners:* Repeat *(a)*. On this occasion the men remain in place while the women dance on in the opposite direction to that taken by the men; they dance around clockwise to the next man, turning anticlockwise as they go.

8   *(d) Swing:* All four couples swing in place.

D. Circle

8   All dancers face to the centre, joining hands in a circle, and advance to the centre and retire, twice.

E. House

8   All four couples dance house around.

Cloneen Jig

A two-hand dance, danced to a jig. Partners cross hands in front facing to the centre, men to the left of partner.

Bars *A. Advance And Change Places*

2   *(a)* Advance two threes.

2   *(b)* Without releasing hands, partners raise right hands and both turn clockwise to face the opposite direction. Right hand in right is held in front and left hand in left is held over the woman's left shoulder.

2   *(c)* Advance two threes.

2   *(d)* Repeat *(b)*, but turning anticlockwise.

B. Side-Step

4   *(a)* Partners take inside hands and side-step to the right, followed by jig step.

4   *(b)* Partners release hands and side-step past each other into their partner's position, finishing with the jig step.

4   *(c)* Partners side-step to the left back to their original position with the woman leading, holding the man's left hand in her right, finishing with the jig step.

4   *(d)* Men side-step anticlockwise to face their partner, while women dance side-step in place, finishing with the jig step.

C. Swing

8   Couples swing in céilí hold.

D. Repeat

Repeat *A–C* as often as desired.

Corca Dhuibhne Set
West Kerry Set

Opening position, except where stated: Couples adopt the standard position.

1ST FIGURE   *(Polkas: 144 bars)*

Bars *A. House*

16   All four couples dance around the house twice.

B. Lead Around

8   With arms behind each other's backs, all four couples lead
       around anticlockwise until they reach their own places.

C. Figure

8   *(a) Women wheel:* All four women join right hands in the centre
       and wheel around clockwise until they reach their own part-
       ners again *[4 bars]* and swing with them *[4 bars]*.

8   *(b) Swing:* All four couples swing in place.

8   *(c) Women chain:* Top women chain in the middle with right
       arms, chain with opposite men with left arms, chain in the mid-
       dle again and dance back to their partners.

8   *(d) House:* Top couples dance around the house inside.

D. Repeat

24   Repeat *A* and *B*.

E. Figure

32   Repeat *C*, with Side women and Side couples dancing at *(c)* and
       (d).

F. Repeat

24   Repeat *A* and *B*.

2ND FIGURE   *(Polkas: 192 bars)*

A. House

16   All four couples dance around the house twice.

B. Lead Around

8   With arms behind each other's backs, all four couples lead around anticlockwise until they reach their own places.

C. Double House

16   1st Tops dance around the house inside twice.

D. Repeat

32   Repeat *A* and *B*.

E. Double House

16   2nd Tops dance around the house inside twice.

F. Repeat

32   Repeat *A* and *B*.

G. Double House

16   1st Sides dance around the house inside twice.

H. Repeat

32   Repeat *A* and *B*.

I. Double House

16   2nd Sides dance around the house inside twice.

J. Repeat

32   Repeat *A* and *B*.

3RD FIGURE   *(Slides: 192 bars)*

A. House

16   All four couples dance around the house twice.

B. Lead Around

8   With arms behind each other's backs, all four couples lead around anticlockwise until they reach their own places.

C. Figure

16   *(a) Swing and show:* 1st Tops man and 2nd Tops woman advance to centre and swing *[8 bars]*; then dance around the house inside, breaking to own places at end of the movement *[8 bars]*.

16   *(b) Women wheel and swing:* All four women wheel around in the centre of the set with right hands until they reach own places *[4 bars]*, and then swing with their partners *[12 bars]*.

8   *(c) Lead around:* With arms behind each other's backs, all couples lead around anticlockwise to own places (walk this movement).

D. Repeat

40   Repeat *C*, 2nd Tops man and 1st Tops woman dancing at *(a)*.

E. Repeat

40   Repeat *C*, 1st Sides man and 2nd Sides woman dancing at *(a)*.

F. Repeat

40   Repeat *C*, 2nd Sides man and 1st Sides woman dancing at *(a)*.

4TH FIGURE   *(Slides: 192 bars)*

A. Slide

16   Couples slide to centre and back to places *[4 bars]*; dance halfway around to opposite places *[4 bars]*. Repeat to return to places.

B. Lead Around

8   With arms behind each other's backs, all four couples lead around anticlockwise until they reach their own places.

C. Figure

8   *(a) Women chain:* Top women chain in the middle with right arms, chain with opposite men with left arms, chain in the middle again and dance back to their partners.

8   *(b) House:* Top couples dance around the house inside.

D. Repeat

24   Repeat *A* and *B*.

E. Figure

16   Top couples repeat *C*.

F. Repeat

24   Repeat *A* and *B*.

G. Figure

16   Side couples dance *C*.

H. Repeat

24   Repeat *A* and *B*.

I. Figure

16   Side couples repeat *C*.

J. Repeat

24   Repeat *A* and *B*.

5TH FIGURE   *(Polkas: 152 bars)*

Opening position: All four couples join hands in front and face anticlockwise around the circle, men on the inside.

A. Lead Around

8   Holding hands in front, all four couples lead around anticlock-wise until they reach their own places.

B. Turn The Lady

8   When each couple reaches their own place the man turns the woman clockwise under his arms and the couples continue leading around till they reach their own places again.

C. Figure

16   *(a) Double house:* 1st Tops dance around the house inside twice.
16   *(b) Slide and change:* Top couples slide to the centre and back to their places *[4 bars]*, dance halfway around to each other's places *[4 bars]*. Repeat to return back to own places *[8 bars]*.

D. Figure

32   Top couples repeat C, with 2nd Tops dancing *(a)*.

E. Figure

32   Side couples dance C, with 1st Sides dancing *(a)*.

F. Figure

32   Side couples repeat C, with 2nd Sides dancing *(a)*.

6TH FIGURE *(see over for alternative)*   *(Slides: 224 bars)*

A. House

16   All four couples dance around the house twice.

B. Lead Around

8   With arms behind each other's backs, all four couples lead around anticlockwise until they reach their own places.

C. Figure

8   *(a) Circle:* All dancers join hands facing the centre and advance and retire twice.

4   *(b) Women wheel:* All women join right hands in the centre and dance three-quarters' way around to the men to the right of their original partners, stopping on the men's right-hand sides.

4   *(c) Men wheel:* All men join left hands in the centre and dance all the way around to their own places again.

8   *(d) Swing:* All four new couples swing in place.

D. Repeat

24   Repeat *A* and *B*.

E. Figure

24   Repeat *C* to bring the women around to the men opposite their original partners.

F. Repeat

24   Repeat *A* and *B*.

G. Figure

24   Repeat *C* to bring the women around to the men to the left of their original partners.

H. Repeat

24   Repeat *A* and *B*.

I. Figure

24   Repeat *C* to bring the women back to their original partners.

J. Repeat

24 Repeat *A* and *B*.

*ALTERNATIVE 6TH FIGURE   (Hornpipes: 120 bars)

A. House

8 All four couples dance around the house.

B. Double

8 All four couples dance around the house, using doubled step.

C. Change Partners

8 The four women walk on to the next men to their right.

D. Repeat

24 Repeat *A–C* to bring the women around to the men opposite their original partners.

E. Repeat

24 Repeat *A–C* to bring the women around to the men to the left of their original partners.

F. Repeat

24 Repeat *A–C* to bring the women back to their original partners.

G. Repeat

16 Repeat *A* and *B*.

Connemara Set
Seit Chonamara (Cor)

1ST FIGURE *(Reels: 160 bars)*

Bars *A. Lead Around*

16 All four couples lead around anticlockwise, holding crossed hands in front; turn the woman and lead around clockwise. All dance the last 2 bars facing their partner.

B. Swing

8 All couples swing in céilí hold *[6 bars]*, dancing out the last 2 bars facing into the set. This swing is danced throughout the set.

C. Advance And Retire

8 Holding crossed hands, Top couples advance and retire twice.

D. House

8 Top couples house around, still holding crossed hands *[6 bars]* and dance facing into the set *[2 bars]*.

E. Swing

8 Top couples swing in place.

F. Repeat

24 Side couples dance *C–E*.

G. Women Chain

8 Top women chain, right hands in the centre, left hand to the opposite man, going around him and turning under his arm; then pass back, right shoulder to right to place. Each man turns anticlockwise with the opposite woman, then turns clockwise in his own corner while his partner is crossing back to face him.

H. Swing

8   Top couples swing in place.

I. Repeat

16   Sides dance *G* and *H*.

J. Repeat

24   Top couples repeat *C–E*.

K. Repeat

24   Side couples dance *C* and *D*, then all couples swing in place.

2ND FIGURE   (Reels: 192 bars)

A. Lead Around

16   All couples lead around anticlockwise, holding crossed hands in front; turn the woman and lead around clockwise.

B. Swing

8   All couples swing in place.

C. Opposites Dance Around

8   Top man and opposite woman dance forward, passing right shoulder to right; move sideways to the right without turning and reverse back, passing left shoulder to left to face each other in the centre.

D. Swing

8   Top man and opposite woman swing in the centre, reversing to place during the last 2 bars.

E. Advance And Retire

8   Top couples advance and retire twice.

F. House

8   Top couples house around each other, holding crossed hands.

G. Swing

8   Top couples swing in place.

H. Repeat

40   Repeat *C–G* with 1st Side man (on the right) and opposite woman leading. This time, Side couples dance *E–G*.

I. Repeat

40   Repeat *C–G* with 2nd Top man and opposite woman leading.

J. Repeat

40   Repeat *C–G* with 2nd Side man and opposite woman leading.

3RD FIGURE   (Reels: 184 bars)

A. Advance And Retire

8   All advance and retire twice in a circle, dancers turning to face their partners as they retire the second time.

B. Swing

8   All couples swing in place.

C. Advance And Retire

8   1st Top couple, with the woman's hand on the man's shoulder and his arm around her waist, advance and retire; then advance and face each other in the centre.

D. Swing

8   1st Top couple swing in the centre *[2 bars]*, then dance into a

circle of four with the opposite couple, who dance in to meet them *[2 bars]*.

E. Swing

8   Top couples swing in four in the centre.

F. Chain

8   Top women chain.

G. Swing

8   Top couples swing in place.

H. Repeat

40   Side couples dance *C–G* with the couple on the right leading.

I. Repeat

40   Tops couples repeat *C–G* with 2nd Top couple leading.

J. Repeat

40   Side couples repeat *C–G* with 2nd Side couple leading. This time, all couples swing at *G*.

4TH FIGURE. *MAGGIE IN THE WOODS*   (Polkas: 96 bars)

A. Advance And Retire

8   All advance and retire twice in a circle.

B. Dance In Place

8   All couples dance in place, turning twice in waltz hold.

C. Advance And Retire And Change Partners

8   All circle, advance and retire twice, women moving on the

inside to the position on the right instead of retiring.

D. Change Position

8   With new partners, all dance to the position on the right, turning twice.

E. Circle And Change Partners

8   All circle again, women moving on to man opposite their own.

F. Change Position

8   All dance on to the next position on the right, turning twice.

G. Circle And Change Partners

8   All circle again, women moving on a third time.

H. Change Positions

8   All couples dance to next position on the right, turning twice.

I. Circle

8   All circle again, women moving back to their own partners.

J. Return To Place

8   All couples dance back to their own places, turning twice.

K. Swing

8   All couples swing in céilí hold to finish.

Corofin Plain Set
Seit Chora Finne

1ST FIGURE *(Reels: 112 bars)*

Bars *A. Lead Around*

8   All lead around anticlockwise, holding hands in front. Turn the woman clockwise under right arm only.

B. Swing

8   All face partner and dance one full turn clockwise around partner *[4 bars]*, then swing in place *[4 bars]*.

C. Cross Over

8   Top couples dance to opposite side, women going first, passing right shoulder to right, followed by men who pass left shoulder to left. All turn in towards partner on opposite side, women clockwise and men anticlockwise, then dance back to place.

D. Chain

8   Top women chain, right hands in centre, left arm around opposite man, right in centre again and back to place.

E. Swing

8   Top couples dance around partner and swing.

F. Pass Through

8   Top couples repeat *C*.

G. Swing

8   All dance around partner and swing.

H. Repeat

32   Side couples dance *C–F*.

I. Swing

8   All dance around partner and swing.

J. House

8   All house around.

2ND FIGURE   (Jigs: 104 bars)

A. Lead Around

8   Lead around as at *1st Figure, A.*

B. Swing

8   All dance around partner and swing.

C. Advance And Retire

8   Holding right hands in front, Top couples advance and retire;
     the man turns the woman clockwise to the opposite position.

D. Repeat

8   Top couples repeat C back to own position.

E. Repeat

16   Side couples dance C and D.

F. Repeat

16   Top couples repeat C and D.

G. Repeat

16   Side couples repeat C and D.

H. Swing

8   All dance around partner and swing.

I. House

8   All house around.

3RD FIGURE   (Reels: 176 bars)

A. Lead Around

8   Lead around.

B. Swing

8   All dance around partner and swing.

C. Opposites Dance Around

8   Top man and opposite woman dance clockwise around each other to opposite side, facing each other as they go *[4 bars]*; swing *[4 bars]* to finish on opposite side facing their own positions.

D. Dance Around

8   From the swing, still holding hands (men left to women's right), they dance back clockwise to their own positions beside their partner, giving their free hand to their partner's near hand *[2 bars]*. All now lead around anticlockwise to opposite position, breaking into couples after 2 more bars and dancing the last 2 bars in the opposite position.

E. Advance And Retire

8   Top man and opposite woman advance and retire twice, bowing on the last beat of the 8 bars.

F. Advance And Retire

8   **Top couples advance and retire once in waltz hold and then dance back to place.**

G. Repeat

32   Top couples repeat *C–F* with the other woman and man leading.

H. Swing

8   All dance around partner and swing.

I. Repeat

64   Side couples dance *C–G*, 1st Side couple on the left.

J. Swing

8   All dance around partner and swing.

K. House

8   All house around.

4TH FIGURE   *(Jigs: 240 bars)*

A. Lead Around

8   All lead around as at *1st Figure, A*.

B. Swing

8   All dance around partner and swing.

C. Chain

8   Top women chain.

D. Swing

8   Top couples dance around partner and swing.

E. House

8   1st Top couple house inside, to leave Top woman beside the opposite couple on the man's left.

F. Advance And Retire

8   Opposite man takes the women's outside hands in front. The three advance as the Top man retires alone. The three retire and advance again, then the man turns the woman on his left clockwise and the other woman anticlockwise to leave them beside the Top man. Women turn on the 6th bar.

G. Advance And Retire

8   The Top man and the women now advance, retire, advance and the women turn again to form a circle of four in the centre.

H. Swing

8   Top couples swing in four in the centre.

I. Repeat

48   Top couples repeat *C–H* with 2nd couple leading.

J. Swing

8   All dance around partner and swing.

K. Repeat

96   Side couples dance *C–I*.

L. House

16   All dance around partner and swing, then all house.

5TH FIGURE   *(Reels: 208 bars)*

A. Lead Around

8   All lead around as at *1st Figure, A*.

B. Swing

8   All dance around partner and swing.

C. Advance And Retire

8   Top couples advance, retire and dance in place.

D. Advance And Retire And Change Places

8   Top couples advance, retire and dance to opposite position.

E. Repeat

16   Top couples repeat *C* and *D* back to own places.

F. Chain

8   Top women chain.

G. Swing

8   Top couples dance around partner and swing.

H. Repeat

32   Top couples repeat *C–E*.

I. Swing

8   All dance around partner and swing.

J. Repeat

80   Side couples dance *C–H*.

K. House

16   All dance around partner, swing and then house.

6TH FIGURE   *(Polkas: 208 bars)*

A. Circle And Swing

16   All circle, advance and retire twice *[8 bars]*, then swing *[8 bars]*.

B. Body

16   In waltz hold, all couples dance in, back and turn on one position. Repeat three times to finish in own place.

C. House

8   All house around.

D. Circle

8   Circle again, advance and retire.

E. Change Partners And Swing

8   All women dance to the man on the right and swing.

F. Repeat

24   Repeat *B* and *C*.

G. Repeat

120   Repeat *D–F* three more times, finishing with own partner.

Cross Reel

(Reels: 328 bars)

Bars **A. Lead Around**

16   Couples take inside hands, make a half-turn to the right and with promenade step, dance round anticlockwise. On the eighth three, release hands and reverse. Partners again take inside hands and dance back in the opposite direction, turning in to original places on the last two threes.

B. Body

16   *(a) Sides:* Men side-step to the right behind their partners, and women side-step to the left in front to finish with two threes. All again side-step on in the same direction as before, and end with two threes. Each man takes the right hand of the woman on his right, both make a half-turn and all chain back as they came, to meet partners with right hand, in starting position and turn in place.

16   *(b) Full chain:* Partners face each other and chain round in a circle, the women going clockwise and the men going anticlockwise, giving right and left hands alternately until they meet in original places. Partners then dance a right-hand full turn in place.

16   *(c) Men interlace:* Men dance to the right in front of partners. They promenade round behind the women on their right and left-hand full turn with the same women. Men give right hands across in the centre and dance full round clockwise; left-hand turn women on the right of their original places, and right-hand turn partners in place.

8   *(d) Back-to-back:* Each man, holding his partner's right hand, side-steps towards the left of the contrary woman while his partner dances towards the left of the contrary man. The man then takes the left hand of the contrary woman while his partner takes the left hand of the contrary man. The four dancers thus form a circle, the men back-to-back and women

facing each other; all dance two short threes in this position. The man releases his partner's right hand, turns around the contrary woman and returns to his own partner, passing the other man right arm to right.

8   *(e) Exchange places:* 1st Tops and 1st Sides exchange places with side-step, while 2nd Tops and 2nd Sides do likewise. Partners all exchange places with one another with side-step. Then all dance back to places in the same manner, exchanging as before. (Note: Partners dance this movement without taking hands.)

C. 1st Figure

16   *(a) Figure of eight and ring:* The men of the Top couples dance in between, Side couples on their left, with promenade step; they circle clockwise round the men, dance in between couples again and circle anticlockwise round the women to their original places. All eight dancers now form a ring and side-step (with two threes) right and then left, falling into their original places on the last two threes.

16   *(b) Repeat:* The Side couples dance *C*.

D. Body

64   Repeat *B*.

E. 2nd Figure

16   *(a) Circle round and hands across:* The two Top couples advance, taking inside hands, and circle clockwise back-to-back, round each other to place. The Top couples now give right hands in the centre and dance full round, clockwise. The two couples then swing round each other and back to original places.

16   *(b) Repeat:* The Side couples dance *(a)*.

F. Body

64   Repeat *B*.

G. Finish

8   *(a) Circle:* All join hands in circle, hands at shoulder height.
16 Advance to the centre with promenade step and retire. Repeat.
    (b) All side-step anticlockwise and finish with two short threes;
    side-step back, finishing as before.
16 *(c)* Repeat *(a)*. All side-step clockwise and back.
8   *(d)* Each couple takes hands and swings around anticlockwise.

Cuchulainn Jig

Formation: Four couples.

(Jigs: 232 bars)

Bars *A. Circle*

16 All catch hands and side-step to the left, ending with rising step. Side-step back to places again, ending with rising step *[8 bars]*; repeat the movement, but begin the side-step to the right.

B. Body

8 *(a) Lines:* 1st Tops and 1st Sides catch hands in line, as do 2nd Tops and 2nd Sides. The dancers advance and retire, advance and pass through. When going through, pass right shoulder to right, and all turn by right.

8 *(b) Lines:* Repeat *(a)* and then back to places.

8 *(c) Side-step and pass partners:* Partners side-step past each other, ending with rising step and then back to places again, ending with rising step.

8 *(d) Slip sides:* Men side-step to the left and women to the right with rising step and back to places.

16 *(e) Lines:* Repeat *(a)* and *(b)*, but lines now comprise 1st Tops and 2nd Sides, and 2nd Tops and 1st Sides.

C. 1st Figure

8 *(a)* Tops advance to the centre and dance rising step *[4 bars]*; catch hands in the centre and side-step to the left, ending with rising step *[4 bars]*.

8 *(b)* Side-step to the right and away from each other, and end with rising step *[4 bars]*; partners turn in places *[4 bars]*.

16 *(c)* Sides dance *(a)* and *(b)*.

D. Body

48 Repeat *B*.

E. 2nd Figure

16 Tops, with hands raised in arch formation, exchange positions with Sides: 1st Tops over 1st Sides, and 2nd Tops over 2nd Sides; all dance rising step (hands should be placed by sides while dancing this step). Continue in circle and back to places. Tops and Sides alternate in raising hands.

F. Body

48 Repeat *B*.

G. Circle

16 Repeat *A* to finish.

Derradda (Co. Mayo) Set
Seit Dhoire Fhada

1ST FIGURE *(Jigs: 192 bars)*

Opening position: Couples face centre, hands crossed, right hands caught in front of left hands. Step: Polka threes.

Bars *A. Advance And Retire*

8   Four couples advance and retire twice.

B. Body

8   *(a)* Top couples exchange places (back-to-back, facing Side couples on left in doing so, women leading); return to own places.

8   *(b)* Top couples swing (céilí swing) in place.

8   *(c)* Top women chain: women advance to centre and each catch right elbows, and continue to opposite man, catching left elbow. Both turn in place. Women return to own partner, both making a full turn in place. Both couples dance a complete circle around each other.

8   *(d)* Top couples swing in place; Side couples, holding hands crossed in front, dance threes on the spot.

C. Body

32   Side couples dance *B*. At *(d)*, Top couples dance threes on the spot.

D. Threes

8   *(a)* Top man and opposite Top woman dance threes to centre and swing, while Top woman and opposite Top man dance threes on the spot.

8   *(b)* Top couples repeat *B (a)*.

E. Repeat

16   Repeat *D*, but at *(a)*, Top woman and opposite Top man swing in the centre.

F. Women Chain And Basket

8   (a) Top women chain. Women advance to centre and each catch right elbows, catch left elbows with opposite man who turns the woman fully around and places her on his left, the four forming a basket on the last two threes (women finish up on their partners' right, placing arms on men's shoulders).

8   (b) Wheel to the left for 6 bars and dance last 2 bars back to place.

G. Repeat

48   Side couples now dance *D–F*. At *D* (a), 1st Side man (on the left of Top man) and 2nd Side woman swing in the centre.

H. Advance And Retire

8   Repeat *A*.

I. Swing

8   All couples swing in place.

2ND FIGURE   (Polkas: 184)

Step: Polka Threes.

A. Slide In And Out

8   All couples, with partners facing each other and in waltz hold, slide sevens in towards centre and out, twice.

B. Lead Around

8   The four women lead around clockwise on the inside dancing threes (right shoulders to centre) and end up facing own partner in own place.

C. Swing

8 All couples swing.

D. Double Sevens

8 (a) Top couples exchange places, dancing two continuous sevens (men back-to-back), and cross back to own positions dancing two continuous sevens (women back-to-back).

8 (b) Top couples house around.

8 (c) Repeat (a).

8 (d) Repeat (b).

8 (e) Top women chain as at *1st Figure, B* (c).

8 (f) Top couples swing in place, while Side couples dance threes in place.

E. Repeat

48 Side couples dance *D*, but all couples swing for (f).

F. Repeat

8 Repeat *A*.

G. House

8 Couples house around slowly to opposite positions.

H. Repeat

16 Repeat *F* and *G*.

I. Slide In And Out

8 Repeat *A*.

J. Lead Around

8 Repeat *B*.

K. Swing

8 Repeat *C*.

3RD FIGURE   *(Reels: 152 bars)*

A. Advance And Retire

8   Forming a circle, all advance and retire twice, dancing hop threes.

B. Women Change

8   The four women catch right hands in the centre and move clockwise for three threes, then catch left hands in the centre, moving anticlockwise to end up facing the man on the right of starting-off position; move into position behind him. Men dance threes in place.

C. Men Star

8   Men dance *B*, but return to their own positions. Women dance threes in place.

D. Swing

8   All four new couples swing in place.

E. Lead Around.

8   With right hands caught over women's right shoulders and left hands caught in front, couples lead around anticlockwise back to starting-off positions.

F. Repeat

96   Repeat *B–E* until women arrive back with their own partner.

G. Advance And Retire

8   Repeat *A*.

Down Caledonian

This set is not danced in the normal way, but the dancers walk the movements in time to the music. During the 8-bar introduction before each figure, all the dancers bow to their own partners and then to the person on the side.

1ST FIGURE *(Single Reels: 80 bars)*

Bars *A. Wheel*

8   Top couples wheel.

   B. Swing

8   Top couples swing.

   C. Women Chain

8   Top women chain: right hand in the centre, left hook with the opposite man and dance around twice anticlockwise, right hand in the centre and back home to partner.

   D. Swing

8   Top couples swing.

   E. Repeat

32   Side couples repeat *A–D*.

   F. The Finish

8   Dancers stand in position, sometimes clapping hands.

2ND FIGURE *(Single Reels: 112 bars)*

   A. Men Dance Around

8   Top men pass left shoulder to left and turn twice anticlockwise while moving towards the Side woman to the left of their original position.

B. Swing

8   Top men swing the Side woman to their left while the Top women swing the Side man to their right.

C. Big Wheel

8   The four men put left hands in a wheel and dance around anti-clockwise with their new partners.

D. Repeat

16   Top men repeat A and B.

E. Big Wheel

8   Repeat C.

F. Repeat

16   Side men repeat A and B.

G. Big Wheel

8   Repeat C.

H. Repeat

16   Repeat A and B, swinging original partner.

I. Big Wheel

8   Repeat C.

J. The Finish

8   Dancers stand in position, sometimes clapping hands.

3RD FIGURE   *(Single Reels: 80 bars)*

A. Wheel

8   Top couples wheel.

B. Swing

8   Top couples swing.

C. Women Chain

8   Top women chain as at *1st Figure, C*.

D. Swing

8   Top couples swing.

E. Repeat

32   Side couples repeat *A–D*.

F. The Finish

8   Dancers stand in position, sometimes clapping hands.

4TH FIGURE   *(Single Reels: 112 bars)*

A. Swing

8   Top woman and opposite man swing in the centre.

B. Pass Through

8   1st Tops, holding inside hands, pass through on the inside with 2nd Tops on the outside, to the opposite position. 1st Top couple turn away from each other, the man turning anticlockwise and the woman turning clockwise while 2nd Tops turn in, the man clockwise and the woman anticlockwise. Both couples

return to their original position with 1st Tops on the outside and 2nd Tops holding hands on the inside.

C. Swing

8   Top men swing the Side woman on their left, while Top women swing the Side man on their right.

D. Repeat

24   Tops repeat *A–C* with 2nd Top woman and opposite man leading.

E. Repeat

24   Sides repeat *A–C* with 1st Side woman (to the right of 1st Tops) and opposite man leading.

F. Repeat

24   Sides repeat *A–C* with 2nd Side woman and opposite man leading.

G. The Finish

8   Dancers stand in position, sometimes clapping hands.

5TH FIGURE   (Single Reels: 224 bars)

A. Around The House

8   Top woman faces Top man with her back to the centre of the set; he reverses her to the centre of the set for 2 bars, then they dance around the house.

B. Advance And Retire

4   (a) The four women advance and retire to the centre, take three steps forward and slightly kick the left foot in the air. Step back on the left and kick the right foot in the air; step back on the

right and kick the left in the air; step back on the left and place it beside the right foot.

4   (b) The four men advance to the centre, turn clockwise and return to their partners.

C. Swing

8   All four couples swing.

D. Chain

8   All four couples, right hand in right, chain half-way around.

E. Lead Around

4   (a) Cross hands; four couples lead around to home.
4   (b) With hands crossed the couples turn clockwise twice in place.

F. Face Out, Face In

4   (a) Partners release left hands and form a circle, men facing out and women facing in. All dance the step starting on the right foot, kick right, kick left, kick right and kick left foot in the air.
4   (b) The men turn the women under their raised right arm into place.

G. Repeat

48   Repeat A–F with 2nd Tops leading.

H. Repeat

48   Repeat A–F with 1st Sides (couple to right of 1st Tops) leading.

I. Repeat

48   Repeat A–F with 2nd Sides leading.

J. The Finish

8   Dancers stand in position, sometimes clapping hands.

Down Quadrilles
Quadrille Co. An Dúin

Introduction for all figures: All dancers bow, first to their partners and then to the person on their other side [8 bars].

1ST FIGURE   (Polkas: 72 bars)

Bars *A. Cross Over*

8   Top couples cross over, women passing between the opposite couple [2 bars], pass left shoulder to left, to change places with their partners at the other side, women turning anticlockwise to face back and men turning clockwise [2 bars]. Pass back to place, women crossing between the opposite couple again [2 bars], pass partners, left shoulder to left. Turn to face partners, men anticlockwise and women clockwise [2 bars].

B. Swing

8   Top couples swing in place.

C. Chain

8   Top women chain, right hands in the centre, turn twice around the opposite man, left arm in left and take right hands in the centre on the way back.

D. Swing

8   Top couples swing in place.

E. Repeat

32   Side couples dance *A–D*.

2ND FIGURE (Polkas: 136 bars)

A. Advance And Retire

8 Top couples advance and retire twice (1-2-3, lift foot in and 1-2-3, lift foot back), holding right hand in right.

B. Cross Over

4 Top couples pass through (cross over) as at *1st Figure, A,* and pass partners, left shoulder to left to change places, men turning anticlockwise and women clockwise, then take right hands again.

C. Repeat

12 Top couples repeat *A* and *B*, dancing back to their own side.

D. Swing

8 Top couples swing in place.

E. Repeat

32 Top couples repeat *A–D*.

F. Repeat

64 Side couples dance *A–E*.

3RD FIGURE (Polkas: 136 bars)

A. Swing

8 Top man and opposite woman swing in the centre.

B. Line Up

8 They finish the swing, taking right hand in right, each of them

with backs to the couple right of their own position, and give their left hands to their own partners who face them, forming a line of four. All now dance (1-2 four times, lifting their foot on 2) on the spot *[4 bars]*; then each couple crosses on the right to the opposite position *[4 bars]*. Top man brings his partner past him into her position, while opposite woman turns slightly anticlockwise to face her partner as she crosses in front of him.

C. Advance And Retire

8 Top man and opposite woman (the swinging couple) advance and retire towards each other twice, bowing before they retire each time.

D. Advance And Retire And Pass Through

8 Both couples advance and retire, right hand in right *[4 bars]*; then pass through back to their own side and pass their partners left shoulder to left, as they cross to their own places.

E. Repeat

32 Top couples repeat *A–D*, Top woman and 2nd man leading.

F. Repeat

64 Side couples dance *A–E*. Man on the left and woman on the right swing first.

4TH FIGURE   *(Jigs: 200 bars)*

A. Chain

8 Top women chain, as at *1st Figure, C.*

B. Swing

8 Top couples swing in place.

C. Swing Into Line

8   While 2nd Top couple stand in place right hand in right, with the woman facing out of the set, 1st Top couple swing, moving across the set as they do so. Top woman finishes facing the 2nd man, on his left-hand side and she takes his left hand in left. He is now facing the two women, holding their hands.

D. Three And One

16   2nd man and the women dance across the set and back, as Top man retires to place *[4 bars]*; then cross again, both women turning in (towards 2nd Top man) to give their free hands to 1st Top man *[4 bars]*. He now crosses over and back with the women, over again and all four form a circle in the centre *[8 bars]*.

E. Christmas

8   Top couples swing in four in the centre.

F. Repeat

48   Top couples repeat A–E, 2nd couple leading.

G. Repeat

96   Side couples dance A–F, couple on the right leading.

5TH FIGURE   *(Jigs: 152 bars)*

A. Advance And Retire

8   All advance and retire twice holding hands in a circle (1-2-3, kick when advancing; 1-2-3, cross free foot over the other when retiring).

B. Swing

8   All couples swing in place.

C. Chain

8 Top women chain, as at *1st Figure, C*.

D. Gallop

8 Top couples dance in *[1 bar]*, back *[1 bar]*; then gallop (1-2-3-4-5-6-7, dancing 1 on the leading foot) across on the right *[2 bars]*. They dance in *[1 bar]* and back *[1 bar]* on the opposite side, moving to their right slightly; then gallop back to place *[2 bars]*.

E. Repeat

32 Repeat *A–D*, Side couples dancing *C* and *D*.

F. Repeat

64 Repeat *A–E*.

G. Repeat

16 All repeat *A* and *B* to finish.

Dublin Set

1ST FIGURE   *(Polkas: 152 bars)*

Bars **A. Lead Around**

8   All lead around.

     B. Swing

8   All swing.

     C. Circles And Arches

8   *(a) Big circle:* Everyone catches hands in a circle; advance and retire twice.

8   *(b) Small circles and arches:* Retiring from the big circle the second time, the dancers break into two small circles, Tops catching hands with the couple on their right (the following movement is danced without releasing hands). Tops make an arch which sides Sides dance under, then Sides dance under their own arch. Everyone marks time. Sides make an arch which Tops dance under, then Tops dance under their own arch. Everyone dances back to place.

8   *(c)* Repeat *(a)*.

8   *(d)* Repeat *(b)* with Tops dancing with the couple on their left.

     D. Swing

8   All swing.

     E. Cartwheel

8   At the end of the swing the men move into the centre with their right shoulder and catch the right arm of the man in front, creating a cartwheel formation; dance backwards until they are back in their own place. Face out. At the same time the women advance one position to the right; mark time. Return, dancing backwards to own position; mark time and face in.

F. Star

32   With everyone back to place, men facing out, women facing in, all catch hands. The following movement is like a slow chain, with the women moving in an anticlockwise direction and the men clockwise:

Everyone advances for 2 bars, releases left hands and moves on in the direction given above; women are now on the inside facing out. Then everyone advances for 2 bars, releases right hands and moves on in the direction given above.

Repeat this whole movement until everyone meets their own partner in their own place; the man turns the woman under into place.

G. Swing

8   All swing.

H. Circles And Arches

32   Repeat C with Sides making the arch first at *(b)*.

I. Swing

8   All swing.

J. House

8   All house around.

2ND FIGURE   *(Jigs: 176 bars)*

A. Circle

8   All dancers catch hands in a circle, advance and retire twice.

B. Arches

24   Men advance and retire, advance again and catch hands, forming arches. Women advance under the arches and everyone

catches hands behind. Everyone dances to the left using jig step until back in place. Men form arches again, women advance and retire under them. Men advance, release hands and retire.

C. Swing

8   All swing.

D. House Around

8   All dance house around.

E. Waves

32   Tops lead around to opposite place and the man turns the woman under with both hands to opposite man. Advance and retire twice with new partner. While retiring the woman dances under the man's arms, to change places with him. Lead around back to own place and turn the woman under back to her own partner. Lead all the way around; Tops and Sides turn the woman under.

F. Repeat

16   Repeat C and D.

G. Waves

32   Sides dance E.

H. Repeat

16   Repeat C and D.

I. Arches

24   Repeat B.

J. Circle

8   Repeat A.

3RD FIGURE   (Hornpipes: 104 bars)

This part of the Dublin Set commences with the four couples facing in at the normal positions but after the first movement the entire dance is conducted from the four corners. The waltz hold is not used; instead, a more informal hold with partners holding both arms just above the elbow, is adopted.

A. Men Lead Off

8   The four men each dance in front of the woman on their left, around behind her and back to their own partner; catch elbows and turn into the corner on their right which will be their position for the rest of the hornpipes.

B. Square

8   Men starting with their backs to the centre, all four couples dance four sevens (seven to each corner) back to place.

C. Change Places

16   Tops hop in, 2-3, hop out, 2-3, and change places; hop in, 2-3, hop out, 2-3, and back to place. Sides repeat.

D. Hands In

16   Tops give right hands in and dance around, then left hands in. For the last 2 bars of left hands in, each Top man takes the opposite woman with his left hand and turns her under into the position that was originally on his left (and originally on the woman's right) so that he is facing in an anticlockwise direction and the woman is facing clockwise. At the same time as Tops put left hands in, Sides vacate their position (which Tops will occupy) by giving left hands to the person opposite them, the man turning the woman under and into the position vacated by Tops (again men go to the Top position on their left, women to the right) so that men are facing in an anticlockwise direction, women clockwise. Everyone dances back to place in a chain movement, except that no-one catches hands and thus it is a

weave rather than a chain, women moving on the inside first. At the end of this movement everyone meets their own partner in the opposite place to their original position. Turn the woman under.

E. Square

8   Repeat *B*.

F. Change Places

16   Repeat *C* with Sides dancing first.

G. Hands In

16   Sides dance *D*.

H. Square

8   Repeat *B*.

I. House Around

8   Everyone houses around to finish, ending up where they started in the usual set-dancing places.

4TH FIGURE   *(Reels: 160 bars)*

A. Lead Around

32   Sides dance clockwise, Tops anticlockwise as follows: Tops face the couple on their right. Advance and retire once and, turning the woman under, swap places with that couple, lining up again in the same direction, i.e. Sides clockwise, Tops anticlockwise. While swapping places, Sides always dance on the inside, Tops on the outside. Facing the next couple, advance and retire again and swap places again, continuing on in this manner until back to place.

B. House And Advance And Retire

16   House in place, and advance and retire twice.

C. House

8   House in place. At the end, Top couples split to join Side couples in two lines, facing in (Top man and 2nd Top woman join 1st Sides, and 2nd Top man and Top woman join 2nd Sides).

D. Advance And Retire

8   (a) Men advance and retire at the same time as women retire and advance; women advance and retire as men retire and advance.

8   (b) Men give right hands to the woman on their left, full turn in place; everyone gives right hands in with the two people opposite and turn the woman under into the opposite place.

8   (c) Men advance and retire at the same time as women retire and advance; women advance and retire as men retire and advance.

8   (d) Men give right hands to the woman on their left; full turn in place. The four dancers in the middle put right hands in, dance back to place and turn the woman (partner) under. At the same time the four dancers on the outside mark time for 2 bars then catch right hands with the person opposite (partner) and turn the woman under into place. Everyone should be back in place.

E. House And Advance And Retire

16   Repeat B.

F. House

8   Repeat C, with Sides splitting. 1st Side man and 2nd Side woman join 2nd Tops; 2nd Side man and 1st Side woman join 1st Tops.

G. Advance And Retire

32   Repeat D.

H. House And Advance And Retire

16   Repeat B.

Duke Reel

A round dance for three couples who stand in a ring holding hands.

(Reels: 264 bars)

Bars **A. Rings**

8 (a) *Rings:* All side-step in a ring anticlockwise, finishing with two short threes. Side-step clockwise, finishing as before.

B. Body

16 (a) *Sides:* Partners side-step past each other, the men passing behind, finishing with two short threes. Side-step back to places, the men dancing in front, and finish as before
The men now do a similar movement with the woman on their left, the woman passing behind when going right, and in front when returning.

8 (b) *Link arms:* Partners link right arms and dance a full turn clockwise [*2 bars*]; each man then links left arm with the woman on left of original position, and turns anticlockwise [*2 bars*]. Repeat to finish in original positions [*4 bars*].

8 (c) *Interlace:* Partners face each other and pass, with promenade step, right shoulder to right; on around circle, passing alternately on either side as in any chain movement, except that the hands are not taken.

16 (d) *Advance and retire:* All join hands in a ring and advance towards the centre. All retire and advance again, but on retiring release non-partners' hands and go into position for *B*.

B. 1st Figure

16 (a) *Figure of eight:* With promenade step, couple 1 advance towards couple 2 while couple 3 stand idle. The woman of couple 1 passes between the other pair, followed by the man; but while the woman makes a figure of 8 by passing round the woman and then the man, the man of couple 1 passes round the man and then the woman. This leaves couple 1 on the inside of couple 2 and they join hands in a ring. All four side-step clock-

wise, finishing with two short threes and the partners take both hands and swing back to places.

16 *(b) Repeat:* (a) is then danced by couple 2, who pass through and dance with couple 3 while couple 1 stand idle.

16 *(c) Repeat:* (a) is then danced by couple 3 who pass through and dance with couple 1.

C. Body

48 Repeat *A*.

D. 2nd Figure

16 *(a) Right and left chain:* Couples 1 and 2 now perform the right and left chain. Each man gives right hand to opposite woman and both move forward in a semi-circle, men clockwise, women anticlockwise. Continue to meet partner with left hand, then opposite woman again with right hand and on to own partner, with left hand to finish in position, thus completing the chain. Both couples then dance complete circle around.

16 *(b) Repeat:* Couples 2 and 3 dance *(a)*.

16 *(c) Repeat:* Couples 5 and 1 dance *(a)*.

E. Body

48 Repeat *A*.

F. Finish

8 Partners hold hands, crossed, and swing round in couples anti-clockwise.

Dungarvan Polka Set

1ST FIGURE   *(Polkas: 72 bars)*

Opening position: Top couples adopt standard hold, Side couples face the centre.

Bars A. Figure

4   (a) *Slide:* Top couples slide to the centre and back once.

4   (b) *Swing:* Top couples swing in place.

8   (c) *Chain:* Top women chain with right hands in the centre, hook left hand with left hand of opposite men who dance around with them. The women then dance back to place, passing right shoulder to right shoulder.

8   (d) *House:* Top couples dance house around inside.

4   (e) *Slide:* Top couples repeat *A*.

4   (f) *Swing:* Top couples swing in place.

B. Figure

32   Side couples dance *A*.

2ND FIGURE   *(Polkas: 104 bars)*

Opening position: Top couples adopt standard hold, Side couples face the centre.

A. Figure

4   (a) *Slide:* Top couples dance to the centre and retire once, with hands crossed in front and facing each other as follows: men dance sevens into the centre (L-R-L-R-L-R-L), the three steps on the right foot being heel-toe-heel. The women dance sevens: R-L-R-L-R-L-R *[2 bars]*. Couples repeat this movement with opposite steps to bring them back to place *[2 bars]*.

4   (b) *Change:* Top couples dance anticlockwise around to each other's place, each woman dancing in front of the man and turning once clockwise under the men's right arms.

4   (c) *Slide:* Top couples repeat *A*.

4   *(d) Change:* Top couples repeat *B*.

8   *(e) Swing:* Top couples swing in place.

B. Repeat

24   Top couples repeat *A*.

C. Repeat

24   Side couples dance *A*.

D. Repeat

24   Side couples repeat *A*.

3RD FIGURE   (Polkas: 120 bars)

Opening position: All four couples face the centre. 1st Sides couple is to the right of 1st Tops couple in this set.

A. Figure

8   *(a) Swing and change places:* 1st Tops man and 2nd Tops woman advance to the centre and swing while their dancing partners exchange places, crossing anticlockwise. 1st Tops man and 2nd Tops woman come out of the swing with their backs to their partners who are now in opposite positions.

8   *(b) Dance around:* 1st Tops man and 2nd Tops woman dance around each other anticlockwise in the centre, bowing to each other before returning to their original partners.

4   *(c) Slide:* Top couples dance to the centre and retire once in waltz hold.

4   *(d) Half house:* Top couples dance half way around the house, to their original positions.

24   *(e) Repeat:* Top couples repeat *(a)–(d)* with 2nd Tops man and 1st Tops woman swinging in *(a)*.

4   *(f) Slide:* Top couples repeat *(c)*.

4   *(g) Swing:* Top couples swing in place.

B. Figure

56 Side couples dance *A*, with 1st Sides man and 2nd Sides woman swinging at *(a)*, and 2nd Sides man and 1st Sides woman swinging in *(e)*.

4TH FIGURE. *BRING UP THE FIGURE* (Polkas: 216 bars)

Opening position: All four couples face the centre. 1st Sides couple is to the right of 1st Tops couple in this set.

A. Figure

8 *(a) Women chain:* Top women chain with right hands in the centre, hook left hand with left hand of opposite men who dance around with them. The women then dance back to place, passing right shoulder to right shoulder.

8 *(b) House:* Top couples dance around the house inside.

16 *(c) Bring up the figure:* 1st Tops slide into the centre and back once *[4 bars]* and dance in place *[4 bars]*, turning once. Repeat this movement once.

8 *(d) House:* Top couples dance house around.

8 *(e) Women chain:* Top women repeat *(a)*.

8 *(f) House:* Top couples dance house around.

16 *(g) Bring up the figure:* 2nd Tops dance *(c)*.

8 *(h) House:* Top couples dance house around.

8 *(i) Women chain:* Top women repeat *(a)*.

8 *(j) House:* Top couples dance house around.

4 *(k) Slide:* Top couples dance to the centre and retire once in waltz hold.

4 *(l) Swing:* Top couples swing in place.

B. Figure

104 Side couples repeat *A*, with 1st Sides dancing *(c)* and 2nd sides dancing *(g)*.

5TH FIGURE   *(Polkas: 88 bars)*

Opening position: All four couples face the centre joining hands in a circle.

A. Circle

8   All four couples advance and retire twice.

B. Swing

8   All four couples swing.

C. Figure

8   *(a) Circle and change partners:* All four couples advance and retire twice in a circle. When retiring the second time each woman leaves her own partner and dances into position on the right-hand side of the man on her right.

8   *(b) Swing:* All four couples swing new partners.

D. Figure

16   Repeat *C*, women moving on one more place.

E. Figure

16   Repeat *C*, women moving on one more place.

F. Figure

16   Repeat *C*, women moving on one more place to return to their original positions.

Dunmanway Set
Seit Dhún Mánmhaí

1ST FIGURE. *SINGLE CHAIN* *(Polkas: 104 bars)*

Bars **A. Body**

16 All couples adopt waltz hold, dance two threes in place and turn to next position. Repeat in each position until back home.

B. Part

8 *(a)* Top couples house around each other.
8 *(b)* Top women chain, right hands in centre, left to opposite man, turn in place, and women return to own partner while men dance in position.
8 *(c)* Top couples swing in place.

C. Body

16 All couples repeat *A*.

D. Part

8 Side couples dance *B*.

E. Body

16 All couples repeat *A*.

2ND FIGURE. *SHOW THE LADY* *(Slides: 144 bars)*

A. Body

16 All couples adopt waltz hold, slide to centre and out again, 1-2 and 1-2-3, and dance to opposite position. All slide to centre and out again, and dance to home.

B. Part

8   (a) Top couple Show the Lady by housing around within the square once until back to home.

8   (b) Top couple slide into centre and out, and turn once in place.

C. Body

16   All couples repeat A.

D. Part

16   Top side couple dance B.

E. Body

16   All couples repeat B.

F. Part

16   Opposite Top couple repeat B.

G. Body

16   All couples repeat A.

H. Part

16   Opposite Side couple dance B.

I. Body

16   All couples repeat A.

3RD FIGURE. BASKET   (Polkas: 288 bars)

A. Body

16   All couples adopt waltz hold, dance two threes (in and out) and turn to next position. Repeat in each position until back home.

B. Part

8   *(a)* Top couples house around each other.

8   *(b)* Top women chain, right hands in centre, left to opposite partner, turn in place, and return to home while man dances in place.

8   *(c)* Top couples swing in place.

8   *(d)* Top couples dance two threes (in and out) twice and turn once in place.

8   *(e)* Top couples take right hand in right. Top couple dance to opposite Tops. Opposite man holds Top woman's left hand in left and turns both women once towards himself into a straight line of three, facing 1st Top man. 1st Top man takes inner hands of both women, and all four dance back to centre of square. Both women turn outwards one full circle, ending with women facing women and men facing men.

8   *(f)* All four hold hands behind backs and swing in basket. All four break circle on last 2 bars of swing and retire to original positions.

8   *(g)* Top women chain, right hands in centre, left to opposite partner, turn in place and return to home while men dance in place.

8   *(h)* Top couples swing in place.

C. Repeat

64   1st Side couples dance *B*. Top Side couple advances (i.e. couple on right of 1st Tops) at *B*, *(e)*.

D. Repeat

64   Top couples repeat *B*. Opposite Top couple advances at *B*, *(e)*.

E. Repeat

64   2nd Side couples repeat *B*. Opposite Side couple advances (i.e. couple on left of 1st Tops) at *B*, *(e)*.

F. Body

16   All couples repeat *A*.

4TH FIGURE (Slides: 144 bars)

A. Body

16 All couples adopt waltz hold and dance as at *2nd Figure, A*.

B. Part

8 (a) All women give right hands in centre, dance around clockwise one-and-a-half times, passing their own partner and advancing to opposite man.

8 (b) All couples swing in place.

C. Body

16 All couples repeat *A*.

D. Part

8 (a) All men give left hands in centre and dance around anticlockwise one-and-a-half times, passing their original position and advance to opposite position.

8 (b) All couples swing in place (with own partner now in opposite positions).

E. Body

16 All couples repeat *A*.

F. Part

8 (a) All women give right hands in centre, dance around, clockwise one-and-a-half times to own position.

8 (b) All couples swing in place.

G. Body

16 All couples repeat *A*.

H. Part

8 (a) All men give left hands in centre and dance around anti-

clockwise one-and-a-half times to original position.

8　*(b)* All couples swing in place.

I. Body

16　All couples repeat *A*.

5TH FIGURE. *ROUND THE HOUSE*　　　*(Polkas: 208 bars)*

A. Lead Around

16　All couples face anticlockwise, with man's right arm around woman's waist and woman's left hand on man's shoulder, and dance two threes on to next position and two threes in place. Continue until back at home

B. Body

16　All couples adopt waltz hold, dance in place two threes and turn to next position. Repeat in each position until back home.

C. Part

8　*(a)* All women give right hands in centre, dance around clockwise *[4 bars]*, turn, give left hands in the dance back, passing own partner and advancing to the next man on the right of original position *[4 bars]*.

8　*(b)* All men give right hands in centre, dance around clockwise, turn, give left hands in and dance back to original position.

8　*(c)* All couples swing in place, now with new partner.

D. Body

16　All couples repeat *B*.

E. Part

24　Repeat *C*.

F. Body

16 All couples repeat *B*.

G. Part

24 Repeat *C*.

H. Body

16 All couples repeat *B*.

I. Part

24 Repeat *C*, bringing women back to original positions.

J. Body

16 All couples repeat *B*.

K. Lead Around

16 All couples repeat *A*.

Durrow Threshing Set
Seit Dharmagh Ua nDuach

1ST FIGURE *(Jigs: 184 bars)*

Bars **A. Lead Around**

16   All couples lead around, holding right hands. Dance 2 bars, battering, in each position on the way around.

B. Turn The Ladies

8   Top couples dance around the centre anticlockwise, women in front, turning clockwise under the men's right hands in each position.

C. Advance And Retire

8   Still holding right hands, Top couples advance to the centre, batter on the spot, retire and batter on the spot.

D. Big Wheel

16   Top men join left hands and lead around the centre again, turning the woman with the right hand and battering in each position.

E. Swing

8   Top couples swing in céilí hold. Men start the swing facing out.

F. Repeat

40   Side couples dance *B–E*.

G. Repeat

80   Repeat *B–F*. All couples swing at *E* during the last 8 bars.

2ND FIGURE   *(Polkas: 136 bars)*

A. House

8   Top couples house around in waltz hold.

B. Chain

8   Top women chain, right arms in the centre, left arms around opposite man, right arms in the centre again and left arms around their own partners.

C. Opposites Swing

8   Top man and opposite woman swing in the centre *[6 bars]*. They finish the swing facing their own partners and dance back to face them *[2 bars]*.

D. Swing

8   Top couples swing in place.

E. Repeat

32   Side couples dance *A–D*, with 1st Side couple on the right. 1st Side man and opposite woman dance *C*.

F. Repeat

32   Top couples repeat *A–D*. Top woman and opposite man dance *C*.

G. Repeat

32   Side couples repeat *A–D*. 1st Side woman and opposite man dance *C*, and all couples swing at *D*.

3RD FIGURE   *(Polkas: 264 bars)*

A. House

8   Top couples house around.

B. Arches

8   Top couples take their partners' near hands. They dance across to the other side, with the 2nd couple passing under an arch made by the Top couple, the 2nd woman dancing in front of the man. In opposite position all turn in to their partners, take their other hands and face back towards home, women now on the left of their partners. Repeat the movements dancing back to home, the 2nd couple making the arch this time and the Top couple passing under.

C. Chain

8   Top women chain. Top woman turns into place beside her partner.

D. Swing Across

8   Top man places his right arm over his partner's shoulder, taking her hand. Opposite couple swing, moving across to leave the woman beside the Top man, who places his arm over her shoulder, taking her hand. 2nd man takes the women's other hands.

E. Three And One

8   The three advance as the 2nd man retires to place [2 bars], then the women turn to join the 2nd man, Top woman clockwise and 2nd woman anticlockwise [2 bars]. All dance back to the centre [2 bars] and the women turn out again to form a circle [2 bars].

F. Swing

8   Top couples swing in four. The men's hands are around the women's waists, and the women's hands on the men's shoulders.

G. Chain

8   Top women chain.

H. Swing

8   Top couples swing in place.

I. Repeat

64 Side couples dance *A–G*, with 1st Side couple on the right leading.

J. Repeat

64 Top couples repeat *A–G*, with 2nd Top couple leading.

K. Repeat

64 Side couples dance *A–F*, with 2nd Side couple leading. All swing for 8 bars at the end.

4TH FIGURE   (Hornpipes: 152 bars)

A. House

8   Top couples house to the other side and double back to place *[4 bars]*; men dance across, clap and stamp facing the opposite woman *[4 bars]*.

B. House

8   Top couples repeat *A* with opposite person.

C. Repeat

16 Repeat *A* and *B*.

D. House

4   Top couples house to the other side and double back to place.

E. Repeat

36 Side couples dance *A–D*.

F. Repeat

72 Top couples, then Side couples repeat *A–D*.

5TH FIGURE   (Polkas: 144 bars)

A. House

8 Top couples house around each other.

B. Advance And Retire And Cross Over

32 With men's arms around the women's waists and women's hands on the men's shoulders, Top couples advance and retire twice *[8 bars]* then cross anticlockwise to the opposite side *[4 bars]*. Side couples advance and retire twice and cross over, starting 2 bars behind Top couples. All repeat the same movements, starting in opposite positions and finishing back at home.

C. Women's Chain

8 All women chain, Side women starting 2 bars behind Top women. They dance back to face their partners in waltz hold.

D. Reverse Polka

16 All couples, with women reversing and men going forward, dance to the position on their right *[2 bars]* and turn once in place there *[2 bars]*. Repeat the movements three more times to get around to home.

E. Repeat

64 All dance *A–D* again, with Side couples leading.

F. Swing

8 All couples swing in place.

6TH FIGURE
(Jigs: 152 bars)

A. Circle

8   All circle, advance battering, retire dancing 1, 2, 1-2-3-4, advance and retire again.

B. Swing

8   All couples swing in place.

C. Lead Around

16   All lead around, moving forward to each position [2 bars] and stopping there while the men batter [2 bars].

D. Women Move On

8   Circle again and women move on to the position on the right.

E. Swing

8   All swing new partners.

F. Repeat

96   Repeat C–E until back in own position; swing own partners.

East Galway Set
Seit Ghaillimh Thoir

This set comes from the Killimor area of Galway. Its formation is different from other sets. The opening position has partners facing each other in the corners of a square, i.e. Front and Back couples rather than Tops and Sides. This set should be seen danced to appreciate the style and footwork.

1ST FIGURE   *(Reels: 56 bars)*

Bars **A. House**

8   All house around, hands crossed at front and keeping square formation.

B. Ducks

8   The women lead around inside the set, followed by men. As they reach home positions the man dances back to his own place and turns clockwise in place to meet the woman, who has danced around to get back to place.

C. Swing

8   All swing own partner.

D. Repeat

24   Repeat *A–C*.

2ND FIGURE   *(Reels: 72 bars)*

A. House

8   House as at *1st Figure, A*.

B. Advance And Retire

4   All advance and retire. This is danced as half set.

C. House

4   House to opposite position.

D. Repeat

8   Repeat *B* and *C* to home.

E. Swing

8   Swing own partner.

F. Repeat

32   Repeat *A–E*.

3RD FIGURE   *(Reels: 88 bars)*

A. House

8   House as at *1st Figure, A*.

B. Advance And Retire

4   Advance and retire as at *2nd Figure, B*.

C. House

4   House to opposite position.

D. Repeat

8   Repeat *B* and *C* to home.

E. House

8   All house.

F. Swing

8   Swing own partner.

G. Repeat

40 Repeat *A–F*.

4TH FIGURE   *(Jigs: 88 bars)*

A. House

8   House as at *1st Figure, A*.

B. Advance And Retire

4   Advance and retire as at *2nd Figure, B*.

C. Home

4   All dance at home, turning once clockwise *[4 bars]* with partner, hands crossed.

D. Advance And Retire

4   Repeat *B*.

E. Home

4   Repeat *C*.

F. House

8   All house.

G. Swing

8   Swing partner.

H. Repeat

40 Repeat *A–G*.

5TH FIGURE *(Reels: 104 bars)*

A. House

8 House as at *1st Figure, A*.

B. Advance And Retire

4 Advance and retire as at *2nd Figure, B*.

C. Women Cross Over

4 Women cross over to opposite man, passing right shoulder to right shoulder. Turn clockwise in centre and turn in to face man who dances, turning once in place.

D. Swing

8 Swing new partner.

E. Repeat

8 Repeat *B* and *C*, back to home.

F. House

8 All house.

G. Swing

8 Swing partner.

H. Repeat

48 Repeat *A–G*.

Eight-Hand Jig

Position of the dancers:

1
B A

4 G   **F 3**
H   **E**

C D
2

A, C, E and G are men; B, D, F and H are women.
AB are leading Tops, CD opposite Tops; EF leading Sides and GH opposite sides.

Bars **A. Lead Round**

8 Dancers half right turn and lead around a complete circle. Release hands, about turn inwards. Man takes partner's right hand in his left and both lead back to place.

B. Body

8 *(a) Sides:* Men side-step to right behind partner, ending with 'rise and grind', while women side-step to the left in front. All side-step back to place, men in front, women behind, ending with rise and grind

16 *(b) Skip across:* The four men cross to opposite women, Tops a fraction before Sides, all passing right arm to right. Turn women with left hand, pass to woman on right of original position and turn with right hand. Men cross to opposite women as before, turn with left hand, pass to own partner and turn with right hand once in place.

16 *(c) Swing into line:* Leading Tops half-turn in place to face outward from the circle; at the same time the other couples swing into line behind leading Tops, the position of the dancers now is as shown over:

New position of the dancers:

> **1** A B
>
> **3** E F
>
> **4** G H
>
> **2** C D

Partners of the leading couple (AB) turn outward from each other, man to left, woman to right, and lead around to place vacated by opposite Tops (CD); the man is followed by the other men, and the woman by the women. Partners of the leading couple turn in towards each other and, taking hands, lead up to place, being followed in like manner by the remaining couples. All release hands, all half turn inwards to face partners and dance rising-step on both feet; partners take hands and turn into original positions.

16   *(d) Set all-round:* Partners take right hands and turn half-round; men, retaining partner's hand, take left hand of woman on left, so that men are then all facing outwards, women facing inwards. All dance rising-step. Release right hands, men turn around woman on left and return to own partner with right hand, and turn once in place. Leading Tops and leading Sides dance around each other while opposite Tops and opposite Sides do likewise.

C. 1st Figure

16   *(a) Advance and retire:* Leading and opposite Tops men take partner's left hands in their right, both advance to meet the opposite couple and retire to place *[4 bars]*. Repeat the movement. Both couples then dance a complete circle around each other.

16   *(b) Repeat:* Sides dance *(a)*.

D. Body

56 Repeat *B*.

E. 2nd Figure

16 *(a) Tops chain:* The man gives his right hand to opposite woman and both move forward in a semi-circle, men clockwise, women anticlockwise. Continue to meet partner with left hand, opposite woman again with right hand and on to own partner with left hand to finish in position, thus completing the circular chain.

16 *(b) Right hand to opposite woman:* Leading and opposite Tops men advance to woman opposite, give right hand and turn once in place; return to own partner, give left hand and turn once in place. Both men advance to centre, take right hand and turn once; advance to opposite woman, give left hand and turn once in place. Return to own partner and take her hands. Both couples dance around each other and back to place.

32 *(c) Repeat:* Side couples dance *(a)* and *(b)*.

F. Body

56 Repeat *B*.

G. Finish

40 All dancers join hands in a circle, forearms bent sharply upwards and elbows held in to the sides. Advance to centre, retire, advance again and retire. All side-step anticlockwise and finish with two short threes; side-step back, ending with two short threes. Advance and retire twice as before. All side-step clockwise and back. All couples take hands and swing around to the right to finish off.

Eight-Hand Reel

Diagram 1. Position of the dancers:

```
                    1
                   B A


        4 G              F 3
          H              E


                   C D
                    2
```

A, C, E and G are men; B, D, F and H are women.
Assume that couple 1 (AB) are nearest the music; they are leading Tops, 2 (CD) are opposite Tops; 3 (EF) are leading Sides, and 4 (GH) opposite Sides. Couples 1 and 4, and 2 and 3, are said to be contrary to each other.

Bars **A. Lead Around**

16 Dancers half right turn and lead around a complete circle. Release hands and about turn inwards. The man takes his partner's right hand in his left and both lead back to place.

B. Body

16 *(a) Extended sides:* Men side-step to right behind partners, women side-step to the left in front; finish with two short threes. All again side-step on in same direction as before; end with two short threes. The dancers' new position is shown in Diagram 2.

Diagram 2.

```
                    1
                   H E


        4 A              B 3
          D              C


                   G F
                    2
```

Each man takes the right hand of woman next to him on his right and both make a full turn; all now chain back as they have come, to meet partners, with right hand, in starting position, and turn in position.

32 (b) *Skip across:* Dancers A and C now exchange places to the side-step, ending with two short threes; E and G follow suit, facing each other, right arm to right when crossing. Turn woman with right hand and pass on to woman on left of original position; give left hand and turn in place. The new positions are shown in Diagram 3.

Diagram 3.

1
B G

4 C   F **3**
H   A

E D
2

A and C again change places to the side-step as before, ending with two short threes; E and G follow suit. Turn women with left hand, pass on to meet own partner, with right hand, in original position and turn in place.

16 (c) *Return chain:* Men are now in original position, holding partner's right hand in own right; men give left hand to woman on right, women give left hand to men on left. All chain around, giving right and left hand alternately until meeting own partner again with right hand at opposite side of the circle. Turn right around partner and chain back to original position, meeting partner with right hand and turning in place.

16 (d) *Back-to-back:* The man, holding his partner's right hand, side-steps towards the left of contrary woman, while his partner dances towards the left of contrary man. The man then takes the left hand of contrary woman while his partner takes the left hand of contrary man, the four dancers thus forming a circle, men being back-to-back, women facing each other. All dance two short threes. The man releases his partner's right hand, turns around contrary woman and returns to his own partner, passing the other man right arm to right. Partners take hands and dance around the couple opposite to contrary couple (i.e. couples 1 and 3 in the diagrams dance around each other, as do couples 2 and 4).

C. 1st Figure: Advance And Retire

16 (a) *Advance and retire:* Leading and opposite Tops men take partner's left hand in their right, both advance to meet opposite couple and retire to place *[4 bars]*. Repeat the movement. Both couples then dance a complete circle around each other.

16 (b) *Repeat:* Sides dance (a).

D. Body

80 Repeat B.

E. 2nd Figure

16 (a) *Women chain:* Top women advance, give right hands in centre and continue to opposite man, giving left hand. Both turn in place. Women return to own partner, both making a full turn in place. Both couples dance a complete circle around each other.

16 (b) *Repeat:* Sides dance (a).

F. Body

80 Repeat B.

G. Finish

40 All dancers join hands in a circle, forearms bent sharply upwards and elbows held in to the sides. Advance to centre, retire, advance again and retire. All side-step anticlockwise and finish with two short threes; side-step back ending with two short threes. Advance and retire twice as before. All side-step clockwise and back, then the couples take hands and swing around to the right to finish off.

Every Man's Chance

Bars *A. Advance And Retire*

8   All dancers advance to the centre and retire twice.

B. Swing

8   All couples swing in place.

C. Women In

8   The women advance to the centre and retire twice.

D. Men In

8   The men advance to the centre and retire twice. The women move on one place to the right while the men are advancing the second time.

E. Repeat

Repeat *A–D*; swing *[8 bars]*.

Fáinne Uladh
The Ring Of Ulster

A reel for four couples. Leading/1st Tops A B; 2nd Tops C D; 1st Sides E F;
2nd Sides G H. (B, C, F and G are men; A, D, E and H are women.)

Bars   **A. Lead Around**

16   Lead around and back to places.

B. Body

8   *(a)* Partners take right hand in right and side-step to the centre,
finishing on two short threes *[4 bars]*. On the second two three
all drop hands and face outwards; re-catch hands and side-step
to the right to complete a semi-circle, again finishing on two
short threes *[4 bars]*.

8   *(b)* Still catching hands, dancers advance to form a large circle
[2 bars]. On second two three drop hands, complete turn
inwards (partners to face) and re-catch hands *[2 bars]*. All side-
step to original places, the circle moving to the right and ending on two short threes *[4 bars]*.

8   *(c)* Men face their partners and side-step to the left between the
women *[2 bars]*. They move backwards to the centre on the first
short three and catch hands in a circle on the second short three
[2 bars]. Advance back to partners, enlarging the circle *[2 bars]*.
Drop hands in the circle, give right hands to partners and turn
once in place *[2 bars]*.

8   *(d)* Women dance *(c)*, but side-step to the right and in the last 2
bars give left hands to partners.

C. 1st Figure

24   *(a)* Tops commence: men advance and turn opposite women
with right hands, turning once in places and back to partners
with left hands. Men advance to meet each other, catching right
hands, and complete full turn to face opposite women again,
advancing to turn once again with left hands and return to

partners with right hands; turn in places. Swing round each other *[8 bars]*.

(b) Sides dance (a).

D. Body

32 Repeat B.

E. 2nd Figure

8 (a) Tops advance to meet each other in the centre, hands by their sides. Tap right and left feet alternately on the ground, clap hands twice, tap right and left feet again and clap hands once *[4 bars]*. Fall back to places and repeat *[4 bars]*.

8 (b) Sides dance (a).

F. Body

32 Repeat B.

G. Lead Around

16 Lead around and back to places.

Fermanagh Set
Seit Fhear Manach

1ST FIGURE. *RAKE THE FIRE* (Polkas: 112 bars)

Bars *A. Slide In And Out*

8 All four couples slide in and out *[4 bars]* and house to the opposite side *[4 bars]*.

B. Slide In And Out

8 Repeat *A* and back to home.

C. Slide In And Out

8 All four couples slide in and out *[4 bars]* and swing *[4 bars]*.

D. Advance And Retire

8 Top couples, hands crossed in front, advance and retire *[4 bars]*; pass through, men on the outside *[4 bars]*.

E. Repeat

8 Side couples dance *D*.

F. Men Chain

8 Top men turn to their left, Side men to their right and chain right hands; give left hand to women and dance around. The same men chain right hands, give left hands to their own partner and acknowledge.

G. Lead To Home

8 Lead back to place, man's right arm around woman's waist, holding hands *[4 bars]*. Dance around in place *[4 bars]*.

H. Swing

8 All four couples swing.

I. Repeat

40 Repeat *D–H*, with Side couples leading.

2ND FIGURE. *SADDLE THE PONY*   (Polkas: 168 bars)

A. Slide In And Out

24 All four couples dance as at *1st Figure, A–C*.

B. Wheel

8 Four women right-hand wheel *[4 bars]* then turn, left-hand wheel, pass their own position and dance to man on the right *[4 bars]*.

C. Swing

8 All four new couples swing.

D. Repeat

120 Repeat *A–C* three more times until partners rejoin.

3RD FIGURE. *STEAL THE LADY*   (Reels: 128 bars)

A. Lead Around

8 Lead around, man's right arm around woman's waist and woman's left arm on man's right shoulder.

B. Advance And Retire

8 All four couples advance and retire in lead-around position. Advance again, Top men steal woman from left and retire in line of three. Side men also retire.

C. Advance And Square

8   The line of threes advance and retire once *[4 bars]*. The women square, passing right to right shoulder, turn and pass right shoulder and form a line of three with the Side men *[4 bars]*.

D. Advance And Square

8   Repeat *C*; women back to own partner.

E. Dance At Home

8   All four couples dance at home.

F. Star

8   Tops to the left, Sides to the right, wheel *[4 bars]*. The men join both hands, lift them over the women and place them around their waist. The women do likewise, but put their hands on men's shoulders. This movement is performed while moving clockwise *[4 bars]*.

G. Basket

8   Swing in four clockwise.

H. Swing

8   Swing out of basket without stopping.

I. Repeat

56   Repeat *B–H*, with Side couples leading.

4TH FIGURE. *ROCK THE CRADLE*   (Hornpipes: 112 bars)

A. Body

32   All four couples sevens to centre and back *[4 bars]*; hop in, 2-3 and out, 2-3 *[2 bars]*. Double to next position *[2 bars]*. Repeat three more times *[24 bars]*.

B. House

8   All four couples house.

C. Lead Around

8   Lead around to opposite place. The women turn twice clockwise and the men dance back to home alone.

D. Repeat

48   Repeat *A–C* with new partner.

E. House

8   House to finish. Double the last 2 bars.

Four-Hand Jig

A four-hand dance. Partners cross hands and face the opposite couple.

(Jigs: 288 bars)

Bars **A. Lead Around**

16 Lead around anticlockwise. On the 8th bar of music, turn and lead back clockwise to original position; turn clockwise around partner into place.

B. Body

8 *(a) Sevens past partners:* Partners side-step past each other and jig step; side-step back to place, finishing with jig step.

8 *(b) Change places and swing:* Partners take right hand in right and dance anticlockwise to opposite position, with the man leading *[2 bars]*; couples swing *[4 bars]* and jig step *[2 bars]*.

8 *(c) Sevens past partners:* Repeat (a).

8 *(d) Change places and swing:* Repeat (b), returning to original position.

C. 1st Figure

8 *(a)* Top couple advance, holding inside hands *[2 bars]*, then turn, the man turning clockwise and the woman anticlockwise. Top man hooks right arm in right with opposite woman, while Top woman hooks left arm in left with opposite man; dance around *[2 bars]*. Top man and woman meet, take inside hands (the woman's right hand in the man's left) and dance back to place *[2 bars]*. Top woman turns clockwise and man anticlockwise into original position *[2 bars]*. Opposite couple dance throughout, performing jig step for the last 2 bars.

8 *(b)* Both couples advance to the centre; Top man hooks opposite woman's left arm in his left and they dance around anticlockwise. Top woman hooks opposite man's right arm in her right and they dance around clockwise *[2 bars]*. Dancers return to original position *[2 bars]*. Couples take hands uncrossed and dance around in original position *[2 bars]*. Finish with jig step *[2 bars]*.

8   (c) *Repeat:* Repeat (a) with opposite couple leading.

8   (d) *Repeat:* Repeat (b); this time the opposite man hooks left arms with the Top woman and the opposite woman hooks right arms with the Top man.

D. Body

32   Repeat *B*.

E. 2nd Figure. Women Chain

8   Women take right hands in the centre and dance past, giving left hand to opposite man's left. Dance under the man's raised arm with the men following the women around; release hands and women dance back to original position, passing right shoulder to right. Give right hand to right with partner; turn into place.

F. Body

32   Repeat *B*.

G. 3rd Figure

8   (a) Top man takes opposite woman's right hand in his right; they side-step to the man's right. When dancing the jig step the Top man turns anticlockwise and the woman turns clockwise. Top man gives left hand to his partner's left and dances around her anticlockwise. At the same time, opposite woman gives her right hand to her partner's right and dances around him clockwise.

8   (b) Top man and opposite woman meet again, holding hands uncrossed; dance side-step to the man's left. The man releases his right hand with the woman's left hand while dancing the jig step; he takes his partner's right hand in his right and they dance clockwise into place. At the same time opposite woman gives left hand in left with her partner and they dance anticlockwise into place.

16   (c) Repeat (a) and (b) with Top woman and opposite man leading.

I. Body

8 Repeat B.

J. 4th Figure. Men Chain

16 Men dance straight across to opposite woman, take right hand in right and dance around; men return to original position, passing left shoulder to left and give left hand to left with partner; dance around. The men meet in the centre, hook right arm in right and dance around clockwise; give left hand to left of opposite woman, pass right shoulder to right and give right hand to right with partner; turn into place.

K. Body

32 Repeat B.

L. Lead Around

16 Lead around as at A.

Four-Hand Reel

Position of the dancers:

B A   *(leading couple)*

C D *(opposite couple)*

A and C are men; B and D are women.

Bars A. Lead Around

16   Dancers half-right turn and lead around a complete circle; release hands and about turn inwards. The man takes his partner's right hand in his left and both lead back to place.

B. Body

16   *(a) The square:* The men side-step a square in anticlockwise direction while the women side-step a square in clockwise direction, all finishing with two short threes after each side-step. This is performed by dancer A side-stepping to the place which was occupied by B, ending with two short threes, proceeding to place which was occupied by C, then on to D's place, and finally to his original position. Meanwhile, B has been side-stepping to A's position, and so on. Similarly with C and D. Thus, each man passes twice in the course of the square, with the woman passing in front on each occasion.

8   *(b) Four sevens:* With the dancers now back in their original position, the man side-steps to the right behind his partner, the woman side-stepping to the left in front; man side-steps back to place in front of his partner, woman side-stepping back to place behind. This movement is repeated. (Note that the two short threes are not performed at the end of each side-step in the movement.)

8   *(c) Hands across:* All four dancers give right hands across in the centre, shoulder high, and dance around clockwise. They then release hands, reverse, give left hands across and dance back to place. Thus, A and C take hands, as do B and D.

8   *(d) Down the centre:* The leading couple (i.e. the couple nearest the music) turn to face each other, take right hands and side-step through the centre to the place occupied by the opposite couple, while the latter sidestep separately up the outside to the place occupied by leading couple. The leading couple half-turn in place and release hands, while the opposite couple take right hands and half-turn. The opposite couple side-step back to place through the centre while the leading couple side-step separately up the outside; each couple take hands and half-turn to original position.

8   *(e) Right and left chain:* The man gives his right hand to the opposite woman and both move forward in a semi-circle, men clockwise, women anticlockwise. They continue to meet their partner with the left hand, opposite woman again with the right hand and on to own partner with left hand to finish in position, thus completing the circular chain.

C. 1st Figure

32   *(a) Figure of eight and Rings of three:* The leading couple take inside hands, advance to the opposite couple and release hands. The leading man retires to place and remains idle while his partner performs the figure of eight by passing between the opposite couple and going first round the woman and then round opposite man. The two women now advance to the leading man and take hands in a ring of three. The leading couple and opposite woman, in the ring of three, dance the side-step to the right (anticlockwise), ending with two threes and then sidestep to left; meanwhile, the opposite man at the same time has been side-stepping to right and left. The leading couple arch arms and allow the opposite woman to pass under to the leading woman's original position, and then advance and form a ring of three with the opposite man. The leading couple and the opposite man dance the side-step in a ring to the left and right; meanwhile, the opposite woman has been side-stepping left and right. The leading couple arch arms and allow the

opposite man to pass under to his partner. Both couples then swing half round, anticlockwise, to their original places.

32 *(b) Repeat:* The opposite couple dance *(a)*.

D. Body

48 Repeat *B*.

E. 2nd Figure

16 Women's chain: The women advance, give right hands in the centre, and continue to the opposite man, giving left hand. Both turn in place and the women return to their own partner, both making a full turn in place. Both couples dance a complete circle around each other.

F. Body

48 Repeat *B*.

G. Lead Around

16 Repeat *A* and finish.

Freres Nantes
(Connemara Jig Set)
Seit Chonamara (port)

1ST FIGURE *(Jigs: 288 bars)*

Bars *A. Circle*

8   All circle, advance and retire twice, doing polka step.

B. Lead Around

16   Lead around anticlockwise, the man's right arm over the woman's shoulder, holding both hands in front. On the last 2 bars, the man brings his right hand over the woman's head as she turns anticlockwise slightly to face him. Both dance one step backwards holding both hands (tug) and swing.

C. Advance And Retire

8   Holding crossed hands in front, Top couples advance facing in and retire facing out, twice.

D. Lead Around

8   Top couples lead around inside, as at *B*.

E. Tug And Cross Over

8   Top couples tug and cross over (change places dancing clockwise with partner, holding hands in front), tug and cross back *[4 bars]*. Then all men swing the woman on their left in the corners *[4 bars]*.

F. Advance And Retire

8   All advance and retire twice with swinging partner (Tops towards their own partner).

G. Lead Around

8 With new partners, all lead around the couple facing them at *F*.

H. Swing

8 Tug and cross back *[2 bars]* to swing own partners *[6 bars]*.

I. Repeat

64 Repeat *B–H*, with Side couples leading.

J. Repeat

128 Repeat *B–I*, Tops and Sides each leading in turn again.

K. Lead And Swing

16 All lead around and swing, to finish the Figure.

2ND FIGURE   *(Jigs: 256 bars)*

A. Circle

8 Circle, advance and retire twice.

B. Lead Around

16 All lead around and swing, as at *1st Figure, B*.

C. Women Chain

8 Top women chain, right arm in centre, left hand to opposite man; dance around outside him as he turns anticlockwise with her, putting his right arm over her shoulder *[4 bars]* and lead back to woman's positions *[4 bars]*.

D. Repeat

8 Repeat the chain to lead back home with own partner.

E. Advance And Retire

8 Top couples advance and retire twice.

F. Lead Around And Swing

16 Top couples lead around inside and swing.

G. Lead Around And Swing

16 All couples lead around and swing.

H. Repeat

40 Side couples dance *B–F*.

I. Repeat

112 Repeat *B–H*.

J. Lead Around

16 All lead around and swing to finish.

3RD FIGURE   *(Jigs or Slides: 264 bars)*

A. Advance And Retire

8 Top couples advance and retire twice.

B. Women Chain

8 Top women chain, right arm, left arm around opposite man, right hand, left hand to partner, turning anticlockwise into lead-around position.

C. Lead Around

16 Top couples lead around inside and swing.

D. Repeat

32   Side couples dance *A–C*.

E. Advance And Retire

8   Top couples advance and retire once, and the man turns the woman across on the right, right hand in right hand in one turn clockwise.

F. Advance And Retire

8   Top couples advance and retire once and the man turns the woman across on the right, left hand in left hand, clockwise, facing into a circle of four on the last 2 bars. The man places the women's left hand on his shoulder and puts his own right arm around his partner's waist.

G. Christmas

8   Top couples swing in four in the centre.

H. Women Chain

8   Top women chain as in *B*.

I. Lead Around

16   Top couples lead around and swing.

J. Repeat

48   Side couples dance *E–I*.

K. Repeat

96   Top couples and side couples repeat *E–I*.

4TH FIGURE (Hornpipes: 184 bars)

A. Advance And Retire

8   All circle, advance arid retire twice.

B. House

8   All house around in waltz hold.

C. Turn The Lady

8   1st Top man turns the woman clockwise four times, right hand in right hand, dancing anticlockwise around inside the set.

D. Advance In Three

8   Top man advances and retires twice, holding inside hands with his own partner and the side woman on his left.

E. Arches

8   Top man and the two women dance the arches or high gates. Side woman passes under the arch first, followed by man, then Top woman, Side woman again and Top woman again. All three finish facing in, holding hands.

F. Repeat

120   Repeat A–E three times with 1st Side couple (on the right), 2nd Top couple and 2nd Side couple leading at C, D and E in turn.

G. Circle And House

16   All circle and house to finish.

5TH FIGURE (Polkas: 144 bars)

A. Advance And Retire

8   All circle, advance and retire twice.

B. Lead Around

8   All lead around in waltz, facing forward.

C. Dance At Home

8   Dance in place, turning twice.

D. Circle

8   Circle again. All advance, retire and advance again. Each man turns to the woman on his left, puts his right arm around her waist and brings her to his position in waltz hold.

E. Lead Around

8   All lead around in waltz hold with new partner.

F. Dance At Home

8   Dance in place with new partner.

G. Repeat

72   Repeat *D–F* three more times, ending with own partner.

H. Circle

16   Circle and swing to finish.

Galway Half Set
Leathsheit Ghaillimh

*This is danced in the Ballinasloe/Killimor area of East Galway.
The basic step is hop 1, hop 2, hop 1-2-3; hands crossed.*

1ST FIGURE   *(Reels: 64 bars)*

Bars **A. Lead**

8   Four positions in square formation, facing partner all the time.

B. Dance Around

8   Singly, dance hop 1-2-3s around clockwise in a circle, the
     women passing in front of their partners. The women (and
     men) end up in the 'wrong' positions, women turning in to face
     men on last two threes.

C. Swing

8   Swing in place.

D. Repeat

24   Repeat A–C.

E. Lead

8   Repeat A.

2ND FIGURE   *(Reels: 80 bars)*

A. Lead

8   Repeat as at *1st Figure, A.*

B. Advance And Retire

8   Couples advance and retire, sideways, once. Instead of dancing

the basic step here, couples could dance hop 1-2-3-4-5-6-7 in and out, and house four threes to opposite positions.

C. Repeat

8   Repeat *B*, ending up in original positions.

D. Swing

8   Swing partners.

E. Repeat

32   Repeat *A–D*.

F. Lead

8   Repeat *A*.

3RD FIGURE   (Reels: 96 bars)

A. Lead

8   Repeat as at *1st Figure, A*.

B. Repeat

16   Repeat as at *2nd Figure, B* and *C*.

C. Lead

8   Repeat *A*.

D. Swing

8   Swing partners.

E. Lead

8   Repeat *A*.

F. Repeat

40   Repeat *B–E*.

4TH FIGURE   *(Jigs: 96 bars)*

A. Lead

8   Use the same step as in the reels: hop 1, hop 2, hop 1-2-3, hands crossed.

B. Advance And Retire And Dance At Home

8   Couples advance and retire once, dancing the usual step, and then turn once clockwise in place, dancing four threes.

C. Advance And Retire And Dance Anticlockwise

8   Couples advance and retire once and then turn anticlockwise once in place.

D. Lead

8   Repeat *A*.

E. Swing

8   Swing partners.

F. Repeat

40   Repeat *A–E*.

G. Lead

8   Repeat *A*.

5TH FIGURE

(Reels: 112 bars)

A. Lead

8   Repeat as at *1st Figure, A*.

B. Advance And Retire

8   Couples advance and retire once, then the women swap places, turning clockwise twice as they pass back-to-back. While the women are exchanging places the men turn in place to the right, clockwise, twice.

C. Swing

8   Swing new partners.

D. Advance And Retire

8   Repeat *B*, ending up in original places.

E. Lead

8   Repeat *A*.

F. Swing

8   Swing partners.

G. Repeat

48   Repeat *A–F*.

H. Lead

8   Repeat *A*.

Gates Of Derry

(Single Jig: 248 bars)

Bars *A. Advance And Retire*

16   The two lines of dancers, holding hands, advance towards each other with promenade step and retire to places. They advance again and the first line raise hands to form arches; the second line, having released hands, pass through to their partners' places, right shoulder to right shoulder. Repeat, with the second line forming arches, and so back to places.

B. The Gates

8   Couples 1 and 3 take crossed hands and side-step to the right down the centre. While dancing two threes, the man turns his partner clockwise under his raised right hand, having dropped his left hand to his side. Again holding his partner's crossed hands, he side-steps back to place, finishing with two short threes. In the meantime, couples 2 and 4 have danced side-step to the left, to the places of couples 1 and 3 respectively, and back to original places.

C. Rings

8   Couples 1 and 2 now take hands to form a ring, as do couples 3 and 4 on their side, and dance side-step and threes to the right and back again.

D. The Gates

8   Couples 2 and 4 dance *B*, dancing to their left and back, while couples 1 and 3 dance to their right outside them.

E. Rings

8   Repeat *C*, but dancing to left first then returning to the right.

F. Telescope

Begin with the couples in the following order: 1 2 3 4.

4   (a) Odd-numbered couples take uncrossed hands and side-step to the men's right down the centre, while at the same time even-numbered couples dance side-step to the men's right on the outside, to take up these new positions: 2 1 4 3. With a continued seven, i.e. without doing two threes, couples 1 and 4 change places so that the new positions now are: 2 4 1 3. (Note: each time the centre couple change places the outside couples dance two threes.)

4   (b) Couples 2 and 1 repeat (a) with couples 4 and 3, leaving the dancers in the order: 4 2 3 1. With a continued seven, couples 2 and 3 change places, leaving the order: 4 3 2 1.

4   (c) In these positions, couples 4 and 2 repeat (a). This leaves the dancers as follows: 3 4 1 2. With a continued seven, couples 4 and 1 change places, leaving the order: 3 1 4 2.

4   (d) In these positions, couples 3 and 4 repeat (a) to leave the positions: 1 3 2 4. Couples 3 and 2 side-step to change places, falling into the positions at the beginning of the Telescope: 1 2 3 4.

G. Right And Left Wheel

8   Couples 1 and 2 join right hands across the centre as do couples 3 and 4 on their side, and with promenade step dance round clockwise, turning on the fourth three. They then take left hands across and dance back to places.

H. Swing Around

8   Each pair of couples who danced *G* together (1 and 2, and 3 and 4) now swing round each other and finish in exchanged places, ready for a repetition of the dance.

I. Repeat

64 (a) *1st repeat:* Repeat *B–H*, the outside couples (2 and 3) standing idle while couples 1 and 4 dance *G* and *H*.

96 (b) *2nd repeat:* Repeat *A–H*, all taking part as the first time, but in new positions. Then repeat *A* again to finish.

Gillen Set
Seit Ghillen

Opening position, except where indicated: All four couples face into the set.

1ST FIGURE   *(Reels: 72 bars)*

Bars *A. Swing*

8   All swing in place in céilí hold.

B. Figure

4   *(a) Pass through:* Top couples advance towards each other and pass through, 1st Tops couple on the outside, 2nd Tops couple on the inside. On reaching opposite positions all turn. 1st Tops couple turn into the set and 2nd Tops couple turn out of the set.

4   *(b) Pass through:* Top couples repeat *(a)* but with 2nd Tops couple dancing on the outside first and 1st Tops couple on the inside. On reaching original positions all turn to face each other.

8   *(c) Tap-it-out:* Top couples face their partners, take right hand in right and 'tap-it-out'.

C. Swing

8   All swing in céilí hold.

D. Figure

16   Side couples repeat *B*, with 1st Sides couple on the right of 1st Tops couple dancing at *(a)*.

E. Tap-It-Out

8   All couples face partners with right hands joined and tap-it-out.

F. Swing

8   All swing in place.

2ND FIGURE
(Reels: 72 bars)

A. Swing

8   All swing in place in céilí hold.

B. Figure

8   (a) *Women chain:* Top women chain with right elbows in the centre, left elbows to opposite men who dance around with the woman, right elbows in the centre again and then chain with left elbows to their own partners, who dance around with them.

8   (b) *Tap-it-out:* Top couples face their partners with right hands joined and tap-it-out.

C. Swing

8   All swing.

D. Figure

16   Side couples dance *B*.

E. Tap-It-Out

8   All couples face partners with right hands joined and tap-it-out.

F. Swing

8   All swing.

3RD FIGURE
(Reels: 120 Bars)

A. Swing

8   All swing in place in céilí hold.

B. Figure

8   (a) *Women chain:* Top women chain with right hands (not arms) in the centre *[2 bars]* and dance past each other to the opposite men *[2 bars]*. They give left hands to opposite men's left hands

and turn clockwise under their arms while dancing around behind the men into the women's position. The men face into the centre and do not turn in to the women *[2 bars]*. Finally the men take the women's right hands in front and place them on the women's shoulders while taking left hands in front *[2 bars]*.

8 *(b) Lead around:* Top couples lead around on the inside of the set and back to the men's position, the men bringing the women's right hands forward over the women's heads during the last 2 bars for tap-it-out position.

8 *(c) Tap-it-out:* Top men, with new partners, tap-it-out.

8 *(d) Women chain:* Top women repeat *(a)*, but dance the last 2 bars facing their partner.

8 *(e) Tap-it-out:* Top couples tap-it-out.

C. Swing

8 All swing.

D. Figure

40 Side couples repeat *B*.

E. Tap-It-Out

8 All tap-it-out.

F. Swing

8 All swing.

4TH FIGURE. *EVERY MAN'S CHANCE*   (Reels: 152 Bars)

Opening position: All face the centre, joining hands in a circle.

A. Advance And Retire

8 All advance and retire twice.

B. Lead Around

8 Holding right hand in right on the women's shoulders and left

hands in front of women, all lead around anticlockwise back to own places. During the last 2 bars men bring women's right hands over their heads as they turn anticlockwise to face men.

C. Tap-It-Out

8 All tap-it-out.

D. Swing

8 All swing in céilí hold.

E. Figure

8 *(a) Change partners and lead around:* All four women dance forwards to the next man on their right, while the men dance on the spot *[2 bars]*. Then, with new partners, all lead around until back in the men's places *[6 bars]*.
8 *(b) Tap-it-out:* All four new couples tap-it-out.
8 *(c) Swing:* All four new couples swing.

F. Figure

24 All repeat *E*, with the women moving on one position at *(a)* to the men opposite their original partners.

G. Figure

24 All repeat *E*, with the women moving on one position at *(a)* to the the men on the left of their original partners.

H. Figure

24 All repeat *E*, with women moving back to original partners at *(a)*.

I. Circle

8 All circle and advance and retire twice.

J. Swing

8 All swing in céilí hold.

Glassdrummond Reel

A six-hand dance. Formation: Dance in threes of one man and two women.

Bars *A. Advance And Retire And Circle*

16 *(a)* Advance and retire twice. On the second retire form a ring and on the last two threes all dancers turn out and dance seven steps to the right, then two threes. On the last of the two threes, all face in and dance to their right to original places.

16 *(b)* Repeat *(a)*, this time going to the left.

B. Arches

8 *(a)* Each man takes inside hands with the woman on the right, forming an arch. Advance with promenade step to opposite woman who dances promenade step under the arch. Continue the movement, completing the square to original place.

8 *(b)* Repeat *(a)*, starting with the woman on the left.

C. Men Swing Right Then Left

8 *(a)* Men face the woman on their right and swing. Meanwhile, the other women beats time with her hands.

8 *(b)* Repeat *(a)* with woman on left, as the first women beats time.

D. Men Change Places While Women Dance Square

8 Men take right hand in right; change places on their two threes. The women dance sevens past each other on their two threes. Men then give left hands and back to place; the women continue sevens. The men take right hands again and change places. Women continue sevens and men give left hands back to place. Women continue sevens and back to place.

E. Men And Women Hook Arms

8 *(a)* Men hook the woman on right, then on left, then right again. All dancers stamp on right foot, then left, and clap hands twice.

8 *(b)* Repeat *(a)*, starting with woman on the left.

8 *(c)* Advance, retire, advance and pass through to next three.

Glencar P...
Seit Ghleann A'Ch...

1ST FIGURE

A. Polka

16 All dancers take their partners in w... back, moving on slightly *[2 bars]*; th... position on the right *[2 bars]*. Repeat ...s three times, dancing on to each position until ...ome *[12 bars]*.

B. House

8 All couples house around.

C. Full Wheel And Swing

16 Top couples join right hands in centre and dance one complete clockwise turn around to home *[8 bars]*; swing in place *[8 bars]*.

D. Chain

8 Top women chain with right hands in the centre, left hands at waist height around opposite man, right hands in the centre again and dance back to place.

E. House

8 Top couples house.

F. Repeat

24 All couples repeat *A* and *B*.

G. Repeat

32 Side couples dance *C–E*.

H. Repeat

24 All couples repeat *A* and *B*.

A. Polka And House

All couples dance the polka and house as at *1st Figure, A* and *B*.

B. Show the Lady

8   1st Top couple house inside the set.

C. Slide And Home

8   1st Top couple slide to the centre and back *[4 bars]*; then turn once in place *[4 bars]*.

D. Repeat

40   Repeat *A–C*, with 2nd Top couple dancing *B* and *C*.

E. Repeat

40   Repeat *A–C*, with 1st Side couple (on the left of 1st Top couple) dancing *B* and *C*.

F. Repeat

40   Repeat *A–C*, with 2nd Side couple dancing *B* and *C*.

G. Polka And House

24   All couples repeat *A*.

3RD FIGURE   *(Polkas: 144 bars)*

A. Polka And House

24   All couples dance the polka and house as at *1st Figure, A* and *B*.

B. Slide And House

8   Top couples slide to the centre and back *[4 bars]*; then house across to opposite positions *[4 bars]*.

C. Slide And House

8   Top couples repeat *B*, dancing back to their own places.

D. Chain

8   Top women chain as at *1st Figure, D*.

E. House

8   Top couples house around each other.

F. Polka And House

24   All couples repeat *A*.

G. Repeat

32   Side couples dance *B–E*.

H. Polka And House

24   All couples repeat *A*.

4TH FIGURE   (Slides: 152 bars)

A. Lead Around

8   Top couples lead around, holding crossed hands in front.

B. House

8   Top couples house around each other.

C. Slide And House

8   Top couples slide to the centre and back *[4 bars]*, then house across to opposite positions *[4 bars]*.

D. Repeat

8   Top couples repeat *C*, dancing back to place.

E. Slide And House

8   Top couples slide to the centre and back *[4 bars]*; then Top women cross, passing right shoulder to right, to opposite man *[4 bars]*.

F. House

8   Top women house around with opposite men.

G. Slide And Top Women Chain

8   Top couples slide in and back with their new partners *[4 bars]*; then Top women chain with right hands as they dance back to turn with left hands around their own partners into place *[4 bars]*. Men turn with the women.

H. Top Women Chain

8   Top women dance a full chain, right hands in the centre *[4 bars]*, then turn with left hand around opposite man, right hands in the centre and dance back to place *[4 bars]*.

I. House

8   Top couples house around each other.

J. Repeat

72   Side couples dance *A–I*.

5TH FIGURE   *(Polkas: 224 bars)*

A. Polka And House

24   All couples dance the polka and house as at *1st Figure, A* and *B*.

B. Slide In And Out

8   1st Top couple slide to the centre and back, then dance in place.

C. Women Wheel And Swing

16   The four women join right hands and dance one clockwise turn around the centre *[8 bars]*; then all couples swing *[8 bars]*.

D. Repeat

24   All couples repeat *A*.

E. Slide In And Out

8   2nd Top couple dance *B*.

F. Men Wheel And Swing

16   The four men join left hands and dance one anticlockwise turn in the centre *[8 bars]*; then all couples swing *[8 bars]*.

G. Repeat

24   All couples repeat *A*.

H. Repeat

48   1st Side couple dance *B*; then all couples dance *C* and *D*.

I. Repeat

48   2nd Side couple dance *B*, then all couples repeat *F* and *G*.

6TH FIGURE   *(Hornpipes: 160 bars)*

A. Body

16 All couples dance one step to the centre and back, then turn clockwise to the position on the right *[4 bars]*. Repeat the movements three times, dancing around to home *[12 bars]*.

B. House

8   All couples dance around the house.

C. Women Move On

8   The four men stand in place as women move on to the position on the right to dance with the next man.

D. Repeat

96 All repeat *A–C* three times as women move around the set, dancing with each man in turn before returning to their partners.

E. Repeat

24 All dance *A* and *B* with their own partners to finish.

Glencree Set
Seit Ghleann Chrí

1ST FIGURE. *PASS THROUGH* (Polkas: 136 Bars)

Bars *A. Pass Through*

8   Both Top couples advance and pass through, women in centre, left shoulder to left shoulder. All turn clockwise in opposite position and pass back again to own place, the women dancing anticlockwise under the men's right arm.

B. Lead Around

8   Both Top couples lead around anticlockwise until back in their own positions. The man has the woman's hands held in front; he turns her right, left, right, left as they lead and, when back in place, turns her anticlockwise.

C. Women Chain

8   Top women give right elbow in the centre, left elbow to opposite man. Dance back to own position, turning anticlockwise under partner's right arm.

D. Swing

8   Top couples swing.

E. Repeat

32 Sides dance *A–D*.

F. Repeat

32 Tops repeat *A–D*.

G. Repeat

32 Sides repeat *A–D*, but with all couples swinging at *D*.

2ND FIGURE. *ADVANCE AND RETIRE*   *(Polkas: 168 Bars)*

A. Women Chain

8 Top women elbow chain, as at *1st Figure, C*.

B. Advance And Retire

8 Top couples advance and retire twice. On the second retire the man turns his partner anticlockwise under his right arm.

C. Lead Around

4 Both Top couples lead around anticlockwise, as at *1st Figure, B*, to opposite position.

D. Advance And Retire

8 Tops repeat *B*.

E. Lead Around

4 Both Tops repeat *C*, to original position.

F. Swing

8 Top couples swing.

G. Repeat

40 Sides dance *A–F*.

H. Repeat

40 Tops repeat *A–F*.

I. Repeat

40 Sides repeat *A–F*.

3RD FIGURE. *SWING OPPOSITE* (Polkas: 168 bars)

A. Women Chain

8 Top women elbow chain, as at *1st Figure, C*.

B. Swing

8 Top men cross to opposite women and swing.

C. Hook

8 Top men hook left arms in centre *[6 bars]* then dance back to partners, turning women anticlockwise under their right arms.

D. Lead Around

8 Top couples lead around anticlockwise until back in own places.

E. Swing

8 Tops swing.

F. Repeat

40 Sides dance *A–E*.

G. Repeat

40 Tops repeat *A–E*.

H. Repeat

40 Sides repeat *A–E*, but with all couples swinging at *E*.

4TH FIGURE. *THE KINGSTOWN* (Polkas: 168 bars)

A. Women Chain

8 Top women elbow chain, as at *1st Figure, C*.

B. Swing Across

8   2nd Top man takes partner's right hand in his, the woman facing out of set, dancing in place. 1st Tops swing up to opposite position, woman placed facing out of set on left of 2nd Top man.

C. Advance And Retire

8   Threes advance, holding hands, as 1st Top man retires; threes retire as 1st Top man dances on the spot; threes advance to 1st Top man who takes their hands and turns the women outwards under his arms to form a circle.

D. Swing

8   Tops swing in four, with hands held behind backs.

E. Repeat

8   Tops repeat A.

F. Repeat

24   Tops repeat B–D, 2nd Tops swinging up.

G. Repeat

8   Tops repeat A.

H. Swing

8   Tops swing.

I. Repeat

80   Sides dance A–H, but with all couples swinging at H.

5TH FIGURE. THE GALLOP   (Jigs: 136 bars)

A. Women Chain

8   Top women elbow chain, as at *1st Figure, C.*

B. Dance At Home

4   Top couples face partners in waltz hold and dance on the spot.

C. Gallop

4   Tops gallop across and back, men back-to-back in both directions.

D. Women Chain

8   Repeat *A*.

E. Swing

8   Top couples swing.

F. Repeat

32   Sides dance *A–E*.

G. Repeat

32   Tops repeat *A–E*.

H. Repeat

32   Sides repeat *A–E*, but with all couples swinging the last 8 bars.

6TH FIGURE. *WALTZ*   *(Waltz: 104 bars)*

A. Advance And Retire

8   All circle, advance and retire.

B. Women Move On

16   Each man takes woman on his left and turns clockwise for 8 bars then anticlockwise for 8 bars, travelling in a clockwise direction.

C. Circle And Women Move On

72   Repeat *A* and *B* three more times until back with own partner.

High-Cauled Cap

(Reels: 576 bars)

Position of the dancers:

1
B A

4 **G**   **F** **3**
H   **E**

C D
2

A, C, E and G are men; B, D, F and H are women.
AB are leading Tops, CD opposite Tops; EF leading Sides and GH opposite Sides.

Bars | ## A. Lead Around

16   Dancers half-right turn and lead around a complete circle; release hands and about turn inwards. The man takes his partner's right hand in his left and both lead back to place.

B. Body

16   *(a) Sides:* Leading and opposite Tops side-step to the right (behind), while leading and opposite Sides side-step to the left, all partners holding hands; all finish with two short threes (leading and opposite Tops have now changed positions with couples on their right). All side-step to the next position, finishing with two short threes. (All are now opposite their starting position.) All side-step on to next position, ending with two short threes, and side-step on to place, ending with two short threes.

16   *(b) Double quarter chain:* Each man takes his partner's right hand in right and both turn once in place. The man chains with left hand to the woman on his left and both turn in place, then chains back to his own partner with right hand, turning her in place. Continue the chain with left hand to woman on right, both turn once in place, chain back to own partner with right hand, both turn once in place.

16 *(c) Women interlace:* Each woman dances in front of her partner towards the man on her left, passes behind and around in front of him, dances back towards own partner and behind him to original position. Men meanwhile remain in position. Women give right hands across in the centre, dance around to the left, drop hands, give left hands to the man on the right of the woman's original position (i.e. B to G; D to E; F to A; H to C), both turn once in place, chain on to own partner with right hand and turn into place.

16 *(d) Men interlace:* Each man now dances in front of his partner towards the woman on his right, passes behind and around in front of her, then dances back towards his own partner and behind her to his original position. Men give right hands across in the centre, dance around to left, drop hands, give left hand to the woman on the right of the man's original position, both turn once in place, chain on to own partner with right hand and turn in place.

16 *(e) Stamp and clap:* All stamp right foot twice to 1 bar, and clap hands three times to second bar; repeat. Partners change places to side-step, ending with two short threes. Mark time with foot and beat palms as before. Side-step back to place, ending with two short threes.

C. 1st Figure

64 Leading Tops take right hands and side-step towards the opposite couple, ending with two short threes; side-step back, ending with two short threes. Both turn once in place. The man dances around the woman on his left, and back, while the woman dances around the man on his right, and back; both take hands and turn into place. Opposite Tops, leading Sides, and opposite Sides then perform the 1st Figure, in that order.

D. Body

80 Repeat *B*.

E. 2nd Figure

96 Circle and cross: Leading Tops advance to the opposite couple and pass through, the woman passing around the opposite man and the man passing around the opposite woman. All four give right hands across and dance around clockwise; release hands, leading Tops dancing back to place opposite. Tops turn once in position. The men advance, passing right arm to right to opposite woman, take her left hand and dance around her; release hands, dance back to place. Take own partner's right hand and turn in place. Both couples dance a circle to the right around each other and back to place. Opposite Tops, leading Sides and opposite Sides then perform the 2nd Figure in that order.

F. Body

80 Repeat B.

G. 3rd Figure

32 *Women's chain:* The women advance, give right hands in the centre, and continue to the opposite man, giving left hand. Both turn in place and the women return to their own partner, both making a full turn in place. Both couples dance a complete circle around each other.

H. Body

80 Repeat B.

I. Finish

40 All dancers join hands in a circle, forearms bent sharply upwards and elbows held in to the sides. Advance to centre, retire, advance again and retire. All side-step anticlockwise and finish with two short threes; side-step back, ending with two short threes. Advance and retire twice as before. All side-step clockwise and back, then the couples take hands and swing around to the right to finish off.

Hooks And Eyes

A long dance, danced to jigs. One couple faces another.

A. Link Arms And Dance Half-Way Around

4   *(a)* Partners link right arms and dance half-way around.

4   *(b)* Partners link left arms and dance back to original position.

8   *(c)* Repeat *(a)* and *(b)*.

B. Circle

8   Circle; four dancers take hands and side-step to the left two threes, then side-step to the right two threes.

C. Change Places

2   *(a)* Women change places, passing right arm to right and dancing side-step.

2   *(b)* Men change places, passing right arm to right.

4   *(c)* Repeat *(a)* and *(b)*.

D. Swing

8   Swing around to opposite place.

E. Repeat

When the dancers swing around to opposite place they face a new couple; repeat *A–D* as often as desired.

Humours of Bandon

Danced to the tune, Humours Of Bandon.   *(312 bars)*

Position of the dancers for this four-hand jig:

<blockquote>

B A   *(leading couple)*

C D   *(opposite couple)*

</blockquote>

A and C are men; B and D are women.

Bars **A. Lead Around**

16   All half-right turn and lead around a complete circle; release hands and about turn inwards. The man takes his partner's right hand in his left and both lead back to place.

B. Body

8   *(a) Sides:* Men side-step to the right behind their partners while women side-step in front, all end with rising step. Side-step back to place, men in front, ending with rising step.

8   *(b) Half-right and left:* Partners take both hands and turn once in place. They release hands, and men and women cross to opposite position, men crossing on the outside, women passing between opposite man and woman as shown:

<blockquote>

B A   *Starting position*

C B D A   *Passing in centre*

C D   *Opposite position*

</blockquote>

Partners take both hands and turn into opposite place.

8   *(c) Sides:* Repeat *(a)*.
8   *(b) Half-right and left:* Repeat *(b)*.

C. 1st Figure

16   *(a) Advance through centre:* Leading man takes his partner's left

hand in his right; they advance towards opposite couple and pass between and beyond them. Release hands, reverse and return to opposite couple, woman's right hand in man's left. Release hands. Woman takes opposite man's left hand in her left; leading man takes opposite woman's right hand in his right; all turn once in place. Leading man takes his partner's right hand in his left and they lead back to place. Release hands, reverse, advance again, woman's left in man's right. Release hands. The man gives his left hand to opposite woman and leading woman gives her right hand to opposite man; all turn once in place. Release hands; leading couple dance back to place and turn once.

32   *(b) Repeat B.*

16   *(c) The opposite couple dance (a).*

32   *(d) Repeat B.*

D. 2nd Figure

16   *(a) Centre meet:* Leading man and opposite woman advance to meet, take right hands, dance side-step to man's right and end with rising step. Woman takes her own partner's right hand in her right, man takes his own partner's left in his left and all turn in place. The same man and woman meet again in the centre, take left hands and dance side-step to man's left, ending with rising step. Release hands; woman gives her left hand to her own partner's left, man gives right to his partner's right; turn in place.

32   *(b) Repeat B.*

16   *(c) The opposite couple dance (a).*

32   *(d) Repeat B.*

E. 3rd Figure

16   *(a) Women's chain:* Women advance, give right hands in the centre and continue to opposite man, giving left hand. Both turn in place; women return to own partner, both making a full turn in place. Both couples dance a complete circle around each other.

32   *(b) Repeat B.*

F. Lead Around

16   Repeat *A* and finish.

Hurry The Jug

An eight-hand dance. 1st Sides are to the left of 1st Tops. All swings are performed in the céilí hold.

(Jigs: 400 bars)

Bars **A. Lead Around**

16   Lead around anticlockwise, hands crossed in front; on the 8th bar men turn clockwise and women turn anticlockwise without releasing hands, and lead around clockwise to home.

B. Body

8   *(a) Quarter chain:* Partners face each other, right hand in right and chain past (the men anticlockwise and the women clockwise), giving left hand to the person coming towards them. Dance around anticlockwise and dance back to original partner, taking right hand in right and turning clockwise into place.

16   *(b) Men cross over and chain:* The four men cross to the opposite woman. Top men a fraction ahead of Side men, pass right shoulder to right and dance around the woman anticlockwise, left hand in left *[4 bars]*. Men move on to the woman on the right of the men's original position and dance around her clockwise, right hand in right *[4 bars]*. Men cross to the opposite women (as danced at the start of *(b)*), returning to original partner and turning clockwise into place *[8 bars]*.

16   *(c) Half chain:* Partners holding right hands, chain (the men anticlockwise and the women clockwise). Partners meet half-way and dance around each other clockwise, the men returning clockwise and the women anticlockwise in the chain.

8   *(d) Tilly:* (1st Tops dance this movement with 2nd Sides, and 2nd Tops dance with 1st Sides.) Men, holding their partner's right hand in their right, side-step to the left in front of their partner, while at the same time the women side-step to the left to meet the men. The men take the women's left hands to form a circle of four, the men facing out and the women facing in *[4 bars]*. Partners release hands and dance around their new partner anticlockwise; release hands and men return to original partners, passing right arm to right, taking right hand in right, and turn into place *[4 bars]*.

8   *(e) The gallop with opposites:* Tops cross over to opposite positions, the men passing back-to-back *[2 bars]*. Sides cross over to opposite positions, the men passing back-to-back *[2 bars]*. Tops cross back to original positions, the women passing back-to-back *[2 bars]*. Sides cross back to original positions, the women passing back-to-back *[2 bars]*.

8   *(f) The gallop to the side:* The men passing back-to-back, 1st Tops and 1st Sides couples gallop past, finishing with two three's. 2nd Tops and 2nd Sides gallop at the same time *[4 bars]*. Gallop back to home, the women passing back-to-back *[4 bars]*.

1ST FIGURE

A. Advance And Retire And Cross Over

4   *(a)* Top couples advance and retire, right hand in right.
2   *(b)* Top women cross over, right shoulder to right.
2   *(c)* Top men cross over, left shoulder to left.
8   *(d)* Tops repeat *(a)–(c)*.
16   *(e)* Side couples dance *(a)–(d)*.

B. Body

64   Repeat *B*.

2ND FIGURE

A. Men Swing

4   *(a)* Top men take right hand in right and dance around clockwise; give left hands in left to the man on the left of their original position and dance around anticlockwise.
4   *(b)* Top men cross to opposite Side woman, passing right shoulder to right and dance around clockwise; release hands and the men dance into the centre of the set.
8   *(c)* Top men swing in céilí hold.
16   *(d)* Side men repeat *(a)–(c)*.

B. Body

64 Repeat B.

3RD FIGURE

A. Arches

4   *(a)* Top couples dance straight across the set with 2nd Tops forming an arch and 1st Tops passing under; the men turn clockwise and the women anticlockwise in the opposite position.

4   *(b)* Top couples cross back to original position with 1st Tops forming the arch and 2nd Tops passing under; this time the men turn anticlockwise and the women clockwise into position.

8   *(c)* Top couples around the house.

16 *(d)* Side couples dance *(a)–(c)*.

B. Body

64 Repeat *B*.

C. Lead Around

16 Repeat *A*.

D. Swing

8   All four couples swing to finish.

Jenny Lind
Seit Jenny Lind

1ST FIGURE. *SLOW WHEEL*   *(Jigs: 264 bars)*

Opening position for each figure, except where indicated: All four couples face anticlockwise around the circle, men on the inside. Each woman and man have an arm around each other's waist, and each man places his left hand on the left shoulder of the man in front of him. This position is called the 'lock'.

Bars **A. Lock**

8   In the opening position, all dancers wheel around until all couples reach their starting places.

B. Square

16   Couples adopt the standard hold. Each couple dances straight over to the next position to their right. Women dance: R-L-RLR-LRL-RLR, and men: L-R-LRL-RLR-LRL. Each couple dances to the next position in 2 bars, and then dances 2 bars in that position, turning slightly clockwise so that they are ready to step off with the 'wrong' feet to reach the next position *[4 bars]*. This movement is then repeated with opposite steps to bring each couple to the position opposite their own, and then twice more to bring all back to their own places.

C. House

8   All four couples dance house around.

D. Figure

8   *(a) Show:* 1st Tops dance around the house inside.
8   *(b) Wheel:* 1st Tops and 1st Sides join right hands and wheel clockwise for 8 bars; the other two couples do likewise.

E. Swing

8   All four couples swing in place.

F. Repeat

56 Repeat *A–E*; 1st Sides dance *D* (*a*).

G. Repeat

56 Repeat *A–E*; 2nd Tops dance *D* (*a*).

H. Repeat

56 Repeat *A–E*; 2nd Sides dance *D* (*a*).

I. Finish

32 Repeat *A–C*.

2ND FIGURE   *(Jigs: 296 bars)*

A. Lock

8 In the opening position, all dancers wheel around until all couples reach their starting places.

B. Square

16 All four couples dance the Square as at *1st Figure, B*.

C. House

8 All four couples dance house around.

D. Figure

8 (*a*) *Show:* 1st Tops dance around the house inside.
4 (*b*) *Balance:* Dancing couple and opposite slide in to the centre towards each other and back out again, once.
4 (*c*) *Cross over:* Top women change places, passing back-to-back in the centre *[2 bars]*; then Top men change places, passing back-to-back in the centre *[2 bars]*.
8 (*d*) *Balance and cross over:* Repeat (*b*) and (*c*).

E. Swing

8   The two couples involved in the figure swing in place.

F. Repeat

64   Repeat *A–E*; 1st Sides dance *D*.

G. Repeat

64   Repeat *A–E*; 2nd Tops dance *D*.

H. Repeat

64   Repeat *A–E*; 2nd sides dance *D*.

I. Finish

32   Repeat *A–C*.

3RD FIGURE. *GRAND CIRCLE*   *(Jigs: 328 bars)*

A. Lock

8   In the opening position, all dancers wheel around until all couples reach their starting places.

B. Square

16   All four couples dance the Square as at *1st Figure, B*.

C. House

8   All four couples dance house around.

D. Figure

8   *(a) Show:* 1st Tops dance around the house inside.

8   *(b) Circle:* All dancers face to centre, joining hands in a circle, and advance and retire twice.

8   *(c) Women circle:* The four women join hands in a circle and ad-

vance to the centre and retire twice. As they go in the second time the whole circle makes a quarter turn anticlockwise so that the four women come out beside the next man to their right.

8   (d) *Men in:* The four men advance to the centre and retire twice.

E. Swing

8   The four men with their new partners swing in place.

F. Repeat

72   Repeat A–E; 2nd Sides (couple to the left of 1st Tops) dance D *(a)*.

G. Repeat

72   Repeat A–E; 2nd Tops dance D *(a)*.

H. Repeat

72   Repeat A–E; 1st Sides (couple to the right of 1st Tops) dance D *(a)*.

I. Finish

32   Repeat A–C.

4TH FIGURE. *CHAIN*   *(Jigs: 296 bars)*

A. Lock

8   All four couples dance as at *1st Figure, A*.

B. Square

16   All four couples dance as at *1st Figure, B*.

C. House

8   All four couples dance house around.

D. Figure

8   (a) *Show:* 1st Tops dance around the house inside.

16 (b) *Chain:* Starting with a right hand to their own partners, each dancer chains all the way around the circle, men going anti-clockwise and women clockwise. Each dancer meets partner half-way around *[8 bars]*; then back to place *[8 bars]*.

E. Swing

8   All four couples swing in place.

F. Repeat

64 Repeat *A–E*; 1st Sides dance *D (a)*.

G. Repeat

64 Repeat *A–E*; 2nd Tops dance *D (a)*.

H. Repeat

64 Repeat *A–E*; 2nd Sides dance *D (a)*.

I. Finish

32 Repeat *A–C*.

5TH FIGURE   (Reels: 216 bars)

Opening position: All couples face anticlockwise around the circle, men on the inside. Partners hold hands crossed in front, men's left hand in women's right.

A. Lead Around

8   In the opening position, all couples wheel around till back in place.

B. Turn The Lady

8   Couples drop right hands. Men raise their partner's left hand above her head and the women turn four times in place.

C. Swing

8   All couples swing in place.

D. Figure

Couples adopt the standard hold.

8   *(a) Square:* Top couples square inside; they dance to the opposite right-hand corner of the square and then on to the other
three corners in turn. Men dance: *HR-L, HR-L, HR-L, HR-turn
clockwise; women dance: HL-R, HL-R, HL-R, HL-turn clockwise. These steps are alternated for the second and third leg of
the square, i. e. men dance HL-R, etc. (*HR = Hop on right leg.)

8   *(b) House:* Top couples house inside.

8   *(c) Swing:* Top men cross and swing opposite women.

8   *(d) Men hook:* Top men advance to the centre and hook left arms,
turning with normal step then doubling up for the last 2 bars.

E. Repeat

56   Repeat *A–D*, with Sides dancing *D*.

F. Repeat

56   Repeat *A–E*.

G. Diamond

8   All couples dance directly to the position of the couple on the
right *[2 bars]*; turn clockwise to point to next position, using
step as at *D (a)*. Repeat till back at home.

H. Square

8   All couples dance full house around.

Jubilee Jig

A four-hand jig. **(Double Jigs: 232 bars)**

Bars **A. Lead Around**

16 Lead around *[8 bars]* and lead back *[8 bars]*.

B. Body

8 *(a) Partners dance side-step:* Side-step past partner. The women change places face-to-face while men dance rising step. Men change places face-to-face while women dance rising step, and all dance sevens back to original place.

8 *(b) Four sevens in a square:* All dance four sevens anticlockwise in the form of a square, facing inwards for the first seven, outwards for the second, inwards for the third and outwards for the fourth. (There are no threes between the sevens.)

8 *(c) Right and left hands across:* Give right hands in a wheel, women's hands on top. Dance around for 4 bars and turn; give left hands in a wheel and dance back to starting position.

24 *(d) The turns and back-to-back:* Men give right hand to opposite woman and dance around *[4 bars]*; left hand in the centre, men dance around *[4 bars]*. Women dance into their partner's place. Partners take right hands and dance around *[2 bars]*. Still holding right hands, men take the left hand of the opposite woman to form a circle, women facing inwards and men outwards *[2 bars]*. Dance side-step anticlockwise, finishing with rising step; release right hands and dance around in place *[2 bars]*. Form the circle again, this time with men facing inwards and women outwards *[2 bars]*. Side-step clockwise, finishing with rising step; release left hand and dance around partner into original place *[8 bars]*.

C. 1st Figure. Men's Figure Of Eight

8 *(a)* Both couples advance, the men passing the women right arm to right. Dance around each other without turning, back-to-back and retire to place.

4   *(b)* The men turn inwards and dance side-step diagonally to the centre, ending up back-to-back, while the women dance seven to their left to form a straight line.

8   *(c) Men's figure of eight:* Women stand idle as the men dance around their partners clockwise; pass each other, left arm to left in the centre, dance around the opposite woman anticlockwise and form a circle of four.

4   *(d) Circle:* Side-step anticlockwise to original positions, dancing rising step on the last bar of music.

D. Body

48   Repeat *B*.

E. 2nd Figure. Women's Figure Of Eight

8   *(a)* Women advance, take right hand in right and dance a full turn in the centre, take left hand in left with partner and dance a full turn in place.

8   *(b)* Women dance past each other in the centre, left arm to left, and circle around the opposite man clockwise. Dance past each other in the centre, left arm to left, circle around their partners anticlockwise and form a circle of four.

8   *(c) Circle:* Side-step anticlockwise two threes; side-step clockwise and retire to original place, dancing rising step on last bar of music.

F. Body

48   Repeat *B*.

G. Lead Around

16   Repeat *A* to finish.

Keadue Lancers
Lannsuidhthe Chéideadha

All figures in this dance are danced in polka step.

1ST FIGURE (Reels: 168 bars)

Bars *A. Tops Pass Through*

8   (a) 1st Top man and opposite woman exchange places, passing right shoulder to right *[4 bars]*, turn around clockwise and dance back again to join up in the centre of the set.

8   (b) Dancing couple swing; reverse to place during the last 2 bars.

8   (c) Top couples pass through, leading couple on the inside, the man's right hand holding the woman's left. Turn around and return to place, this time with leading couple on the outside.

16   (d) All dancers turn to their corner and house with new partner, using walking step, and finish in original place.

B. Pass Through

40   Repeat *A*, with 2nd Top man and opposite woman leading.

C. Sides Pass Through

40   Repeat *A*, with 1st Side man (on the left) and opposite woman leading.

D. Pass Through

40   Repeat *A*, with 2nd side man and opposite woman leading.

2ND FIGURE (Jigs: 200 bars)

A. The Lines

8   (a) Top couples advance and retire once (or batter in place), holding right hand in right and left in left, then exchange places, going to the left, women in front.

8   (b) Top couples repeat (a), returning to place.
8   (c) Top couples swing using céilí hold while Side couples divide to form two lines with Top couples.
8   (d) Lines advance and retire twice (or batter in place).
16 (e) All couples house, using walking step.

B. The Lines

48 Repeat A.

C. The Lines

48 Repeat A, with Side couples leading and Top couples dividing to form lines with Side couples.

D. The Lines

48 Repeat C.

3RD FIGURE   (Jigs: 104 bars)

A. Swing In Four

8   (a) Top couples advance and retire, and exchange places going to the left, women in front, and then on to the couple on the right of their original position.
8   (b) With right hands in, dance around to the left for 4 bars, and then to the right for 4 bars, women holding hands overhead, men underneath.
8   (c) The same couples swing in four, the men holding their hands behind the women's backs while the women place their hands on the men's shoulders. Return to place during the last 2 bars.

B. Swing In Four

8   (a) Top couples advance and retire, and exchange places going to the right, men in front, and then on to the couple on the left of their original position.

8   *(b)* Dance around as at *A (b)*.

8   *(c)* Swing in four, as at *A (c)*.

C. Swing In Four

24   Repeat *A*, Side couples leading and exchanging places going to the right, men in front, and dancing with couple on the left of original position.

D. Swing In Four

24   Repeat *A*, Side couples leading and exchanging places going to the left, women in front, and dancing with couple on the right of original position.

4TH FIGURE. *THE HORSESHOE*   *(Reels: 232 bars)*

A. Horseshoe

8   *(a)* Grand chain.

16   *(b)* All couples swing.

8   *(c)* 1st Top couple advance and retire once. The man turns the woman under, they release hands, the man dances in beside the man on his right while the woman dances in beside the woman on her left and all join hands, forming a horseshoe.

8   *(d)* Advance and retire twice (or batter in place).

16   *(e)* All couples house, using walking step.

B. Horseshoe

56   Repeat *A*, with 2nd Top couple leading.

C. Horseshoe

56   Repeat *A*, with 1st Side couple leading.

D. Horseshoe

56   Repeat *A*, with 2nd Side couple leading.

5TH FIGURE. *THE FILLING IN* (*Polkas: 128 bars*)

A. Circle

8 (a) Circle, and advance and retire twice.
16 (b) All couples house, using walking step.

B. Change Partners

8 (a) Circle, advance and retire twice and change partners, each woman moving on to the next man on her right.
16 (b) All couples house.

C. Change Partners

24 Repeat *B* with new partner.

D. Change Partners

24 Repeat *B* with new partner.

E. Change Partners

24 Repeat *B*, women returning to original partners.

Kenmare Polka Set
Seit Neidín (Polca)

1ST FIGURE. *WHEEL*   *(Polkas: 144 bars)*

Bars   *A. Polka*

16   Reverse the woman for 2 bars; turn into next place to the right. Repeat to home.

B. House

8   All four couples house, reversing the woman for two threes at the start.

C. Wheel And Swing

16   Top couples wheel and swing.

D. Women Chain

8   Top women chain.

E. House

8   Top couples house, reversing the woman for two threes at the start.

F. Polka

16   Repeat *A*.

G. House

8   Repeat *B*.

H. Repeat

32   Sides dance *C–E*.

I. Polka

16   Repeat *A*.

J. House

8   Repeat *B*.

2ND FIGURE. *SQUARE*   *(Polkas: 112 bars)*

A. Polka

16   All four couples polka as at *1st Figure, A*.

B. House

8   All four couples house.

C. House

8   Top couples house.

D. Square

8   Top couples square.

E. Polka

16   Repeat *A*.

F. House

8   Repeat *B*.

H. Repeat

16   Sides dance *C* and *D*.

I. Polka

16   Repeat *A*.

J. House

8   Repeat *B*.

3RD FIGURE. *WOMEN WHEEL*   **(Polka: 128 bars)**

A. Polka

16   All four couples polka as at *1st Figure, A*.

B. House

8   All four couples house.

C. House

8   Top couples house.

D. Women Wheel

8   All four women wheel half-way and dance around the opposite man back into the wheel to home.

E. Swing

8   All four couples swing.

F. Polka

16   Repeat *A*.

G. House

8   Repeat *B*.

H. House

8   Sides dance *C*.

I. Women Wheel

8   Repeat *D*.

J. Swing

8   Repeat *E*.

K. Polka

16   Repeat *A*.

L. House

8   Repeat *B*.

4TH FIGURE. *SQUARE AND CHANGE*   (Polkas: 152 bars)

A. Polka

16   All four couples polka as at *1st Figure, A*.

B. House

8   All four couples house.

C. Lead Around

8   Top couples lead around, men with right arm around women's waist and women with left arm on men's right shoulder.

D. House

8   All four couples house.

E. Square The House

8   Top couples slide to position on their right, taking a quarter turn on the second bar. Reverse to opposite position *[2 bars]* and house to home *[4 bars]*.

F. Slide In And Out

8   All slide in and out once; women change places.

G. House

8   Repeat *B*.

H. Slide In And Out

8 Repeat *F*; women come home.

I. Repeat

48 Side couples repeat *C–H*.

J. Polka

16 Repeat *A*.

K. House

8 Repeat *B*.

5TH FIGURE. *CHANGE PARTNERS* (Hornpipes: 160 bars)

A. Polka

16 Polka as at *1st Figure, A*; use hornpipe step.

B. House

8 All four couples house.

C. Circle

8 All circle; step, hop in, 2-3, stamp, hop out, 2-3, stamp. Repeat four times, the fourth time taking the woman from the left home.

D. Repeat

96 All repeat *A–C* until own woman comes home.

E. Polka

16 Repeat *A*.

F. House

8 Men house with own woman.

Kildare Set
Seit Cill Dara

This set was danced in most parts of Kildare from 1918–20 onwards. This version was given to the Kilcullen Set Dancers by Ann Gill of Clane.

1ST FIGURE *(Slides: 104 bars)*

Bars *A. Slide In And Out And Lead Around*

8 Top couples take their partners in waltz hold. They slide to the centre and back *[4 bars]*, then each man places his right arm over the woman's shoulder and both couples lead around to opposite positions *[4 bars]*.

B. Slide In And Out And Lead To Home

8 Top couples slide to the centre and back again, then with the man's arm over the woman's shoulder, they lead across to their own positions.

C. Swing

8 Top couples swing in place.

D. Repeat

24 Side couples dance *A–C*.

E. Repeat

48 Repeat *A–D*.

2ND FIGURE *(Slides: 72 bars)*

A. Opposites Swing

8 Top man and opposite woman advance to the centre, dance clockwise around each other to the other side and swing, reversing to their partners after the swing.

B. Swing

8   Top woman and opposite man dance *A*.

C. Women Chain

8   Top women chain, right hands in the centre, link left arms around opposite man, right hands in the centre again and dance back to place.

D. Swing

8   Top couples swing in place.

E. Repeat

32   Side couples dance *A–D*.

3RD FIGURE   *(Slides: 104 bars)*

A. Arches

8   Each Top man takes his partner's left hand in his right. Both Top couples advance to the centre, 1st couple making an arch and 2nd couple passing under it as they cross to opposite positions *[4 bars]*. All face their partners, take the other hands and dance back to place, Top couple making an arch again and opposite couple passing under it on the way back *[4 bars]*.

B. Swing And Circle

8   1st Top couple swing, moving into the centre as they do so and during the last 2 bars, opposite couples advance to join them in a circle of four.

C. Christmas

8   Top couples swing in four in the centre *[6 bars]* and reverse to place at the end of the swing *[2 bars]*.

D. Repeat

24 Top couples repeat *A–C*, 2nd Top couple leading.

E. Repeat

48 Side couples dance *A–D*.

4TH FIGURE   (Polkas: 104 bars)

A. Slide In And Out

8   All couples take waltz hold. Top couples slide forward, men meeting left shoulder to left and retire to place *[4 bars]*; Side couples repeat the movement *[4 bars]*.

B. Slide In And Out

8   Repeat *A*.

C. Gallop

8   Top couples slide or gallop to the opposite side, turning clockwise to face in there *[4 bars]*; Side couples repeat, dancing across to face in from opposite side position *[4 bars]*.

D. Repeat

24 All couples repeat *A–C*, dancing back to place.

E. Repeat

48 All couples dance *A–D*.

5TH FIGURE   (Reels: 112 bars)

A. Advance And Retire

8   All advance and retire twice in a circle.

B. Lead Around

8   All couples lead around, the man's arm around the woman's waist and her arm on his shoulder.

C. Swing

8   All couples swing. From the swing, women move to join the man on the right of their own position.

D. Repeat

16   Repeat *B* and *C* with new partners, the women moving on to the next man on the right.

E. Repeat

16   Repeat *B* and *C*, the women moving on to the third man.

F. Repeat

16   Repeat *B* and *C*, the women moving back to their own partners after the swing this time.

G. Repeat

16   All dance *B* and *C* with their own partners.

H. Advance And Retire

8   All advance and retire twice in a circle.

I. Swing

8   All couples swing to finish.

Kilkenny Lancers Set

This set was made famous by the Slate Quarry Dancers in Kilkenny. It is written here as described by Stephen Quigley. The batter is danced during the last 2 bars of each introduction. 1st Side couple are on the right of 1st Top couple.

1ST FIGURE   (Polka: 104 bars)

Bars   *A. Swing*

8   Top man and opposite woman swing in céilí hold in the centre.

B. Swing Behind

8   All swing in the corners: men turn left and women right away from own partners; they batter *[2 bars]* and swing *[6 bars]*.

C. Swing

8   All dance to their partners *[2 bars]* and swing *[6 bars]*.

D. Repeat

72   Repeat *A–C* with each man and opposite woman leading in turn. Dancing from the last swing, all circle (huddle), arms around each other in the centre.

2ND FIGURE   (Polka: 104 bars)

A. House

8   Top couples house around each other in waltz hold, hands low.

B. Advance And Retire

8   All line up in Top positions; Side dancers move to the nearest side. All advance and retire twice, dancing the batter when advancing and a swinging step when retiring (1-2-3-4 or 1-2, 1-2-3).

C. Swing

8   All swing their own partners.

D. Repeat

24 Repeat *A–C* with Top couples leading again.

E. Repeat

48 Repeat *A–D* with Side couples leading.

3RD FIGURE   *(Polkas: 104 bars)*

A. Tops House

8 Top couples house around each other, the woman turning clockwise under the man's left arm during the last 2 bars. While turning, she moves into the man's position and he stays in hers.

B. Swing

8 Top couples swing for 6 bars and dance out (batter) for 2 bars.

C. Lead Around

8 All lead around, men on the inside, arm around the woman.

D. Repeat

24 Repeat *A–C* with Top couples leading again.

E. Repeat

48 Repeat *A–D* with Side couples leading.

4TH FIGURE   *(Polkas: 120 bars)*

A. Chain And Swing

16 Starting by giving right hands to their partners, all chain to the opposite position and swing their partners there.

B. Chain

8 Taking their partner's right hand again, all chain back to place.

C. Dance In The Corner

16 1st Top couple and 1st Side couple (on the right) house around each other *[8 bars]*; then advance and retire towards each other twice, dancing the lancer batter when advancing *[8 bars]*.

D. Dance In The Corner

16 2nd Top couple and 2nd Side couple dance C.

E. Repeat

32 Repeat C and D.

F. Repeat

24 All repeat A and B.

5TH FIGURE   (Polkas: 104 bars)

A. Chain And Lead

16 All take partner's right hand in right and chain. In the opposite position each woman dances anticlockwise without turning, around the man, under his right arm and into the lead-around position, facing anticlockwise. Men do not turn *[8 bars]*. All couples lead anticlockwise back to place with each man's arm around woman's waist *[8 bars]*.

B. Dance In The Corner

16 1st Top couple and 1st Side couple (on the right) house around each other *[8 bars]*, then advance and retire towards each other twice, dancing the lancer batter when advancing *[8 bars]*.

C. Dance In The Corner

16 2nd Top couple and 2nd Side couple dance B.

D. Repeat

32 Repeat B and C.

E. Chain And Lead

16 All couples repeat *A*. Chain across and lead back.

6TH FIGURE (Polka: 152 bars)

A. Lead Around

8 All lead around, men on the inside, arm around women's waists.

B. House

8 Top couples house around each other.

C. House Across

16 Top couples dance (batter) in and out, house across to opposite positions *[8 bars]* and repeat, dancing back to place *[8 bars]*.

D. House

8 Repeat *B*.

E. Repeat

32 Side couples dance *B–D*.

F. Repeat

64 Repeat *B–E*.

G. Lead Around

8 All lead around again.

7TH FIGURE (Hornpipes: 144 bars)

A. Throw The Lady

8 1st Top couple dance sevens into the centre and back *[4 bars]*. Turn clockwise so the man has his back to the couple on the right

[2 bars] and double, 'throwing' the woman to the man on the right as the next woman moves out slightly to join the Top man.

B. Dance The Ladies

24   Top man repeats A with each woman, each of them moving on to the right of their own positions. He keeps the fourth woman.

C. Repeat

96   Repeat A and B with 1st Side man, 2nd Top man and 2nd Side man leading, each of them starting with 1st Top woman.

D. Diamond

8   All dance diamond sevens forward to the position on right and diamond sevens backwards to the next position *[4 bars]*; turn clockwise to home *[2 bars]* and double in place.

8TH FIGURE   *(Jigs: 120 bars)*

A. Circle

16   All circle, advance (battering) and retire twice; swing in place.

B. Lead Around

8   Women move to the right and all lead around with new partners.

C. Repeat

72   Repeat A and B until women lead around with own partners.

D. Circle

8   All circle again, advance and retire twice.

E. Swing

8   All swing their own partners, finishing in the circle.

Kilkenny Quadrilles

This set was recorded in 1990 in the Springhill Hotel, Kilkenny, from the late Paddy Staunton, musician and dancer. The meeting was arranged by Phil Curran. According to Paddy, it was usually danced as a half set, with two lines of dancers facing each other in half sets across the hall. It is described here as a half set (but can also be danced as a full set, with Side couples dancing after Top couples).

1ST FIGURE   (Polkas: 48 bars)

Bars *A. Pass Through*

8   Pass through to the other side, women passing between the opposite couple. All turn right, pass back to own side and face partner.

B. Swing

8   Swing in place in waltz hold.

C. Women Chain

8   Women chain with right hands in the centre, turn with left hand under the opposite man's left arm while he stays facing in, and chain back to partner.

D. Lead Around

8   Lead around, with the man's right arm over the woman's shoulder, holding both hands.

E. Swing

8   Swing in place.

2ND FIGURE   (Polkas: 56 bars)

A. Arch

8   Advance and retire holding right hands; then leading couple

make an arch and 2nd couple pass under as both dance to the opposite side. As they turn into place, the leading woman turns anticlockwise under her partner's arm and the 2nd couple, holding hands, turn clockwise into place without turning the woman.

B. Arch To Home

8   Repeat *A*, dancing back to place.

C. Swing

8   Both couples swing.

D. Repeat

24   Dance *A–C* again, with 2nd couple forming the arch at *E*.

3RD FIGURE   *(Single Jig: 72 bars)*

A. Swing

8   Top man and opposite woman swing in the centre.

B. Turn The Lady

8   Both couples advance and retire holding right hands; then cross on the right-hand side, each woman turning clockwise twice under her partner's right arm.

C. Turn The Lady

8   Repeat *B*, dancing back to place.

D. Swing

8   Both couples swing.

E. Repeat

32   Dance *A–D* again, with 2nd man and Top woman swinging.

4TH FIGURE *(Jigs: 144 bars)*

A. Women Chain

8   Women chain as at *1st Figure, C*.

B. Lead Around

8   Lead around anticlockwise, as at *1st Figure, D*.

C. Swing

8   Both couples swing.

D. Gallop

8   Top couple gallop across and back *[4 bars]*, across again *[2 bars]* and turn once *[2 bars]* to leave the woman beside the opposite man, who places an arm over each woman's shoulder.

E. Three And One

8   The man and two women advance as the other man retires alone *[2 bars]*; they retire while he dances in place *[2 bars]*; then all advance again *[2 bars]* and form a circle of four in the centre *[2 bars]*.

F. Swing

16   Swing in four, first to the left *[8 bars]*, then to the right *[8 bars]*.

G. Repeat

56   Repeat *A–F*, with 2nd couple leading.

H. Repeat

24   Repeat *A–C*.

5TH FIGURE
(Jigs or Polkas: 128 bars)

When this set is danced as a half set, two half sets or more join together for the 5th Figure.

A. Circle

8 Circle, advance and retire twice.

B. Lead Around

8 Lead around, with each man's arm around his partner's waist.

C. Swing

8 All swing.

D. Women Move On

8 Circle, advance and retire again, women moving on to the right.

E. Repeat

72 Repeat *B–D* until women are back with their own partners.

F. Lead Around

16 All lead around with own partners and swing to finish.

King's Head

Danced to the tune, The Soldier's Joy.

Bars *A. Circle*

16   Dancers form a circle. All dance side-step and two threes clockwise and back to place *[8 bars]*; side-step anticlockwise with threes and back as before *[8 bars]*.

B. Body

8   *(a) Three-cornered hook:* 1st and opposite Tops men advance towards each other with promenade step, hook right arms, pass on to the man on the right of original position, hook left arms and pass behind own partner back to place *[6 bars]*. All clap alternate hands on legs above the knees four times *[1 bar]* and clap hands three times *[1 bar]*, keeping time with the tune.

8   *(b)* Side men repeat *(a)*.

C. 1st Figure. All Round Arch

8   *(a)* 1st Tops and opposite Tops exchange places, 1st Tops making an arch and opposite Tops passing under; then Sides exchange places, 1st Sides making an arch and opposite Sides passing under. All dance Sides Under Arms, 1st Tops passing under the arms of opposite Sides while opposite Tops make an arch for 1st Sides. Tops are now in Sides' original places and vice versa.

8   *(b)* From that finishing position, repeat *(a)*, Sides moving first.

D. 2nd Figure. Hook And Chain

16   Men hook the woman on their left with left arm, then hook own partner with right arm. Chain back to the woman on the left with left hand, and continue the chain movement until all dancers regain their former places.

E. 3rd Figure. All In, Or Thread The Needle

8   *(a)* All form a ring and take hands except 1st Tops man and the woman on his left. Top couple raise hands to make an arch. The

woman on the left passes through and round to her place, taking all the dancers in line after her.

8 *(b)* Repeat *(a)*, 1st Tops man passing under the arms of the couple on his left, and the other dancers following.

F. Body

16 Repeat *B* to complete the dance.

Labasheeda Reel Set
Seit Leada Sioda

Opening position for all figures, except where indicated: All four couples join hands in front and face anticlockwise around the circle, men on the inside.

1ST FIGURE

(Reels: 192 bars)

Bars | **A. Lead Around**

8   All four couples dance anticlockwise around until back in their original places. During the last 2 bars each man turns his partner clockwise under both arms, then adopts the standard hold.

B. Swing

8   All four couples swing in place.

C. Figure

8   *(a) Show each woman:* 1st Tops couple dance house around inside. During the last 2 bars the woman of the couple to the left of 1st Tops moves aside to allow the 1st Tops man to leave his partner in her place.

24   *(b) House:* 1st Tops man then dances house around with 1st Sides woman, and each successive woman, leaving each woman one place to the left of her original position.

D. Swing

8   All four new couples swing in place.

E. Figure

32   Repeat *C* with 1st Sides man dancing the Figure and each woman finishing opposite her original position.

F. Swing

8   Repeat *D*.

G. Figure

32   Repeat *C* with 2nd Tops man dancing the Figure and each woman finishing to the right of her original position.

H. Swing

8   Repeat *D*.

I. Figure

32   Repeat *C* with 2nd Sides man dancing the Figure and each woman finishing in her original position.

J. Swing

8   Repeat *D*.

K. House

8   All four couples dance house around.

2ND FIGURE   *(Reels: 128 bars)*

A. Lead Around

8   All four couples lead around as at *1st Figure, A*.

B. Swing

8   All four couples swing in place.

C. Figure

8   *(a) House:* 1st Tops couple dance house around inside, finishing in front of 1st Sides woman.

8   *(b) High gates:* The man takes his partner's left hand in his right hand and the 1st Sides woman's right hand in his left; this hold is maintained for 6 bars. The man then raises his left arm to form an arch, under which his partner dances, followed by the

man turning in place *[2 bars]*. The man drops his left and raises his right arm again forming an arch, under which the 1st Sides woman dances, followed by the man turning in place *[2 bars]*. The first arch is repeated *[2 bars]* and all three dancers dance back to place *[2 bars]*.

D. Swing

8   All four couples swing in place.

E. Figure

16   Repeat C with 1st Sides couple dancing *(a)* and 1st Sides couple and 2nd Tops woman dancing *(b)*.

F. Swing

8   Repeat D.

G. Figure

16   Repeat C with 2nd Tops couple dancing *(a)* and 2nd Tops couple and 2nd Sides woman dancing *(b)*.

H. Swing

8   Repeat D.

I. Figure

16   Repeat C with 2nd Sides couple dancing *(a)* and 2nd Sides couple and 1st Tops woman dancing *(b)*.

J. Swing

8   Repeat D.

K. House

8   All four couples dance house around.

3RD FIGURE   *(Reels: 128 bars)*

A. Lead Around

8   All four couples lead around as at *1st Figure, A*.

B. Swing

8   All four couples swing in place.

C. Figure

8   *(a) House:* 1st Tops couple dance house around inside to finish facing the couple on their left.

8   *(b) Little Christmas:* Both couples form a tight circle with arms behind each other's backs. They swing in a circle clockwise.

D. Swing

8   All four couples swing in place.

E. Figure

16   Repeat *C* with 1st Sides couple dancing *(a)*.

F. Swing

8   Repeat *D*.

G. Figure

16   Repeat *C* with 2nd Tops couple dancing *(a)*.

H. Swing

8   Repeat *D*.

I. Figure

16   Repeat *C* with 2nd Sides couple dancing *(a)*.

J. Swing

8   Repeat *D*.

K. House

8   All four couples dance house around.

4TH FIGURE   *(Reels: 192 bars)*

A. Lead Around

8   All four couples lead around as at *1st Figure, A*.

B. Swing

8   All four couples swing in place.

C. Figure

8   *(a) Show each man:* 1st Tops couple dance house around inside.
     During the last 2 bars the man of the couple to the left of 1st
     Tops moves aside to allow the 1st Tops woman to leave her
     partner in his place.

24   *(b) House:* 1st Tops woman then dances house around with 1st
     Sides man, and each successive man, leaving each man one
     place to the left of his original position.

D. Swing

8   All four new couples swing in place.

E. Figure

32   Repeat *C* with 1st Sides woman dancing the Figure and each
     man finishing opposite his original position.

F. Swing

8   Repeat *D*.

G. Figure

32 Repeat *C* with 2nd Tops woman dancing the Figure and each man finishing to the right of his original position.

H. Swing

8 Repeat *D*.

I. Figure

32 Repeat *C* with 2nd Sides woman dancing the Figure and each man finishing up in his original position.

J. Swing

8 Repeat *D*.

K. House

8 All four couples dance house around.

*5TH FIGURE *(see opposite for alternative)*   *(Jigs: 176 bars)*

A. Lead Around

8 All four couples lead around as at *1st Figure, A*.

B. Swing

8 All four couples swing in place.

C. Figure

8 *(a) House:* Top couples dance house around inside.
4 *(b) Advance and retire:* Top couples advance and retire once.
4 *(c) Change partners:* Top women dance straight across to opposite men, who dance in place.
8 *(d) House:* New couples dance house around inside.
4 *(e) Advance and retire:* New couples advance and retire once.
4 *(f) Change partners:* Top women dance straight back to their

original places. Top men move to the side while the women on their left join them by dancing clockwise into place, the woman passing in front of the man.

32   *(g) Repeat:* Top men repeat *(a)–(e)* with new women, and both Top men and Side women dance back to their own partners at *(f)*.

D. Home

8   All four couples dance around at home.

E. Figure

64   Repeat *C* with Side couples dancing the Figure.

F. Home

8   All four couples dance around at home.

G. House

8   All four couples dance house around.

*ALTERNATIVE 5TH FIGURE   (Flings: 168 bars)

A. Lead Around

8   All four couples lead around as at *1st Figure, A*.

B. Swing

8   All four couples swing in place.

C. Figure

4   *(a) Slide and home:* Top couples dance 1 bar into the centre, 1 bar back to place, then dance at home for 2 bars, doubling the step.

4   *(b) Slide and change:* Top couples dance 1 bar into the centre, 1 bar back to place, then dance half-way around the house to each other's positions, doubling the step.

4   *(c) Slide and home:* Top couples repeat *(a)*.

4   *(d) Slide and change:* Top couples repeat *(b)*, finishing in their original positions.

4   *(e) Left-hand chain:* Top men dance straight across to the opposite women, hook left arm in left, dance around each other and then dance back to their original partners.

4   *(f) Slide and home:* Top couples repeat *(a)*.

8   *(g) House:* Top couples dance house around, doubling the last 2 bars only.

D. Figure

32   Side couples dance *C.*

E. Figure

32   Top couples repeat *C.*

F. Figure

32   Side couples repeat *C.*

G. Home

8   All four couples dance around at home.

H. House

8   All four couples dance house around, doubling the last 2 bars.

6TH FIGURE   *(Hornpipes: 160 bars)*

Opening position: All four couples adopt the standard hold.

A. Body

16   All four couples dance 1 bar into the centre and 1 bar back to place, then dance on to the position of the couple on their right *[4 bars]*. This movement is repeated three more times *[12 bars]*, the couples ending up in their original positions.

B. House

8   All four couples dance house around.

C. Figure

8   Change partners: All four couples dance 1 bar into the centre and 1 bar back to place [2 bars]. Couples then separate: the men dance clockwise in place while the women dance clockwise to the men on their right; the women dance into place passing in front of the men [2 bars]. All four new couples dance around at home [4 bars].

D. Body

16   Repeat A.

E. House

8   Repeat B.

F. Figure

8   Repeat C with the women moving one more place to the right.

G. Body

16   Repeat A.

H. House

8   Repeat B.

I. Figure

8   Repeat C with the women moving one more place to the right.

J. Body

16   Repeat A.

K. House

8   Repeat *B*.

L. Figure

8   Repeat *C* with women moving into their original positions.

M. Body

16   Repeat *A*.

N. House

8   Repeat *B*.

Leitrim Set

Steps: Jig
Normal step: *treble, 1-2-3, treble, 1-2-3, etc.*
Step-it-out: *hop, heel, toe; hop, heel, toe; change, heel, toe; hop, heel, toe, etc.*
Swing: *swing for 6 bars, and treble 1, treble 2, treble 1-2-3, for 2 bars.*
Steps: Reel
Normal step: *and 1-2-3, and 1-2-3, etc.*
Step-it-out: *skip, hop 1-a-2-a-3, skip, hop 1-a-2-a-3, etc. Hop back, hop back, hop back and stamp.*
Advance and retire: *1-2, 1-2-3, 1, 2, 1-2-3, etc.*
Swing: *swing for 6 bars, down 1 and 2 and 1-2-3 for 2 bars.*

1ST FIGURE   *(Jigs: 120 bars)*

Bars   *A. Change Places*

8   *(a)* Top couples change places, women leading, men crossing in front of women at opposite side.

8   *(b)* Tops repeat, returning to place.

8   *(c)* All dancers 'step-it-out', facing partner.

8   *(d)* All couples swing.

B. Sides Change Places

32   Repeat *A*, with Side couples leading.

C. Chain And Swing

8   *(a)* Top women chain.

8   *(b)* All dancers step-it-out, facing partner.

8   *(c)* All couples swing.

D. Sides Chain And Swing

24   Repeat *C*, with Side couples leading.

2ND FIGURE   *(Reels: 88 bars)*

A. All Change Places

8   *(a)* Top couples advance, holding hands *[2 bars]*; Tops retire and Sides advance *[2 bars]*; Tops advance and Sides retire *[2 bars]*; Tops retire and Sides advance *[2 bars]*.

4   *(b)* Tops change places, keeping to the right, woman in front *[2 bars]*; Sides change places *[2 bars]*.

12 *(c)* Repeat *(a)* and *(b)*, from opposite side.

8   *(d)* All dancers step-it-out, facing partner.

8   *(e)* All couples swing.

B. All Change Places

40 Repeat *A*, with Side couples leading.

3RD FIGURE   *(Jigs: 168 bars)*

A. Dance Opposites

8   *(a)* 1st Top woman and opposite man change places, passing right shoulder to right, and reverse back to place, passing left shoulder to left.

8   *(b)* They both swing.

8   *(c)* Pick up partners, make a circle, and dance anticlockwise back to place.

8   *(d)* All dancers step-it-out, facing partner.

8   *(e)* All couples swing.

B. Dance Opposites

40 Repeat *A*, with Top man and opposite woman leading.

C. Repeat

80 Sides repeat *A* and *B*.

4TH FIGURE   *(Reels: 168 bars)*

A. Swing Opposite Woman

8   *(a)* 1st Top couple, with right hand in right, advance, retire and advance again, leaving the woman with the opposite couple, on the man's left. Meanwhile, opposite couple dance in place, the woman with her back to the centre of the set for the first 6 bars.

8   *(b)* All four advance and retire twice.

8   *(c)* Both men swing the opposite women for 6 bars, then the women return to place *[2 bars]*.

8   *(d)* All dancers step-it-out, facing partner.

8   *(e)* All couples swing.

B. Swing Opposite Woman

40 Repeat *A*, with opposite Top couple leading.

C. Repeat

80 Sides repeat *A* and *B*.

5TH FIGURE   *(Jigs: 104 bars)*

A. Swing Behind

8   *(a)* All dancers form a circle, advance and retire, holding hands down *[2 bars]*, hands up *[2 bars]*, hands down *[2 bars]*, hands up *[2 bars]*.

8   *(b)* Step-it-out, each man facing the woman on his left.

8   *(c)* All swing new partners in man's place.

B. Swing Behind

48 Repeat *A* with each new partner.

C. Circle And Swing

24 Repeat *A* with original partner.

6TH FIGURE
(Reels: 136 bars)

A. Women Move On

8   *(a)* All couples advance and retire twice, partners holding right hand in right.

8   *(b)* Each woman dances on to the man on her right, then all house, finishing in the woman's place.

8   *(c)* Step-it-out, with new partner.

8   *(d)* Swing with new partner.

B. Repeat

64   Repeat A with each new partner.

C. Circle And Swing

32   Repeat A with original partner.

Longford Set
Seit Longfoirt

This set was taught by Francis Bolger at the 1995 Galway International Set Dancing weekend.

1ST FIGURE (Reels: 152 bars)

Bars **A. Advance And Retire**

8   Top couples advance and retire holding right hands. As they retire, man brings his arm back over woman's head and places his hand on her shoulder *[4 bars]*. They lead across on the left, woman turning clockwise and man anticlockwise to face in on the other side as man's arm comes off woman's shoulder *[4 bars]*.

B. Tops Change Places

8   The man brings his arm back over the woman's head to place his hand on her shoulder again and Top couples lead across on the left to home, turning as before to face each other in place *[4 bars]* and dance facing each other *[4 bars]*.

C. Swing

8   Top couples swing in céilí hold *[6 bars]* and dance out *[2 bars]*.

D. Repeat

24   Side couples dance *A–C*.

E. Women Chain

8   Top women chain with right hands in the centre and turn clockwise under opposite man's left arm as they dance anticlockwise around each other *[4 bars]*. They chain back and turn clockwise under their partner's arm as he stays facing into the set *[4 bars]*.

F. Dance Out

8   Top couples dance out facing each other.

G. Swing

8 Top couples swing and dance out.

H. Repeat

24 Side couples dance *E–G*.

I. Repeat

24 Top couples repeat *A–C*.

J. Repeat

24 Side couples repeat *A–C*. Top couples join in at the end to dance out *[4 bars]* and swing *[8 bars]*.

2ND FIGURE   (Reels: 272 bars)

A. Pass Through

8 Top couples pass through, dancing across with men on the outside and moving sideways to reverse back with men in the centre. All pass the opposite person right shoulder to right on the way over and left shoulder to left on the way back.

B. Dance Out In The Centre

8 Top couples advance to dance out facing the opposite woman or man in the centre.

C. Swing

8 Top men swing the opposite women in the centre *[6 bars]*, dancing into a circle of four with each woman on her own partner's right-hand side *[2 bars]*.

D. Circle

8 Top couples dance clockwise in the circle *[4 bars]*, then dance back anticlockwise to finish facing their own partners in their own places *[4 bars]*.

E. Dance Out

8   Top couples dance out facing their partners.

F. Swing

8   Top couples swing.

G. Repeat

48   Top couples repeat *A–F*.

H. Repeat

96   Side couples dance *A–G*.

I. Women Chain

8   Top women chain as at *1st Figure, E*.

J. Dance Out

8   Top couples dance out facing their partners.

K. Swing

8   Top couples swing, moving to the centre to join the opposite couple at the end of the swing.

L. Christmas

8   Top couples swing in four in the centre *[6 bars]*, breaking back to place after the swing *[2 bars]*.

M. Repeat

32   Side couples dance *I–L*.

N. Advance And Retire

8   All advance and retire twice in a circle.

3RD FIGURE   (Polkas: 96 bars)

A. Advance And Retire

8   All advance and retire twice in a circle.

B. House

8   All house around with their own partners.

C. Advance And Retire

8   All advance and retire in the circle again, women moving on to
     the man on their right.

D. House

8   All house around with their new partners.

E. Advance And Retire

8   Repeat C.

F. House

8   All house around with their new partners.

G. Advance And Retire

8   Repeat C.

H. House

8   All house around with their new partners.

I. Advance And Retire

8   Repeat C, women moving on to rejoin their original partners.

J. House

16   All house around twice with their own partners.

Mallon's Reel

Diagram 1. Position of the dancers:

```
                1
               B A

        4 G            F 3
          H            E


                C D
                 2
```

Couple 1 are leading Tops, couple 2 opposite Tops, couple 3 leading Sides and couple 4 opposite Sides.

Bars **A. Lead Around**

16   All lead around *[8 bars]* and back *[8 bars]*.

B. Body

8   *(a) Double side-step and return in figure of eight:* Men side-step to the right and women to the left, finishing with two threes. Continue in the same direction with side-step and two threes. The position of the dancers after this movement is as follows:

Diagram 2

```
             H E

        A            B
        D            C


             G F
```

Men and women dance around each other, right shoulder to right, left shoulder to left with the person coming towards you, and right shoulder to right with your partner; turn into place.

16   *(b) The Sides and back to place:* Couples cross hands. Tops to the right, Sides to the left, side-step, finishing with two threes. Couples 1 and 4 dance around each other as do couples 3 and 2, back to starting position *[8 bars]*. Repeat, this time Sides to the right and Tops to the left, and dance around *[8 bars]*.

16   *(c) Women back-to-back and left hands across:* The women dance side-step, turning anticlockwise to face partner and dance two threes in place. Partners take right hand in right and dance clockwise around each other. The four women give left hands in the centre and hold right hand in right in front of partner to form a wheel. Lead around for 6 bars and turn 2 bars in place.

16   *(d) Men back-to-back and left hands across:* Men dance *C*, but dance side-step clockwise.

8   *(e) Swing:* All four couples swing.

C. 1st Figure. The Three Rings

16   *(a)* Leading and opposite Tops dance side-step and face the Side couples to their right; all dance two threes. Form two rings and side-step clockwise two threes. Side-step anticlockwise two threes, with Top couples ending up back-to-back as follows:

Diagram 3

G B C F

H A D E

Top couples take hands in a back-to-back ring and dance side-step clockwise to end up facing own position. Each man releases hands with the opposite woman and, holding his partner's left hand in his right, dances a half-turn into place.

16   *(b)* Leading and opposite Sides repeat.

D. Body

64   Repeat *B*.

E. 2nd Figure. Swing Around And Turn Around

8   *(a)* Top couples cross hands and dance around each other.

8   *(b)* Top couples release left hands, dance a full turn around their partner and release hands. The women dance around the Side man to their right and Top men dance around the Side woman to their left, and dance to centre.

8   *(c)* Top couples give right hands in a wheel and dance around clockwise. Top men give left hands to woman on their left and Top women give left hand to men on their left; dance around once. Release hands. Give right hand to own partner and turn into place.

24   *(d)* Leading and opposite Sides dance *(a)–(c)*.

F. Body

64   Repeat *B*.

G. 3rd Figure. Men And Women Cross And Swing Back To Place

16   *(a)* Top women change places passing face-to-face using side-step and two threes. Top men change, face-to-face using side-step and two threes. Top couples cross hands and dance around the opposite couple to their original starting position.

16   *(b)* Leading and opposite Sides dance *(a)*.

H. Body

64   Repeat *B*.

I. Finish

40   All dancers join hands. Advance and retire twice in a circle *[8 bars]* and side-step to the right, two threes; side-step to the left, two threes back in place *[8 bars]*. Advance and retire twice in circle *[8 bars]* and side-step to the left, two threes; side-step to the right two threes *[8 bars]*. All swing *[8 bars]*.

Mazurka Set
Seit Masúrca

1ST FIGURE. *LITTLE CHRISTMAS*   *(Reels: 144 bars)*

Opening position for all figures: Dancers face centre, joining hands in a circle.

Bars *A. Circle*

8   Advance and retire twice.

B. Figure

8   *(a) Swing:* All four couples swing in place.

8   *(b) House:* 1st Tops dance around the house inside.

8   *(c) Little Christmas:* The couple who have danced house turn to the couple on their left and form a tight circle with them, arms behind each other's backs. They dance in a circle clockwise, and the other two couples do likewise.

8   *(d) House:* All four couples dance house around.

C. Figure

32   Repeat *B*; 1st Sides dance house at *(b)*.

D. Figure

32   Repeat *B*; 2nd Tops dance house at *(b)*.

D. Figure

32   Repeat *B*; 2nd Sides dance house at *(b)*. Double the last 2 bars of *(d)*; i.e. women, instead of dancing: RLR-LRL-R, should dance: R-L-R-L-R. Men, instead of dancing: LRL-RLR-L, should dance L-R-L-R-L.

2ND FIGURE. *ADVANCE AND RETIRE*   *(Reels: 144 bars)*

A. Circle

8   Advance and retire twice.

B. Figure

8   *(a) Swing:* All four couples swing in place.

8   *(b) House:* 1st Tops dance around the house inside.

8   *(c) Advance and retire:* The couples who have danced house face the couple to their left. These two couples advance towards each other and retire, twice. The other two couples do likewise.

8   *(d) House:* All four couples dance house around.

C. Figure

32   Repeat *B*; 1st Sides dance house at *(b)*.

D. Figure

32   Repeat *B*; 2nd Tops dance house at *(b)*.

E. Figure

32   Repeat *B*; 2nd Sides dance house at *(b)*. Double the last 2 bars of the final house around, as at *1st Figure, D*.

3RD FIGURE. *HIGH GATES*   *(Reels: 144 bars)*

A. Circle

8   Advance and retire twice.

B. Figure

8   *(a) Swing:* All four couples swing in place.

8   *(b) House:* 1st Tops dance around the house inside.

8   *(c) High gates:* The man of the couple who have danced house raises his partner's right hand with his left hand and reaches under the raised arms with his right hand to take the right hand of the woman from the couple to their left and bring her through. She in turn keeps dancing around 1st Tops couple anticlockwise until it is her turn to pass through again. Then 1st Tops woman passes under her partner's right arm, followed by her partner. Dancing around, 1st Tops woman again passes

under her partner's right arm, followed by her partner. Finally the woman from the other couple, still holding the hand of the 1st Tops man, passes under the man's left, and woman's right arms of 1st Tops couple. Having danced completely around 1st Tops she should pass through this time in the opposite direction to the first time, heading back towards her partner.

8   (d) *House:* All four couples dance house around.

C. Figure

32   Repeat *B*; 1st Sides dance house at *(b)*.

D. Figure

32   Repeat *B*; 2nd Tops dance house at *(b)*.

E. Figure

32   Repeat *B*; 2nd Sides dance house at *(b)*. Double the last 2 bars of final house around, as at *1st Figure, D*.

4TH FIGURE. SWING   (Reels: 128 bars)

A. Circle

8   Advance and retire twice.

B. Figure

8   (a) *Swing:* All four couples swing in place.
8   (b) *House:* 1st Tops and 2nd Tops dance around the house inside.
32   (c) *Swing:* 1st and 2nd Tops men swing with all four women in turn, starting with the women to their left. All four couples swing for the last 8 bars.
8   (d) *House:* All four couples dance house around.

C. Figure

56   Repeat *B*; Side couples and Side men dance *(b)* and *(c)*. Double the last 2 bars of final house around, as at *1st Figure, D*.

5TH FIGURE. *CHAIN* (Reels: 176 bars))

A. Circle

8   Advance and retire twice.

B. Figure

8   *(a) Swing:* All four couples swing in place.

8   *(b) House:* 1st Tops dance around the house inside.

16   *(c) Chain:* Women dancing clockwise and men anticlockwise, all dancers chain around, starting with right hands to their own partners, until they reach home *[12 bars]*; partners swing *[4 bars]*.

8   *(d) House:* All four couples dance house around.

C. Figure

40   Repeat *B*; 1st Sides dance house at *(b)*.

D. Figure

40   Repeat *B*; 2nd Tops dance house at *(b)*.

E. Figure

40   Repeat *B*; 2nd Sides dance house at *(b)*. Double the last 2 bars of final house around, as at *1st Figure, D*.

6TH FIGURE. *FACE THE WALL* (Reels: 208 bars)

A. Circle

8   Advance and retire twice.

B. Figure

8   *(a) Swing:* All four couples swing in place.

16   *(b) House and line-up:* 1st Tops and the couple to their left (1st Sides) dance house around each other and end up facing out of

the set in 1st Tops' direction, with 1st Tops first and 1st Sides behind them *[8 bars]*. The other two couples repeat this movement and end up lined up behind the first two couples *[8 bars]*. (Starting from the couple in whose direction the line is facing, the other three couples should always be lined up behind them in the order that they come. Going clockwise around the set from that couple, men are on the left, women on the right.)

16   *(c) Arch:* Men circle off to the left and women to the right, making a tight circle. They pass through their starting positions once and go around again. When the leading couple come around to the starting position the second time they face each other and form an arch with their arms *[8 bars]*. As the other couples reach the arch they adopt the normal hold and dance under it and around anticlockwise to their own positions *[8 bars]*.

8   *(d) House:* All four couples dance house around.

C. Figure

48   Repeat *B*; 1st Sides and 2nd Tops dance house at *(b)*. Line faces out of the set in the direction of 1st Sides.

D. Figure

48   Repeat *B*; 2nd Tops and 2nd Sides dance house at *(b)*. Line faces out of the set in the direction of 2nd Tops.

E. Figure

48   Repeat *B*; 2nd Sides and 1st Tops dance house at *(b)*. Line faces out of the set in the direction of 2nd Sides. Double the last 2 bars of the final house around, as at *1st Figure, D*.

Mealagh Set
Seit Mhealaigh

1ST FIGURE. WOMEN CHAIN
(Polkas: 72 bars)

Bars *A. Advance And Retire*

8   Top couples advance and retire twice with hands held behind partners' backs, right hand in right, left hand in left.

B. Swing

8   Top couples swing.

C. Women Chain

8   Top women chain, right arm in centre, link left arm with opposite man. The man follows the woman around; women link right arm in centre and return to partner.

D. Swing

8   Top couples swing in place.

E. Repeat

32   Side couples dance *A–D* to finish.

2ND FIGURE. SLIDE AND SWING
(Slides: 56 bars)

A. Slide

16   All four couples slide in and out and house to opposite side *[8 bars]*; slide in and out and house to home *[8 bars]*.

B. Swing

8   All four couples swing.

C. Repeat

24   Repeat *A* and *B* to finish.

3RD FIGURE. *ADVANCE AND SWING*   *(Polkas: 136 bars)*

A. Swing

8   Top man and opposite woman advance to centre and swing. Return to own partner on the last 2 bars.

B. Lead Around

8   The man takes his partner's left hand in his left, right hand in right, behind her shoulder; lead around to opposite position. Women turn clockwise under man's right arm on last 2 bars.

C. Swing

8   Top man and opposite woman repeat *A*.

D. Lead Around

8   Top couples repeat *B*.

E. Swing

8   Opposite Top man and Top woman advance and swing.

F. Repeat

24   Tops repeat *B–D*.

G. Swing

8   1st Side man and opposite Side woman advance and swing.

H. Repeat

24   Sides dance *B–D*.

I. Swing

8   2nd Side man and 1st Side woman advance and swing.

J. Repeat

24   Sides repeat *B–D* to finish.

4TH FIGURE. *THE BASKET*   **(Polkas: 168 bars)**

A. Women Chain

8   Top women chain as at *1st Figure, C*.

B. Swing

8   Top couples swing.

C. Slide In And Out

8   Top couples slide in and out in place twice. Top men take right hands in right and advance to the centre. 1st Tops woman crosses over to opposite couple, turning clockwise into line of three and giving left hand to opposite man at shoulder while the opposite man turns his partner clockwise into line of three.

D. Three And One

8   1st Top man holds his partner's right hand in right and opposite woman's left hand in left. Top man reverses and the line of three advances for 2 bars; line of three reverses and Top man advances; Top man reverses and line of three advance for 2 bars. On the last 2 bars the women turn inwards to form a basket.

E. Basket

8   Top couples swing in basket *[6 bars]*; reverse to place *[2 bars]*.

F. Repeat

40   Top couples repeat *A–E*, opposite Tops advancing.

G. Repeat

40   Side couples dance *A–E*, 1st Sides advancing.

H. Repeat

40 Side couples repeat *A–E* to finish, 2nd Sides advancing.

5TH FIGURE. *WOMEN WHEEL*   (Slides: 96 bars)

A. Lead Around

8 All couples lead around anticlockwise to home, man's right arm around woman's waist, woman's left hand on man's right shoulder.

B. Body

16 All couples adopt waltz hold, slide in and out and house around to opposite position *[8 bars]*. Repeat to home *[8 bars]*.

C. Wheel

8 Women right-hand wheel, left arm to opposite man, dance around; right hand back in wheel, back to partner.

D. Swing

8 All swing.

E. Repeat

40 Repeat *A–D*.

F. Lead Around

8 Repeat *A* to finish.

6TH FIGURE. *WHEEL*   (Polkas: 232 bars)

A. Lead Around

8 All couples lead around anticlockwise to home, man's right arm around woman's waist, her left hand on his right shoulder.

B. Body

16 All couples adopt waltz hold, jump on two feet. The man kicks with right foot *[1 bar]*; couples dance in place *[1 bar]*. The woman does the same, but kicking with left foot. Dance to next position on right *[2 bars]*. Repeat three times until couples return home *[4 bars]*.

C. House

8 All house.

D. Women Wheel

8 Women right-hand wheel around *[4 bars]*. Turn left hand; dance past own place to end up with man to the right of own position.

E. Men Wheel

8 Men wheel all the way round.

F. Swing

8 Swing new partner.

G. Repeat

56 Repeat *A–F*.

H. Repeat

56 Repeat *A–F*.

I. Repeat

56 Repeat *A–F* to finish.

Melleray Lancers Set
Lannsuidhthe Phort Láirge

This lively set comes from the Melleray area of Co. Waterford.

1ST FIGURE (Polkas: 200 bars)

Bars *A. Swing*

8   1st Top man and opposite woman swing in céilí hold in centre.

B. Swing

8   Top couples swing in place.

C. Women Chain

8   Top women chain, right hands in the centre; turn with left arm around opposite man, right hands in the centre again and back to place.

D. Swing

8   Top couples swing again.

E. Steps And Circle

16   Men face the woman on the left, taking right hands. All dance R-L-R; L-R-L; R-L; R-L-R *[4 bars]* and swing *[3 bars]*. Dance from the swing *[1 bar]* into a circle, women facing out and men facing in, all holding their partner's right hand and the other person's left hand. All now dance R-L-R; L-R-L; R-L; R-L-R *[4 bars]* in the circle and swing partners *[4 bars]*.

F. Repeat

48   Repeat *A–E* with Top woman and opposite man dancing.

G. Repeat

96   Repeat *A–F* with Side couples leading; 1st Side couple are on the right of 1st Top couple.

2ND FIGURE   (Polkas: 168 bars)

A. Slide In And Out And Dance At Home

8   Top couple, in céilí hold, slide in, back and turn once in place.

B. Steps And Circle

8   Top couple take right hands and dance steps as at *1st Figure, E*
     [4 bars] and swing *[4 bars]*.

C. Chain And Swing

16   Top women chain *[8 bars]* and Top couples swing *[8 bars]*.

D. House

8   All couples house around in céilí hold.

E. Repeat

120 Repeat *A–D* with 2nd Top couple, 1st Side couple and 2nd Side
     couple leading in turn.

3RD FIGURE   (Polkas or Slides: 200 bars)

A. Kiss And Swing

8   Top man and opposite woman advance, kiss each other in the
     centre *[4 bars]*, then reverse back to swing own partners *[4 bars]*.

B. Kiss And Swing

8   Repeat *A*.

C. Chain And Swing

16   Top women chain *[8 bars]* and Top couples swing *[8 bars]*.

D. Steps And Circle

16   All dance the steps and circle, as at *1st Figure, E*.

E. Repeat

48 Repeat *A–D* with 2nd Top man and opposite woman leading.

F. Repeat

96 Repeat *A–E* with Side couples leading in turn.

4TH FIGURE   *(Polkas: 256 bars)*

A. Chain

16 All take partner's right hand and, starting on the right foot, chain all round, women clockwise and men anticlockwise. In opposite position, all dance R-L; R-L-R, holding partner's right hand; then continue the chain back to place. Dance R-L; R-L-R, facing partner in place.

B. Swing

8 All couples swing.

C. Chain And Swing

16 Top women chain and Top couples swing.

D. Lead Off

8 Top man dances to his left, Top woman to her right. They dance around outside the set to meet in opposite position; then, holding right hands, dance up the centre to place. The others follow the lead off in this order: couple to the right of 1st Top position are second (the man follows Top man and the woman follows Top woman); couple left of 1st Top position are third; and opposite Top couple are fourth. All dance up the centre to finish in lines, with women facing men.

E. Line Up And Swing

8 In lines, all dance the steps and swing partners back to place.

F. Repeat

56   Repeat *A–E* with 2nd Top couple leading.

G. Repeat

56   Repeat *A–E* with 1st Side couple leading.

H. Repeat

56   Repeat *A–E* with 2nd Side couple leading.

I. Chain And Swing

24   All chain all round again and swing partners to finish.

5TH FIGURE   *(Jigs: 200 bars)*

A. Gallop

8   Each Top man places both hands on his partner's waist while she places her hands on his shoulders. 1st couple gallop diagonally from the right-hand side of their own position to the opposite corner *[2 bars]*, 2nd couple gallop diagonally from the left-hand side of their own position to the opposite corner *[2 bars]*; 1st couple gallop back and 2nd couple gallop back.

B. Gallop

8   Top couples repeat *A*.

C. Chain And Swing

16   Top women chain, dancing polka step, and Top couples swing.

D. Steps And Circle

16   Dance steps and circle, as at *1st Figure, E*.

E. Repeat

48   Repeat *A–D* with 2nd Top couple leading.

F. Repeat

96   Repeat *A–E* with Side couples leading in turn.

6TH FIGURE   *(Polkas: 264 bars)*

A. Slide In And Out And Dance At Home

8   1st Top couple, in céilí hold, slide to the centre and back *[4 bars]*, then dance one full turn to face the couple on their right *[4 bars]*.

B. Dance And Swing Opposites

8   Taking right hands with the opposite woman or man, they dance the steps as at *1st Figure, E*, then swing the opposite person.

C. Repeat

40   Top man dances *A* and *B* twice more, bringing each woman to the next position *[32 bars]*; then, with the fourth woman, he slides to the centre, slides back and turns into his own place *[8 bars]*.

D. House

8   All house around with new partners.

E. Repeat

192   Repeat *A–D* with 1st Side man, 2nd Top man and 2nd Side man leading in turn.

7TH FIGURE   *(Polkas: 88 bars)*

A. Advance And Retire

8   All circle, holding hands and advance and retire twice.

B. Swing

8   All swing partners in place.

C. Circle And Women Move On

8   All circle again and women move on to join the man on the
    right.

D. Swing

8   All swing with new partners.

E. Repeat

48 Repeat *C* and *D* until the women are back swinging their own
    partners.

Monaghan Set
Seit Mhuineachain

1ST FIGURE. *WHEEL AND WOMEN CHAIN* *(Reels: 104 bars)*

Opening position: Couples face anticlockwise around the circle, men on the inside. Each man holds his partner's left hand in his left hand, and with his right arm over the woman's shoulder holds her right hand in his right hand.

Bars **A. Lead Around**

8 *(a)* All four couples dance anticlockwise around until they reach their own positions. On the last bar the four couples turn in place to face clockwise. They turn clockwise, out of the circle without releasing hands. Men remain on the inside of the circle but with left arms over the women's shoulders. Partners do not turn around each other; each dancer turns on the spot.

8 *(b)* All four couples dance clockwise back around to their own places again. On the last bar the men release their partners' left hands, take their partners' right hands with their left hands and adopt the standard position.

B. House

8 All four couples dance house around.

C. Home

8 All four couples dance around at home.

D. Figure. Women Right-Hand Chain

8 The four women dance around inside the circle in a chain. To begin, the Top women give their right hands across their bodies to the women on their left, and Side women give their right hands out to the women on their right. Top women never touch each other, nor do Side women.

E. Swing

8 When the women rejoin their partners all couples swing in place.

F. Lead Around

16 Repeat *A*.

G. House

8 All four couples dance house around.

H. Home

8 All four couples dance around at home.

I. Figure. Women Left-Hand Chain

8 Repeat *D*, but substituting left for right and vice versa.

J. Swing

8 When the women rejoin their partners all couples swing in place.

2ND FIGURE. *CROSS OVER*   (Jigs: 128 bars)

Opening position: All dancers face to centre, joining hands in a circle.

A. Circle

8 Advance and retire twice.

B. House

8 All four couples dance house around.

C. Home

8 All four couples dance around at home.

D. Figure

4 (a) *Advance and retire:* Top couples advance to centre and retire.
4 (b) *Cross over:* Top women dance across to each other's places while Top men dance in place *[2 bars]*; then Top men dance across to each other's places while Top women dance in place.

8   *(c) Swing:* Top couples swing in place.
4   *(d) Advance and retire:* Top couples advance to centre and retire.
4   *(e) Cross over:* Top couples repeat *(b)* to bring them back to their own places again.
8   *(f) Swing:* Top couples swing in place.

E. House

8   All four couples dance house around.

F. Home

8   All four couples dance around at home.

G. Figure

32   Side couples repeat *D*.

H. House

8   All four couples dance house around.

I. Home

8   All four couples dance around at home.

3RD FIGURE. *BACK-TO-BACK AND REEL OF THREE*
(Reels: 152 bars)

Opening position: All dancers face to centre, joining hands in a circle.

A. Circle

8   Advance and retire twice.

B. Figure

8   *(a) Pass through:* Top couples advance and pass through, 1st Tops on outside, and then retire and pass through, 1st Tops on inside. 1st Tops separate for the last 2 bars: the woman turns clockwise and dances in beside 2nd Sides man, and the man

turns anticlockwise and dances in beside 1st Sides woman. 2nd Tops dance in place for last 2 bars.

Each couple should take 2 bars to pass through, dance 2 bars while they change from the inside to the outside or vice versa, take 2 bars to pass back through, and 2 bars to dance in place or turn in beside the other couples.

8   *(b) Advance and retire:* The two groups of three dancers facing each other join hands, advance to the centre and retire twice.

8   *(c) Swing:* The two groups of three swing in place, arms around each other's backs. They should make sure to come out of the swing in time for the next movement.

C. Circle

8   Reform the circle and advance and retire twice.

D. Figure

24   Repeat *B*, with 2nd Tops dancing forward on the outside, back on the inside and turning to make the threes with the Side couples.

E. Circle

8   Reform the circle and advance and retire twice.

F. Figure

24   Side couples repeat *B*; 1st Sides dance the Figure.

G. Circle

8   Reform the circle and advance and retire twice.

H. Figure

24   Side couples repeat *B*; 2nd Sides dance the Figure.

I. Circle

8   Reform the circle and advance and retire twice.

J. Swing

8 All four couples swing in place.

4TH FIGURE. *CHANGE PLACES* *(Polkas: 104 bars)*

Opening position: Couples adopt the standard position.

A. Change Places

4 *(a) Tops:* 1st Tops and 2nd Tops dance half-way around the house to each other's place while the Side couples dance in place.

4 *(b) Sides:* 1st Sides and 2nd Sides dance half-way around the house to each other's place while the Top couples dance in place.

4 *(c) Tops:* 1st Tops and 2nd Tops dance half-way around the house back to their own places while the Side couples dance in place.

4 *(d) Sides:* 1st Sides and 2nd Sides dance half-way around the house back to their own places while the Top couples dance in place.

B. Home

8 Top couples dance around at home.

C. House

8 Top couples dance house around.

D. Home

8 All four couples dance around at home.

E. House

8 All four couples dance house around.

F. Change Places

16 Repeat *A;* this time the Side couples change first.

G. Home

8 Side couples dance around at home.

H. House

8 Side couples dance house around.

I. Home

8 All four couples dance around at home.

J. House

8 All four couples dance house around.

5TH FIGURE. *CHANGE ALL AROUND* (Hornpipes: 128 bars)

Opening position: All dancers face to centre, joining hands in a circle.

A. Circle

8 Advance and retire twice.

B. House

8 All four couples dance house around.

C. Home And Change

8 All four couples dance around at home. During the last 2 bars
the men, keeping their partners' right hands in their left hands,
turn their partners under their left arms so that when the circle
forms again the men have their original partners to their left,
and they have new partners to their right.

D. Circle

8 Reform the circle and advance and retire twice.

E. House

8   All four couples dance house around.

F. Home And Change

8   Repeat C. The women move one place around again.

G. Circle

8   Reform the circle and advance and retire twice.

H. House

8   All four couples dance house around.

I. Home And Change

8   Repeat C. The women move one place around again.

J. Circle

8   Reform the circle and advance and retire twice.

K. House

8   All four couples dance house around.

L. Home And Change

8   Repeat C. The women move on to rejoin their original partners.

M. Circle

8   Reform the circle and advance and retire twice.

N. House

8   All four couples dance house around.

O. Home

8   All couples dance around at home, doubling the last 2 bars.

Mullabawn Reel

A round dance.   **(Reels: 408 bars)**

Bars **A. Lead Around**

16   Four couples cross hands and lead around anticlockwise in a
     circle. When couples arrive in original positions the men turn
     clockwise and the women anticlockwise without releasing hands
     [8 bars]; lead around clockwise to original positions *[8 bars]*.

     B. Body

16   *(a) Side-step:* Top couples side-step to the left while Side couples
     side-step to the right, finishing with two threes; repeat side-
     step to original positions *[8 bars]*. Repeat, with Top couples
     dancing to the right and Side couples dancing to the left *[8 bars]*.

16   *(b) Men wheel and big wheel:* The four men give right hands in a
     wheel and dance around clockwise *[4 bars]*. Release hands and
     turn clockwise to grip left hands in the wheel; men take part-
     ner's left hand in their right and dance around anticlockwise to
     original position *[8 bars]*. Partners swing *[4 bars]*.

8   *(c) Men chain:* Each Top man dances to the woman on his left
     while Side men dance to the woman on their right. The men
     pass left shoulder to left and each gives left hand to the woman's
     left; dance around and return to partner with the right hand,
     men passing right shoulder to right. Dance around into place.

8   *(d) Men circle:* The four men dance around anticlockwise in a
     circle without taking hands, dancing for 1 bar on the spot oppo-
     site their own position.

     C. 1st Figure. Advance And Retire

8   *(a)* Top couples cross hands, advance and retire twice.

8   *(b)* Top couples, hands still crossed, dance around each other.

16   *(c)* Side couples dance *(a)* and *(b)*.

     D. Body

48   Repeat **B**.

E. 2nd Figure. Women Chain And Wheel

4   (a) Top women dance to the centre, take right hands and dance around clockwise; as the women dance towards their partners, the men dance in front of them, taking right hands above the women's hands to form a wheel.

12   (b) Top couples continue clockwise in the wheel *[4 bars]*, then turn clockwise, put left hand in the wheel and dance anticlockwise to original position *[4 bars]*; Top couples swing *[4 bars]*.

16   (c) Side couples dance (a) and (b).

F. Body

48   Repeat B.

G. 3rd Figure. Men Chain And Wheel

32   Repeat E, with the men dancing the movements first.

H. Body

48   Repeat B.

I. 4th Figure. Men's Chain

16   (a) Top men dance across to the opposite women, taking right hands and dance around clockwise; dance straight back across to partner, taking left hands and dancing around anticlockwise. Men then dance to the centre, grip right hands and dance a full turn clockwise; release hands and dance to opposite woman, taking left hands and dance around anticlockwise; return to original position.

16   (b) Sides dance (a).

J. Body

48   Repeat B.

K. Lead Around

16   Repeat A to finish.

Newmarket Plain Set
Seit Soiléir Bhaile Nua

1ST FIGURE *(Polkas: 280 bars)*

Bars *A. Lead Around*

16   Lead around three-quarters' way *[8 bars]*, finishing with men's
      backs to the centre, holding hands in front *[4 bars]* and slide to the
      corner *[2 bars]*; slide to home *[2 bars]* and dance at home *[4 bars]*.

B. Show The Lady

8   1st Top couple show the woman (house inside).

C. Advance And Retire And Cross Over

8   Top couples advance and retire, holding right hands and dance
      to opposite side. Women move ahead of their partners, pass
      right shoulder to right and turn clockwise into opposite posi-
      tions. Men pass left shoulder to left and turn anticlockwise into
      opposite positions.

D. Swing

8   Both couples swing in opposite positions.

E. Repeat

16   Top couples repeat *C* and *D* from opposite positions.

F. Women Chain

8   Top women chain right hands in centre; link left arms with op-
      posite man, turning twice around him; dance back to partners.

G. Swing

8   Top couples swing.

H. Square

8   Top couples square to opposite side and house back to place.

I. Repeat

64   2nd Top couple house inside; both Top couples repeat *C–H*.

J. Repeat

128   Side couples dance *B–I*; 1st Side couple are on the left.

2ND FIGURE   *(Polkas: 216 bars)*

A. Lead Around

16   Lead around and square the corner to home.

B. House

8   1st Top couple house inside.

C. Advance And Retire

8   Both Top couples advance and retire holding right hands and turn the woman twice to opposite side.

D. Swing

8   Top couples swing.

E. Repeat

16   Top couples repeat *C* and *D*.

F. Square

8   Top couples square around each other.

G. Repeat

48   Top couples repeat *B–F*; 2nd couple dance *B*.

H. Repeat

96   Side couples dance *B–G*.

3RD FIGURE

(Polkas: 280 bars)

A. Lead Around

16   Lead around and square the corner to home.

B. House

8   1st Top couple house inside.

C. Swing

8   Top man and opposite woman swing in the centre.

D. Advance And Retire

8   Top couples advance, retire and turn the woman twice to other side.

E. Swing

8   Top couples swing.

F. Swingers

8   Top man and opposite woman, advance, retire, then advance sideways and bow with the man's left arm over the woman's shoulder. (An alternative to this is to dance around each other clockwise and bow to each other.)

G. Repeat

16   Top couples repeat *D* and *E*.

H. Square

8   Top couples square around each other.

I. Repeat

64   Top couples dance *B–H* with 2nd couple leading.

J. Repeat

128 Side couples dance *B–I*.

4TH FIGURE   *(Polkas: 216 bars)*

A. Lead Around

16 Lead around and square the corner to home.

B. Show The Lady

8 1st Top couple house.

C. Crowning

8 Top couples advance to the centre (Top man barely moves forward) and both women retire with the 2nd man, facing him; 2nd woman holds his right hand in her right and Top woman holds his left in her left *[4 bars]*. All four advance to the centre and the women give free hands (underneath) to Top man, who pulls the women towards him, raising all hands in the air over the women's heads. This is the 'crowning'. The men then lower their hands to place them around the women's waists, and the women place their hands on the men's shoulders *[4 bars]*.

D. Christmas

8 Top couples swing in four.

E. Women Chain

8 Top women chain.

F. Swing

8 Top couples swing.

G. Square

8 Top couples square around each other.

H. Repeat

48 Top couples repeat *B–G* with 2nd couple leading.

I. Repeat

96 Side couples dance *B–H*.

5TH FIGURE   (Slides: 200 bars)

A. Square

8 Top couples square around each other.

B. Slide And Change

16 Top couples slide and change to other side, slide and change back.

C. Slide And Change

16 Top couples repeat *B*.

D. Square

8 Top couples square around each other again.

E. Repeat

48 Side couples repeat *A–D*.

F. Repeat

96 Repeat *A–E*.

6TH FIGURE   (Hornpipes: 160 bars)

A. Body And House

24 All couples, in waltz hold, dance the Body and House.

B. Women Move On

8 Facing into the centre, not holding hands, all dance in and back,

men four times and women three times. As men dance in the fourth time, women move on to the next position on the right.

C. Repeat

96 Repeat *A* and *B* until back with own partner.

D. Body And House

24 Dance the Body and House, as at *A*, to finish.

7TH FIGURE   *(Reels: 120 bars)*

A. Lead Around And Swing

16 All couples lead around holding hands in front and swing.

B. Lead Across And Back

8 Top couples, holding hands in front, lead across on the right, turn towards partner to face back and lead back on same side.

C. Dance Away From Partners

16 Top couples face partners, with men facing out of the set. They side-step to the left (away from partner), dance two threes, then side-step back, passing partner back-to-back and swing.

D. Men Chain

8 Top men chain right hands in the centre, dancing a full turn around each other; chain left hands around opposite woman and pass right shoulders back to partner.

E. Repeat

48 Repeat *A–E* with Side couples leading.

F. Lead Around

16 Lead around and swing to finish.

Newmarket Set Of Mazurks
Meiseart An Bhaile Nua

Opening position for all figures, except where indicated: all four couples face anticlockwise around the circle, men on the inside with left arms around their partner's waists and women's right hands on men's right shoulders.

1ST FIGURE   *(Jigs: 256 bars; flat sliding polka step)*

Bars **A. Lead Around**

8   All four couples dance anticlockwise around until back in original places.

B. Square

8   All four couples slide to positions on their right, then pivot in place *[2 bars]*; slide to next position then pivot *[2 bars]*. Repeat until home (slide or slide, 1-2-3).

C. Figure

8   *(a)* 1st Tops dance house around the inside.
8   *(b)* 1st Tops swing *[6 bars]*, then 1st Top man drops his partner off at home and, turning one time, moves on to pick up the woman on his left *[2 bars]*.
8   *(c)* 1st Top man swings new woman *[6 bars]*, then drops her off in front of her original partner and, turning one time, moves on to pick up the next woman *[2 bars]*. As the man swings each new woman, the previous woman walks around to take the position of the woman to her left.
16   *(d)* 1st Top man repeats *(c)* until he returns home with the last woman he swings.

D. Lead Around And Square

16   All repeat *A* and *B*.

E. Figure

40   1st Sides repeat *C*.

F. Lead Around And Square

16   All repeat *A* and *B*.

G. Figure

40   2nd Tops repeat *C*.

H. Lead Around And Square

16   All repeat *A* and *B*.

I. Figure

40   2nd Sides repeat *C*.

J. Lead Around And Square

16   All repeat *A* and *B*.

K. Sevens Around

8   All couples dance sevens around the square.

2ND FIGURE *SWINGIN' THREES*
(Jigs: 224 bars; flat sliding polka step)

A. Lead around

8   All four couples dance anticlockwise around until back in original places.

B. Square

8   All four couples slide to positions on their right, then pivot in place *[2 bars]*; slide to next position then pivot *[2 bars]*. Repeat until home (slide or slide, 1-2-3).

C. Figure

8   *(a)* 1st Tops house three-quarters of the way around the inside

of the square *[6 bars]*, then with man's left arm and woman's right arm lifted, encircle woman on the left *[2 bars]*.

8 *(b)* 1st Tops swing with new woman *[6 bars]*, then couple drops woman off at home and, turning once, moves on to pick up the next woman to the left *[2 bars]*.

16 *(c)* 1st Tops repeat *(b)* until they return home.

D. Lead Around And Square

16 All repeat *A* and *B*.

E. Figure

32 1st Sides dance *C*.

F. Lead Around And Square

16 All repeat *A* and *B*.

G. Figure

32 2nd Tops dance *C*.

H. Lead Around And Square

16 All repeat *A* and *B*.

I. Figure

32 2nd Sides dance *C*.

J. Lead Around And Square

16 All repeat *A* and *B*.

K. Sevens Around

8 All couples dance sevens around the square.

3RD FIGURE. *UNDER THE FINGER*
(Jigs: 160 bars; flat sliding polka step)

A. Lead Around

8   All four couples dance anticlockwise around until back in original places.

B. Square

8   All four couples slide to positions on their right, then pivot in place *[2 bars]*; slide to next position then pivot *[2 bars]*. Repeat until home (slide or slide, 1-2-3).

C. Figure

8   *(a)* 1st Tops dance house around the inside.

8   *(b)* Right hand in right hand, 1st Tops man turns his partner clockwise four times under his right arm, while battering in place himself.

D. Lead Around And Square

16   All repeat *A* and *B*.

E. Figure

16   1st Tops and 1st Sides repeat *C*.

F. Lead Around And Square

16   All repeat *A* and *B*.

G. Figure

16   1st Tops, 1st Sides and 2nd Tops repeat *C*.

H. Lead Around And Square

16   All repeat *A* and *B*.

I. Figure

16   All four couples repeat *C*.

J. Lead Around And Square

16   All repeat *A* and *B*.

K. Sevens Around

8   All couples dance sevens around the square.

4TH FIGURE. *HIGH GATES*
(Jigs: 160 bars; flat sliding polka step)

A. Lead Around

8   All four couples dance anticlockwise around until back in original places.

B. Square

8   All four couples slide to positions on their right, then pivot in place *[2 bars]*; slide to next position then pivot *[2 bars]*. Repeat until home (slide or slide, 1-2-3).

C. Figure

8   (*a*) 1st Tops dance house around the inside.

8   (*b*) Left hand in left, 1st Tops dance 1 bar in to centre and 1 bar towards couple on left *[2 bars]*. Top man, still holding partner's left hand, raises the arms to form an arch. With his right hand, he takes woman on the left under the arch; he turns anticlockwise, while both women turn simultaneously (1st Top woman clockwise and 1st Side woman anticlockwise); both women travel around man (1st Top woman anticlockwise under arch into lead-around position; 1st Side woman clockwise behind man, home to partner and into lead-around position).

D. Lead Around And Square

16   All repeat *A* and *B*.

E. Figure

16   1st Sides dance C.

F. Lead Around And Square

16   All repeat A and B.

G. Figure

16   2nd Tops dance C.

H. Lead Around And Square

16   All repeat A and B.

I. Figure

16   2nd Sides dance C.

J. Lead Around And Square

16   All repeat A and B.

K. Sevens Around

8   All couples dance sevens around the square.

5TH FIGURE. *STALLING*

(Jigs: 112 bars; flat sliding polka step)

A. Lead Around

8   All four couples dance anticlockwise around until back in original places.

B. Square

8   All four couples slide to positions on their right, then pivot in place *[2 bars]*; slide to next position then pivot *[2 bars]*. Repeat until home (slide or slide, 1-2-3).

C. Figure

8   (a) Top couples dance around in the space in front of them and line up in couples, 2nd Tops a little behind 1st Tops and facing the direction of 1st Tops (1st Tops/space/2nd Tops/space).

8   (b) Side couples dance around in the space left in front of them and line up, 1st Sides behind 1st Tops and 2nd Sides behind 2nd Tops (1st Tops/1st Sides/2nd Tops/2nd Sides).

16   (c) Couples lead off twice, men to the left and women to the right *[8 bars]*, then the couple meet up and lead around to home *[8 bars]*.

D. Lead Around And Square

16   All repeat *A* and *B*.

E. Figure

16   Repeat *C* with Side couples dancing around first and lining up facing in the direction of 1st Sides (1st Sides/2nd Tops/2nd Sides/1st Tops).

F. Lead Around And Square

16   All repeat *A* and *B*.

G. Sevens Around

8   All couples dance sevens around the square.

6TH FIGURE   (Hornpipes: 160 bars)

Opening position: couples adopt standard waltz-hold position.

A. Body

16   All couples dance together 1 bar into the centre and 1 bar back to their own positions with a battering hornpipe step, then dance 2 bars around to the position of the couple to their right, doubling up and turning clockwise as they go.

B. House

8   All couples dance house around, doubling the last 2 bars.

C. Women Change

8   While the men dance in place, the women advance and retire three times *[6 bars]*; men then advance and retire once while the women move on to the man on their right, turning anti-clockwise into place *[2 bars]*.

D. Body And House

24   All repeat *A* and *B*.

E. Women Change

8   All couples repeat *C*.

F. Body And House

24   All repeat *A* and *B*.

G. Women Change

8   All couples repeat *C*.

H. Body And House

24   All repeat *A* and *B*.

I. Women Change

8   All couples repeat *C*.

J. Body And House

24   All repeat *A* and *B*.

Newport Set
Seit Phort An Aonaigh

1ST FIGURE *(Jigs: 272 bars)*

Note: Dance 1-2-3, 1-2-3 on advance and retire, and 1, 2, 1-2-3 on the spot all during the 1st Figure.

Bars *A. Advance And Retire*

8   All couples take hands in front, advance *[2 bars]*, dance on the spot *[2 bars]*, retire *[2 bars]* and dance in place *[2 bars]*.

B. Lead Around

8   Lead around to next position, dance 2 bars in place, lead on to opposite position, dance 2 bars again.

C. Swing

8   Men finish facing out of the set, women facing in; all swing.

D. Lead Back

8   Lead back to place as at *B*.

E. Line Of Three

8   Top man advances holding his partner's right hand and takes the other woman's left hand as both women face him *[4 bars]*. He retires to place both arms over the women's shoulders as they turn in beside him *[4 bars]*.

F. Women Cross And Swing

16   Top man and both women advance to the centre *[2 bars]* and dance on the spot *[2 bars]*. The women cross and turn to face opposite man *[4 bars]* and swing in the men's position.

G. Repeat

24   Repeat *E* and *F* with opposite couple leading.

H. Repeat

48   Side couples dance *E–G*.

I. Diagonal Lines

8   Top couples, hands in front, dance to the right of centre, forming a diagonal line with opposite couple *[2 bars]*, dance on the
spot *[2 bars]*, retire *[2 bars]* and dance in place *[2 bars]*.

J. Diagonal Lines

8   Repeat *I*, going to the left. Top man and opposite woman stay
in the centre and face each other.

K. Swing

8   Top man and opposite woman swing *[6 bars]* and retire *[2 bars]*.

L. Repeat

24   Repeat *I–K* with other man and woman swinging.

M. Repeat

48   Side couples dance *I–L*.

N. Women Chain

8   Top women chain right hands with full turn in the centre
around each other, left-hand half-turn around opposite man.
Women keep turning until facing into circle of four.

O. Swing

8   Swing in four.

P. Repeat

16   Side couples dance *N* and *O*.

Q. Advance And Retire

8   All advance dance on the spot, retire, dance at home.

2ND FIGURE   *(Hornpipes: 184 bars)*

Note: All dance hop 1 hop 2 hop 1-2-3 all the time during the 2nd Figure.

A. Advance And Retire

8   Holding right hands, all couples advance, dance on the spot, retire and dance in place.

B. Turn The Women In The Circle

16   Women dance to left in front of partners; all dance clockwise in a circle, each woman in front of partner. Women turn anticlockwise, right hand in right in first position *[4 bars]*, turn clockwise, left hand in left in opposite position *[8 bars]*; repeat back to place. On the last turn clockwise, men pass on inside back to place, turning clockwise as partners turn under their left arms.

C. Square Inside

16   Holding hands in front, Top couples dance to face the couple on the left, dance on the spot for 2 bars *[4 bars]*, reverse into opposite position and dance in place there *[4 bars]*. Repeat to home.

D. Square Inside

16   Side couples dance *C*.

E. Women Face The Men

8   Women dance a half turn anticlockwise to face partners (and out of set) *[2 bars]*; both dance on spot *[2 bars]* then dance, holding joined hands and turning anticlockwise to finish back in place.

F. Men Face The Women

8   Repeat *E* with men moving in, turning clockwise.

G. Top Women Chain

8   Top women dance forward, right shoulder to right *[2 bars]*, take right hands and dance a full turn around each other *[2 bars]*. Dance forward, left shoulder to left of opposite man, take left hands and dance around him to face in again.

H. Top Women Chain

8   Repeat G back to place.

I. Side Women Chain

16   Repeat G and H.

J. Gates

8   Top couples dance forward into a line with 1st couple in centre, Side and opposite couples on either side. Turn around opposite woman or man, holding hands (Top man turns anticlockwise, Top woman clockwise) *[4 bars]*. Dance back to place; turn in to face forward again (man turns anticlockwise, woman clockwise).

K. Gates

8   Repeat J with opposite couple in the centre.

L. Repeat

16   Side couples dance J and K.

M. Chain

32   Straight from the gates, men dance left on the outside, women right on the inside to form diagonal lines at the corners of the set. Dance a full clockwise turn, right hand in right, move on to first positions left or right with men inside and dance a full anticlockwise turn, left hand in left. Repeat three more times to get back home. On the last turn, men turn clockwise into place on the inside as women turn clockwise under partners' arms.

N. Advance And Retire

8 Holding right hands, all couples advance, dance on the spot, retire and dance in place.

3RD FIGURE   (Polkas: 240 bars)

A. Circle

8 Circle, hands low, advance and retire twice.

B. House

8 All house.

C. Long Slide Or Gallop

8 Top couples dance the long slide, or gallop: couples in waltz hold, men leading with left foot and women with right, give a slight hop forward, landing on the foot in front. Keeping the weight on the foot in front, dancers propel themselves forward with the other foot for 14 steps *[4 bars]* across to the opposite position. Reverse the footwork when coming back to original position.

D. House

8 Top couples house.

E. Repeat

8 Side couples dance *C* and *D*.

F. Circle

8 Circle again and women move to the right.

G. House

8 All house.

H. Repeat

144 Repeat C–G until finished housing with partner.

I. Advance And Retire And Chain

16 Advance and retire, holding right hands *[4 bars]* and chain all round *[12 bars]*.

J. Swing

8 Swing to finish.

Paris Set
Seit Pharais

1ST FIGURE *(Reels: 160 bars)*

Bars **A. Lead Around**

8 All couples lead around and turn the woman under.

B. Swing

8 All couples swing in place.

C. Set Left, Set Right

8 *(a)* Leading couple dance house around inside.
8 *(b)* Top couples dance house around each other.
16 *(c)* All couples set left and set right, i.e. each man dances to the woman on his left, turning once, while she also turns once in place *[2 bars]*, and they both dance at home *[6 bars]*; this movement is repeated with his own partner.

D. Set Left, Set Right

32 Repeat *C* with opposite Tops leading.

E. Set Left, Set Right

32 Repeat *C* with 1st Sides leading.

F. Set Left, Set Right

32 Repeat *C* with 2nd Sides leading.

G. House

8 All couples dance house around.

2ND FIGURE   *(Reels: 224 bars)*

A. Lead Around

8   All couples lead around and turn the woman under.

B. Swing

8   All couples swing in place.

C. Clap And Wheel

8   *(a)* Leading couple dance house around, and everybody clap hands on the last beat of the 8th bar of music.

8   *(b)* All men give right hands in the centre and dance around half-way to the left, while all women dance around half-way to the right on the outside. All women and men reverse and dance back to place.

8   *(c)* All couples dance at home.

8   *(d)* Top couples dance house around each other.

16   *(e)* All couples set left and set right.

D. Clap And Wheel

48   Repeat *C*, with opposite Tops leading and women dancing in the centre while men dance on the outside.

E. Clap And Wheel

48   Repeat *C*, with 1st Sides leading and men dancing in the centre while women dance on the outside.

F. Clap And Wheel

48   Repeat *C*, with 2nd Sides leading, and women dancing in the centre while men dance on the outside.

G. House

8   All couples dance house around.

3RD FIGURE   *(Reels: 288 bars)*

A. Lead Around

8   All couples lead around and turn the woman under.

B. Swing

8   All couples swing in place.

C. Dance All The Ladies

32   *(a)* Leading couple dance house around. During the last 2 bars the man leaves his partner back to her place and dances on to the woman on his left, who dances out to meet him. Leading man repeats this movement with each woman in turn.

8   (b) Top couples dance at home.

8   (c) Top couples dance house around each other.

16   (d) All couples set left and set right.

D. Dance All The Ladies

64   Repeat *C* with 1st Sides leading.

E. Dance All The Ladies

64   Repeat *C* with opposite Tops leading.

F. Dance All The Ladies

64   Repeat *C* with 2nd Sides leading.

G. House

8   All couples dance house around.

4TH FIGURE   *(Jigs: 224 bars)*

A. Lead Around

8   All couples lead around and turn the woman under.

B. Swing

8   All couples swing in place.

C. Women Chain

8   *(a)* Top women chain with right hands in the centre and dance over to opposite men. They are followed immediately by Side women *[2 bars]*. Each woman gives left hand to opposite man, turns clockwise under his left arm and dances around behind him, the man turning with the woman. Women return to the centre, Top women slightly in front of Side women. Give right hands and back to partner.

8   *(b)* All couples dance at home.

8   *(c)* Leading couple dance house around inside.

8   *(d)* Top couples dance house around each other.

16   *(e)* All couples set left and set right.

D. Women Chain

48   Repeat *C* with Side women starting the chain and opposite Tops leading.

E. Women Chain

48   Repeat *C* with Top women starting the chain and 1st Sides leading.

F. Women Chain

48   Repeat *C* with Side women starting the chain and 2nd Sides leading.

G. House

8   All couples dance house around.

5TH FIGURE *(Hornpipes/March: 160 bars)*

A. Advance And Retire

8 All couples form circle, advance and retire twice.

B. Chain All Around

12 *(a)* All couples chain; women go left, men go right.
4 *(b)* All couples dance at home.

C. Line Up

8 *(a)* Leading couple dance house around inside, ending up just inside their original position, and facing out of the set.
8 *(b)* The other three couples dance house around, and line up behind the leading couple.
8 *(c)* All couples march around in opposing circles, women to the right, men to the left. (March.)
8 *(d)* All couples dance house around and back to place.

D. Line Up

32 Repeat *C* with 1st Sides leading.

E. Line Up

32 Repeat *C* with opposite Tops leading.

F. Line Up

32 Repeat *C* with 2nd Sides leading.

Peeler And The Goat

Opening position: The man's right arm is around the woman's waist while the woman's left arm is on the man's right shoulder.

Bars **A. Advance And Retire**

8 Advance and retire twice (the man starts on the left foot, the woman on the right): heel 1, heel 2, heel 1-2-3 (advance); heel 1, heel 2, heel 1-2-3 (retire). 8 bars

B. Hook

8 Partners hook right arms, dance around *[4 bars]*; then they turn, hook left arms and dance back *[4 bars]*.

C. Turn Your Partner

8 Face each other with hands crossed, right hand in right, left hand in left. Turn the woman under *[2 bars]*, turn the man under *[2 bars]*; turn the woman under *[2 bars]* and waltz hold *[2 bars]*.

D. House

8 All house.

E. Repeat

Repeat the dance as often as required.

Plain Polka Set
Seit Pholca

This original version of the Plain Set from West Clare was danced to polkas played in the Clare style of music. The men danced battering steps to the polkas.

1ST FIGURE *(Polkas: 112 bars)*

Bars **A. Lead Around**

16   Lead around with men on the inside, holding hands in front. Turn the woman with right hand only and all couples swing.

B. Cross Over

8   Top couples cross, women passing between the opposite woman and man. At the other side, partners pass left shoulder to left, women turning anticlockwise, then men turning clockwise into place. Dance back the same way.

C. Swing

8   Top couples swing.

D. Chain

8   Top women chain, right hands in the centre, left hands with opposite man, going around him, and right hands on the way back.

E. Lead And Pass Through

8   Top couples lead across on the right, holding hands in front, turn the woman clockwise and pass through back to place as at *B*.

F. Swing

8   All couples swing.

G. Repeat

40   Repeat *B–F* with Side couples leading.

H. House

8   All couples house.

2ND FIGURE   (Polkas: 128 bars)

A. Lead Around

16 All couples lead around and swing as at *1st Figure, A*.

B. Advance And Retire And Cross Over

16 Top couples take right hands, advance, retire and turn the woman across. Women turn clockwise twice under their partner's right arm. Advance, retire and turn the woman across to home positions.

C. Swing

8   Top couples swing.

D. Repeat

24 Repeat *B* and *C*.

E. Repeat

48 Repeat *B–D* with Side couples leading.

F. House

8   All couples house.

3RD FIGURE   (Polkas: 170 bars)

A. Lead Around

16 All couples lead around and swing as at *1st Figure, A*.

B. Opposites Dance Around Each Other

8   Top woman and opposite man dance across, passing right shoulder to right and turn clockwise in opposite positions; dance back, right shoulder to right and turn clockwise into place.

C. Lead To Opposite Place

8   Top woman and opposite man take left hands, dancing around each other anticlockwise; both take partner's right hand also, and all lead around to the opposite side and turn the woman. All bow to partner.

D. Advance And Retire

8   Top woman and opposite man advance and retire twice, bowing to each other the second time.

E. Gallop

8   Top couples, in waltz hold, gallop in and back *[4 bars]*; then gallop across to their own side with the men passing back-to-back *[2 bars]*, and dance in place *[2 bars]*.

F. Repeat

32   Top couples repeat *B–E*, 2nd woman and Top man leading.

G. Swing

8   All couples swing in place.

H. Repeat

64   Side couples dance *B–F*. The woman on the left is first to dance.

I. Swing And House

16   All couples swing; then house around.

4TH FIGURE

(Polkas: 240 bars)

A. Lead Around And Swing

16   Lead around and swing as at *1st Figure, A*.

B. Chain And Swing

16   Top women chain and Top couples swing.

C. House

8   1st couple house across to leave the woman beside 2nd man.

D. Advance And Retire In Three

16   2nd man takes both women's outside hands. They advance, retire, advance and the women turn out under the man's arms to finish beside Top man, alone in his own position. He takes the women's other hands *[8 bars]*. With all four holding hands, the line of three now advance, retire, advance again, and the women turn again to form a circle *[8 bars]*.

E. Christmas

8   Top couples swing in four in the centre.

F. Repeat

48   Top couples repeat *B–E*; 2nd Top couple dance *C*.

G. Swing

8   All couples swing in place.

H. Repeat

104   Repeat *B–G* with Side couples leading *B–F*.

I. House

8   All couples house around.

5TH FIGURE *(Jigs: 128 bars)*

A. Lead Around And Swing

16   Lead around as at *1st Figure, A*, with skip step, and swing.

B. House

8   All couples house around.

C. Gallop

8   Top couples gallop across, Side couples repeat; Top couples gallop back and Side couples repeat back.

D. Women Chain

8   Top women chain ahead of Side women: right hands in centre, left hand around opposite man, moving to the man on his left.

E. House

8   All house with new partners.

F. Repeat

24   Dance *C–E*, Side couples leading the gallop and chain.

G. Repeat

48   Repeat *C–F*, all finishing with their own partners.

6TH FIGURE *(Fling: 120 bars)*

A. Double At Home And Double Across

8   Top couples hop in, back and turn, doubling in place *[4 bars]*; hop in, back and double house to opposite position *[4 bars]*.

B. Double At Home And Double Across

8   Top couples repeat *A* to finish in home positions.

C. Dance Opposite And House

12   Top men turn around opposite woman with left hands *[4 bars]*; then Top couples house *[8 bars]*, doubling the last 2 bars.

D. Repeat

28   Side couples dance *A–C*.

E. Repeat

56   Top couples and Side couples both repeat *A–C*.

7TH FIGURE   *(Hornpipes: 160 bars)*

A. Polka

16   In waltz hold, all couples dance in and back; then turn to the position on the right *[4 bars]*. Repeat three times to home.

B. House

8   All couples house around.

C. Women Move To The Right

8   All couples dance in and back *[2 bars]*, women move on inside to the right while men turn clockwise in place *[2 bars]*; then all dance one turn in place with the new partners *[4 bars]*.

D. Repeat

96   Repeat *A* and *B* until back with own partners.

E. Repeat

24   All dance *A* and *B* again with their own partners.

plain Set (Co. Clare)
Seit Shoiléir (Co. An Chláir)

Opening position for all figures: all four couples join hands in front and face anticlockwise around the circle, men on the inside.

1ST FIGURE   *(Reels: 112 bars)*

Bars   *A. Lead Around*

8   All four couples dance anticlockwise around until back in their original places. During the last bar each man, without releasing hands, turns his partner clockwise under both arms and then adopts the standard hold.

B. Home

8   All four couples dance around at home.

C. Figure

4   *(a) Pass through:* Top couples advance towards each other and pass through, women at the centre passing left shoulder to left shoulder. After passing, each couple joins right hands, each woman dances under the man's right arm and the woman and man dance around each other into place, facing into the centre.

4   *(b) Pass through:* Top couples repeat *(a)* to bring them back to their original places again.

8   *(c) Home:* Top couples dance around at home.

8   *(d) Women chain:* Top women dance to centre, chain with right hands and pass each other, give left hands to opposite men, turn clockwise under their left arms and dance around behind them, the men turning with the women. Women then dance straight back to own partners, join right hands with them and turn clockwise, then join left hands for lead-around position.

4   *(e) Lead around:* 1st Tops and 2nd Tops lead around inside. They dance anticlockwise half-way around to reach each other's places and then face into the centre.

4   *(f) Pass through:* Top couples repeat *(a)* to bring them back to their original places again.

D. Home

8   All four couples dance around at home.

E. Figure

32   Side couples dance *C*.

F. Home

8   All four couples dance around at home.

G. House

8   All four couples dance house around.

2ND FIGURE   *(Reels: 128 bars)*

A. Lead Around

8   All four couples dance anticlockwise around until back in original places. During last bar each man, without releasing hands, turns his partner clockwise under both arms and then adopts the standard hold.

B. Home

8   All four couples dance around at home.

C. Figure

4   *(a) Slide:* Top couples advance to centre and retire, with right hands joined.

4   *(b) Change:* Top couples dance around to each other's place. Each woman turns twice clockwise under the man's right arm as they dance around; she should dance ahead of the man.

4   *(c) Slide:* Top couples advance to centre and retire, with right hands joined.

4   *(d) Change:* Top couples repeat *(b)* to return to their own places.

8   *(e) Home:* Top couples dance around at home.
16 *(f) Repeat:* Top couples repeat *(a)–(d)*.

D. Home

8   All four couples dance around at home.

E. Figure

40 Side couples dance *C*.

F. Home

8   All four couples dance around at home.

G. House

8   All four couples dance house around.

3RD FIGURE   *(Reels: 176 bars)*

A. Lead Around

16 Lead around, turn the woman and dance in place.

B. Women Cross Over

8   Top women cross over and dance in place with opposite men.

C. Men Cross Over

8   Top men cross to the opposite woman's side and, taking their own partner's right hand in right, they turn the woman anticlockwise once. Then, taking left hand in left, they turn the woman anticlockwise twice, crossing inside to change places with her.

D. Advance And Retire

8   Top couples advance and retire twice, holding crossed hands.

E. Advance And Retire And House

8   Top couples advance and retire in waltz hold, then house across.

F. Repeat

32   Top couples repeat *B–E*.

G. Dance In Place

8   All couples dance in place.

H. Repeat

72   Repeat *B–G* with Side couples leading.

I. House

8   All couples house around.

4TH FIGURE   (*Reels: 256 bars*)

A. Lead Around

16   All couples lead around, turn the woman and dance in place.

B. Women Chain

16   Top women chain and Top couples dance in place.

C. House

8   1st Top couple house across, leaving the woman on the left-hand side of the opposite man, who takes her left hand in his left and his own partner's right hand in his right. The Top man then takes the women's free hands, underneath the other arms.

D. Three And One

8   The line of three advance as the Top man retires, retire again, then advance a second time and women turn, the Top woman anticlockwise and the 2nd woman clockwise, in beside the other man, all still holding hands.

E. Three And One

8   Repeat *D* from the other side. When the women turn this time, the dancers form a circle of four, arms around each other's backs.

F. Christmas

8   Top couples swing in four in the centre.

G. Repeat

48   Repeat *B–F* with the 2nd Top couple leading.

H. Women Chain

16   Top women chain again, then all couples dance in place.

I. Repeat

112   Repeat *B–H* with Side couples leading. (1st Side couple are on the left of 1st Top couple.)

J. House

8   All couples house around.

5TH FIGURE   *(Jigs: 160 bars)*

A. Lead Around

8   All four couples dance anticlockwise around until back in original places. During the last bar each man, without releasing

hands, turns his partner clockwise under both arms, and then adopts the standard hold.

B. Swing

8   All four couples swing in place.

C. House

8   All four couples dance house around.

D. Figure

8   (a) *Gallop:* Top couples cross straight over to each other's place without turning, men on the inside *[2 bars]*; Side couples do likewise *[2 bars]*. Top couples cross back to their original places, women on the inside *[2 bars]*; Side couples do likewise *[2 bars]*.

8   (b) *Women chain:* Top women chain with right hands in the centre and dance over to opposite men. They are followed immediately by Side women *[2 bars]*. Each woman gives left hand to opposite man, turns clockwise under his left arm and dances around behind him, the man turning with the woman. Each woman then dances to the left across in front of her opposite man, giving right hands to the man in the position one place to the right of their starting positions. They join right hands with this man and dance anticlockwise under his right arm into place.

E. Swing

8   All four couples swing in place.

F. House

8   All four couples dance house around.

G. Figure

16   Repeat *D*. The original Top dancers are always first to cross at (a) and (b).

H. Swing

8   All four couples swing in place.

I. House

8   All four couples dance house around.

J. Figure

16   Repeat *D*. The original Top dancers are always first to cross at *(a)* and *(b)*.

K. Swing

8   All four couples swing in place.

L. House

8   All four couples dance house around.

M. Figure

16   Repeat *D* to bring the women back to their original partners again. The original Top dancers are always first to cross at *(a)* and *(b)*.

N. Swing

8   All four couples swing in place.

O. House

8   All four couples dance house around.

6TH FIGURE   *(Reels: 192 bars)*

A. Lead Around

8   All four couples dance anticlockwise around until back in original places. During the last bar each man, without releasing

hands, turns his partner clockwise under both arms and then adopts the standard hold.

B. Home

8   All four couples dance around at home.

C. House

8   All four couples dance house around.

D. Figure

8   *(a) Home:* All four couples dance around at home.

8   *(b) Women in:* The four women advance to the centre and retire twice.

8   *(c) Men wheel and change partners:* The four men join right hands in the centre and dance around clockwise *[4 bars]*, then turn, join left hands in the centre and dance around anticlockwise *[4 bars]*. At the same time each woman dances around to the next position to her right.

8   *(d) Home:* The women join up with new partners and all four couples dance around at home.

E. House

8   All four couples dance house around.

F. Figure

32   Repeat *D*. At *(c)* the men join left hands first.

G. House

8   All four couples dance house around.

H. Figure

32   Repeat *D*.

I. House

8 All four couples dance house around.

J. Figure

32 Repeat D. At (c) the men join left hands first.

K. House

8 All four couples dance house around.

Portmagee Jig Set (Meserts)
Seit Phort Mhic Aoidh

This set, as remembered by Joseph Falvey of Portmagee, Co. Kerry, was recorded by Muiris O'Brien.

1ST FIGURE
(*Jigs: 248 bars*)

Bars *A. Lead Around*

8   All couples lead around, the man's arm around the woman's waist and her hand on his shoulder.

B. House

8   All couples house around, doubling the last 2 bars.

C. Sevens And Home

8   1st Top couple figure in, dance sevens in and back *[4 bars]*, then dance in place, turning once *[4 bars]*.

D. Swing

8   1st Top couple swing in waltz hold.

E. Top Man Swings Left

8   Top man swings with 1st Side woman (on his left) after she crosses to change places with his partner, passing left shoulder to left.

F. Top Man Swings Left

8   Top man swings in (his) place with 2nd Top woman. The two women change places, passing left shoulder to left.

G. Top Man Swings Left

8   Top man swings with 2nd Side woman. Again the two women change places, passing left shoulder to left. All now have new partners.

H. Repeat

168 Repeat *A–G* three times, with 1st Side man, 2nd Top man and 2nd Side man leading in turn. All of them figure in with 1st Top woman.

I. Repeat

16 All repeat *A* and *B* with their own partners.

2ND FIGURE *(Jigs: 152 bars)*

A. Lead Around And House

16 All couples lead around and house, as at *1st Figure, A* and *B*.

B. Sevens And Home

8 1st Top couple figure in.

C. Basket Of Three

8 1st Top couple swing in three with the woman on the left (1st Side woman).

D. Repeat

96 Repeat *A–C* three times, with 1st Side couple, 2nd Top couple and 2nd Side couple leading in turn. All of them swing with the woman on their left at *C*.

E. Lead Around And House

16 All couples lead around and house again.

3RD FIGURE *(Jigs: 152 bars)*

A. Lead Around And House

16 All couples lead around and house, as at *1st Figure, A* and *B*.

B. Sevens And Home

8 1st Top couple figure in.

C. Turn The Lady

8 Top woman turns clockwise four times, right hand in right, under her partner's arm as he dances on the spot.

D. Lead Around And House

16 Repeat A.

E. Sevens And Home

8 1st Side couple figure in.

F. Turn The Women

8 1st Top woman and 1st Side woman turn four times under the men's arms.

G. Lead Around And House

16 All lead around and house again.

H. Sevens And Home

8 2nd Top couple figure in.

I. Turn The Women

8 1st Top woman, 1st Side woman and 2nd Top woman turn four times.

J. Lead Around And House

16 All lead around and house again.

K. Lead Around And Home

8 2nd Side couple figure in.

L. Turn The Women

8 All women turn clockwise four times under their partners' arms.

M. Lead Around And House

16 All lead around and house again.

4TH FIGURE (Jigs: 152 bars)

A. Lead Around And House

16 All couples lead around and house, as at *1st Figure, A* and *B*.

B. Sevens And Home

8 1st Top couple figure in.

C. High Gates

8 Top man takes right hand in right with his partner and left hand in left with the woman on his left. Top woman dances under the arch he makes with Side woman *[4 bars]*; then Side woman dances under the arch he makes with Top woman *[4 bars]*.

D. Repeat

96 Repeat *A–C* three times with 1st Side couple, 2nd Top couple and 2nd Side couple leading in turn.

E. Lead Around And House

16 All lead around and house again.

5TH FIGURE (Jigs: 224 bars)

A. Lead Around

16 All couples lead around and house, as at *1st Figure, A* and *B*.

B. Sevens And Home

8   1st Top couple figure in, to finish facing out of their own position.

C. Sevens And Line Up

8   1st Side couple figure in and line up behind Top couple.

D. Sevens And Line Up

8   2nd Top couple figure in and line up in third position.

E. Sevens And Line Up

8   2nd Side couple figure in as follows: they dance sevens towards the back, turn slightly clockwise, dance sevens, leading on the other foot, through 2nd Top position *[4 bars]*; then turn once in place there and line up *[4 bars]*.

F. Lead Off And Lead Around

16   With Top man and woman leading, men circle to the left and women to the right. They go around once, meeting their partners at the back and dancing up the centre with them, the man's arm around the woman's waist *[8 bars]*. Then all couples lead around *[8 bars]*.

G. Repeat

144   Repeat *B–F* three times, with 1st Side couple, 2nd Top couple and 2nd Sides leading in turn.

H. House

8   All couples house around, doubling the last 2 bars.

Quadrilles (Co. Fermanagh)
Quadrille Fhear Manach

This set of quadrilles from Co. Fermanagh is as danced in the Cashel, Belcoo and Beleek areas.

1ST FIGURE *(Reels: 120 bars)*

Bars *A. Lead Around*

8   All lead around, and turn the woman under on the last 2 bars.

B. Swing

8   All swing in céilí hold.

C. Advance And Retire

8   Tops advance and retire twice, right hand in right.

D. Change

4   Top women change, right shoulder to right, followed by men.

E. Change

4   Top women change back, right to right, followed by men.

F. Swing

8   Tops swing in céilí hold.

G. Repeat

24   Sides dance *C–F*.

H. Women Chain

8   Top women chain; men turn the woman under into position.

I. House

8   Tops house around with hands crossed.

J. Swing

8   Tops swing.

K. Repeat

24   Sides dance *H–J*, but all swing at *J*.

2ND FIGURE. *LOOK IN, LOOK OUT*   *(Jigs: 152 bars)*

A. Lead Around

8   All lead around.

B. Swing

8   All swing.

C. Advance And Retire

8   Tops advance and retire once. Men and women face each other, right hand in right; dance in, 2-3, out, 2-3; in, 2-3 (look in, look out).

D. Dance Half-Way

4   Top men, with right hand over their partners' right shoulders, dance half-way around.

E. Repeat

12   Repeat *C* and *D* back to place.

F. Swing

8   Tops swing.

G. Repeat

32   Sides dance *C–F*.

H. Women Chain

8 Top women chain.

I. Swing

8 Tops swing.

J. House

8 Tops house with hands crossed.

K. Swing

8 Tops swing.

L. Repeat

32 Sides dance *H–K*, but all swing at *K*.

3RD FIGURE   *(Reels: 184 bars)*

A. Lead Around

8 All lead around.

B. Swing

8 All swing.

C. Opposite Dance

32 Top man and opposite woman dance in and pass each other, right shoulder to right; turn right again, ending with backs to their own positions *[8 bars]*, swing *[8 bars]*, and finish the swing facing their own partners. The swinging couple then hook left arms and dance around *[4 bars]*, turn, hook right arms *[4 bars]*, and dance back to swing their own partners *[8 bars]*.

D. Opposite Dance

32 1st Sides (on the left) dance *C*.

E. Opposite Dance

32 2nd Tops dance C.

F. Opposite Dance

32 2nd Sides dance C.

G. Chain And Swing

16 Top women chain and Top couples swing.

H. Chain

8 Side women chain.

I. Swing

8 All swing.

4TH FIGURE   (Jigs: 184 bars)

A. Lead Around And Swing

16 All lead around and swing.

B. Body

24 1st Tops swing in place *[8 bars]*, while 2nd Tops dance in place *[6 bars]*, right hand in right, the woman facing out of set. On the 7th bar the opposite couple advance to take the Top woman; all three retire *[2 bars]* and turn her under *[2 bars]*. The opposite man advance with both women *[2 bars]*, the Top man advances towards the three, and they swing in four.

C. Chain And Swing

16 Top women chain and swing.

D. Repeat

40 1st Sides dance B and C.

E. Repeat

40   2nd Tops dance *B* and *C*.

F. Repeat

40   2nd Sides dance *B* and *C*, but all swing for the last 8 bars.

5TH FIGURE. *GATHERING UP*   *(Jigs: 104 bars)*

A. Circle

8   Circle, advance and retire, twice.

B. House

8   All house.

C. Circle

8   Circle, advance and retire; the woman moves on to the man on the right.

D. House

8   House with new partners.

E. Repeat

40   Repeat until back to original partners; house.

F. Circle

8   The four men dance to centre. Top men take hands uncrossed and Side men take hands under Top men's *[4 bars]*. The women advance and link arms; left arm to her partner's right and right arm to the left arm of the man to her right *[4 bars]*. (This movement should be seen prior to dancing.)

G. Christmas

8   All swing.

Quadrilles Half Set
Leathsheit Quadrille

1ST FIGURE
(Polkas: 48 bars)

Opening position: The two couples face each other.

Bars **A. Pass Through**

8   The two couples advance and pass through, Top couple passing through centre. On reaching opposite side each dancer turns in place without crossing to correct side *[4 bars]*; repeat to return.

B. Lead Around

8   Each couple join right hands, with the men's right arms over their partners' shoulders. In this position each couple dances around anticlockwise until back in their original places.

C. Swing

8   Both couples swing in place.

D. Women Chain

8   Women dance to centre, chain with right hands and pass each other; give left hands to opposite men and dance around behind them (men do not turn with women). Women then chain in centre again with right hands and dance back to own partners.

E. Swing

8   Both couples swing in place.

2ND FIGURE
(Polkas: 72 bars)

Opening position: The two couples join hands in front and face each other.

A. Advance And Retire

8   The two couples advance to the centre and retire twice.

B. Change

4   Keeping the same hold, the two couples dance half-way around the house to each other's place.

C. Advance And Retire

8   The two couples advance to the centre and retire, twice.

D. Change

4   Keeping the same hold, the two couples dance half-way around the house to each other's place.

E. Swing

8   Both couples swing in place.

F. Repeat

32   Repeat A–E.

3RD FIGURE   (Polkas: 72 bars)

Opening position: The two couples face each other.

A. Advance And Link

4   *(a)* 1st woman and 2nd man dance to the centre and pass each other left side to left, then turn anticlockwise to face each other.

4   *(b)* The two dancers link left arms and dance around each other, ending up, still linked, next to their own partners.

B. Line Up And Wheel

8   The two dancers in the centre take their partners' right hands with their right and the line (in which each dancer should now be facing a different direction from those beside them) dances in the direction in which the centre woman is facing *[2 bars]*, dances back in the other direction *[2 bars]* and then wheels around so that each couple is in their opposite position *[4 bars]*.

C. Advance And Retire

8   The dancing woman and man advance to centre and retire twice.

D. Advance And Retire

4   Both couples join hands in front, advance to centre and retire once.

E. Lead Around

4   Each couple join right hands, with the men's right arms over their partner's shoulders. In this position each couple dances around anticlockwise until back in their original places.

F. Repeat

32   1st man and 2nd woman repeat *A–E*.

4TH FIGURE   (Jigs: 104 bars)

Opening position: The two couples face each other.

A. Women Chain

8   Women dance to centre, chain with right hands and pass each other; give left hands to opposite men and dance around behind them (men do not turn with women). Women then chain in centre again with right hands and dance back to own partners.

B. Swing

8   Both couples swing in place.

C. Figure

4   *(a) Advance and retire:* 1st couple join hands in front, advance to the centre and retire once.

4   *(b) Home:* Keeping same hold, 1st couple dances around at home.

8   *(c) Advance and retire:* 2nd couple join right hands, with man's arm over his partner's shoulder. They advance to 1st couple and 2nd man takes 1st woman's left hand in his left. The three

dancers retire and 1st woman turns clockwise in under 2nd man's arm *[4 bars]*. The three dancers advance again to 1st man and he takes the women's free hands in his, right to right and left to left. As they retire again he advances with them *[4 bars]*.

D. Christmas

8   The four dancers form a tight circle in the centre, arms around each other's backs and dance around clockwise.

E. Women Chain

8   The two women repeat *A*.

F. Swing

8   Both couples swing in place.

G. Repeat

40   Repeat *C–F* with opposite dancers.

5TH FIGURE   (Polkas: 88 bars)

Opening position: The two couples join hands in front and face each other.

A. Advance And Retire

8   The two couples advance to the centre and retire, twice.

B. Change

4   Keeping the same hold, the two couples dance half-way around the house to each other's places.

C. Advance And Retire

8   The two couples advance to the centre and retire, twice.

D. Change

4   Keeping the same hold, the two couples dance half-way around the house back to their own places.

E. Women Chain

8   Women dance to centre, chain with right hands and pass each other; give left hands to opposite men, turn clockwise under their left arms and dance around behind them; men turn with women. Women then dance straight back to own partners, join right hands with them and turn clockwise under their right arms.

F. Swing

8   Both couples swing in place.

G. Repeat

40   Repeat *A–F*.

6TH FIGURE. *EVERY MAN'S CHANCE*   (Polkas: 144 bars)

Opening position: All dancers on the floor join hands in a big circle with alternating women and men.

A. Advance And Retire

8   All dancers advance to the centre and retire, twice.

B. Swing

8   All couples swing in place.

C. Women In

8   Women advance to the centre and retire, twice.

D. Men In

8   Men advance to centre and retire twice; women move on one place to the right while the men are advancing the second time.

E. Repeat

104   Repeat *A–D* until partners rejoin and swing.

Rosscahill (West Galway) Set
Seit Ros Chathail (Ghaillimh Thiar)

1ST FIGURE *(Polkas: 192 bars)*

Bars **A. Advance And Retire**

8   All couples in waltz hold, facing into set, advance *[2 bars]* and retire *[2 bars]*; repeat.

B. House

8   All couples house around half-way.

C. Repeat

16   Repeat *A* and *B* to get back to place.

D. Women Chain

16   Top women chain, right hand to centre, left to opposite man; both turn. Women pass back to partner *[8 bars]*; all couples swing *[8 bars]*.

E. Women Chain

16   Sides dance *D*.

F. Line Up

16   Line up in centre: Top couples in waltz hold, advance and retire *[4 bars]*; advance *[2 bars]*, release hand and make line across, men outside, women inside *[2 bars]*. The opposite women and men link right arms and turn once on the spot *[4 bars]*; link left arms with partner and turn into opposite position (one-and-a-half turns) *[4 bars]*.

G. Line Up

16   Repeat *F* to get back to place.

H. Repeat

32 Sides dance *F* and *G*.

I. Women Swing All Round

32 Women swing each man: the four women dance in front of their partners to the man on their left *[2 bars]* and swing for 6 bars. Repeat with the remaining three men *[24 bars]*.

J. Repeat

32 Repeat *A–C* to finish.

2ND FIGURE. *WAVES*   *(Jigs: 104 bars)*

A. Waves And Swing

16 (a) All couples face each other, in waltz hold. Dance 1 bar in to the centre and 1 bar out to their own positions. All turn once to position on the right, turning clockwise as they go *[2 bars]*. Repeat three times to get back to place *[12 bars]*.
8   (b) All swing.

B. Women Cross Over

8   Top women dance across to opposite place *[4 bars]*; Side women do the same *[4 bars]*.

C. One Wave And House

8   All couples face each other, dance 1 bar in to the set and 1 bar out. Top couples house with couples on the right *[6 bars]*.

D. Repeat

16 Repeat *B* and *C*.

E. Men Wheel

8   The four men hold right hands in centre and dance clockwise

for 4 bars; hold left hands and dance anticlockwise *[4 bars]*.

F. Big Wheel

16 Men retain left hands in centre and put right arm over their partner's shoulder. Women's left arm goes around their partner's waist and right hand holds men's right hand on the right shoulder. All lead around *[8 bars]*. Men take right arm over woman's head *[8 bars]*.

H. Swing

8 All swing.

I. Waves And Swing

24 Repeat *A* to finish.

3RD FIGURE   (Polkas: 88 bars)

A. Circle

8 All dancers join hands in a big circle, advance and retire twice.

B. Back-To-Back

8 Partners face each other and pass left shoulder to left *[2 bars]*, dance to the left *[2 bars]*; pass back without turning, right to right *[2 bars]*, to face each other *[2 bars]*.

C. Circle

8 Repeat *A*.

D. Swing

8 Couples swing.

E. Full Chain

16 Women chain clockwise, men anticlockwise. Pause for 2 bars when partners meet on the opposite side, then continue back to place.

F. Swing

8   All swing.

G. Repeat

24   Repeat A–C.

H. Big Christmas

8   All dancers place arms around each other's backs and swing around in a large circle.

Roscommon Lancers Set
Lannsuidthe Ros Comáin

This lancer set is taught by Martin and Francis Bolger. The Roscommon reel and jig steps are danced for all movements except the house around.

1ST FIGURE

(Reels: 168 bars)

Bars **A. Opposites Dance**

8   Top man and opposite woman cross, passing right shoulder to right *[4 bars]*, reverse back without turning, left shoulder to left shoulder, and face each other in the centre.

B. Swing

8   Top man and opposite woman swing in céilí hold *[6 bars]* and reverse to join their partners *[2 bars]*.

C. Advance And Square

16   Holding crossed hands, Top couples advance and retire *[4 bars]*, dance towards couple on their left *[2 bars]* and reverse to the opposite (Top) position *[2 bars]*. They advance and retire there, dance to their left again and reverse back to own positions.

D. House

8   All men house with the woman on their left, dancing ordinary reel step. Men start on right foot, women on left, women moving forward on first bar and all couples on second bar. They turn four times; men turn into own positions during the last bar.

E. Repeat

40   Repeat *A–D* with Top couples leading again. The other woman and man dance *A* and *B*.

F. Repeat

80   Repeat *A–E* with Side couples leading. (1st Side couple are left of 1st Top couple.)

2ND FIGURE *(Reels: 136 bars)*

A. Advance And Retire

8   Holding crossed hands, Top couples advance, retire, advance; during the last 2 bars Top men take hands in the centre and raise them over the women's heads, to place them on the women's waists. Women place their hands on the men's shoulders.

B. Christmas

8   Top couples swing in four in the centre *[6 bars]* and break away from the circle and their partners to join the Side couples in two lines of four, facing each other *[2 bars]*.

C. Advance And Retire

8   The lines advance and retire twice, Top couples staying in facing their partners the second time.

D. House

8   All house around in ordinary reel step with their own partners.

E. Repeat

32   Repeat *A–D* with Side couples leading.

F. Repeat

64   Repeat *A–E*.

3RD FIGURE *(Jigs: 88 bars)*

A. Circle

8   Holding hands in a circle, all dance in place, moving in and back slightly. A battering step is danced, all stepping on to the left foot and battering twice with the right to start.

B. House

8   All house around with partners in ordinary reel step.

C. Circle

8   All circle again and women move on to the right.

D. House

8   All house with their new partners.

E. Repeat

48   Repeat *C* and *D* until women house with their own partners again.

4TH FIGURE   *(Reels: 168 bars)*

A. Change Places

8   Holding right hands, Top couple advance to the centre and change sides, turning to face back, the man dancing clockwise around the woman as she turns anticlockwise under his arm *[4 bars]*. They dance back to place and turn as before, then move away from each other to join the Side couple nearest their own position. All, except the Top couple who are apart from each other, take hands, forming a semi-circle.

B. Semi-Circle

8   All dance on the spot in the semi-circle.

C. Chain

16   All face their partners and chain around, men going to the right.

D. House

8   All couples house around, dancing the ordinary reel step.

E. Repeat

40   Repeat *A–D* with 2nd Top couple leading.

F. Repeat

40   Repeat *A–D* with 1st Side couple leading.

G. Repeat

40   Repeat *A–D* with 2nd Side couple leading.

5TH FIGURE   *(Reels: 168 bars)*

A. Three And One

16   Holding right hands, Top couple dance across the set. Top man takes opposite woman's left hand and turns both women in towards him, bringing his hands back on to their shoulders. Opposite man takes women's free hands *[4 bars]*; all dance across to 1st Top position *[4 bars]*. 2nd man now pulls both women towards him, placing his hands on their shoulders, as they turn to face Top man. All dance to 2nd position *[4 bars]*, back to centre *[2 bars]*; women turn in towards Top man to form a circle *[2 bars]*.

B. Christmas

8   Top couples swing in four *[6 bars]*, break back to place *[2 bars]* and all turn to face their partners.

C. Dance In Place And Swing Partner

16   All dance opposite partners *[8 bars]* and swing *[8 bars]*.

D. Repeat

40   Repeat *A–C* with 2nd Top couple leading.

E. Repeat

80   Repeat *A–D* with Side couples leading.

6TH FIGURE   *(Jigs: 136 bars)*

A. Advance And Retire

8   Holding hands in front, Top couples advance and retire twice.

B. Change Places

8   Top couples dance to face couple on their left *[2 bars]*, reverse
     to the opposite position *[2 bars]* and dance facing their partners
     there *[4 bars]*; they dance the battering step all the time *[8 bars]*.

C. Swing

8   Top couples swing.

D. House

8   All couples house, dancing the ordinary reel step.

E. Repeat

32   Side couples dance *A–C* and all house again.

F. Repeat

32   Top couples repeat *A–C* from opposite side and all house.

G. Repeat

32   Side couples repeat *A–C* from opposite side and all house.

7TH FIGURE   *(Reels: 168 bars)*

A. Advance And Retire

8   Top couples advance and retire twice, holding crossed hands.

B. Square

8   Top couples square: dance to face the couple on the right *[2
     bars]*, reverse into opposite position *[2 bars]*, dance to face the

other Side couple *[2 bars]* and reverse back to place *[2 bars]*.

C. Star

8   Top couples face the couple on their right, join right hands in a star with them and dance around *[4 bars]*; then turn, join left hands and dance back to place *[4 bars]*.

D. Swing

16   All swing in fours *[6 bars]* then break back to place *[2 bars]*. All couples house around, dancing the ordinary reel step.

E. Repeat

40   Repeat *A–D* with Side couples leading. Side couples turn right for the hands in and swing.

F. Repeat

40   Repeat *A–D* with Top couples leading again. This time, they square to their left at *B* and turn left for the star at *C*.

G. Repeat

40   Repeat *A–D* with Side couples leading.

8TH FIGURE   (Reels: 168 bars)

A. Women Chain

8   Top women chain with right hands in the centre and dance around the opposite man, turning clockwise under his left arm *[4 bars]*. Women chain back, each woman turning under her partner's left arm and going around behind him into place as he moves forward turning clockwise to face in on her left *[4 bars]*.

B. Circle

8   Top couples take hands in a circle and dance a full clockwise turn around the centre to place.

C. Dance In Place And Swing Partner

16 All dance opposite their partners *[8 bars]* and swing *[8 bars]*.

D. House

8 All couples house around, dancing the ordinary reel step.

E. Repeat

40 Dance A–D with Side couples leading.

F. Repeat

80 Repeat A–E.

9TH FIGURE   (Jigs: 136 bars)

A. Change Places

8 Top women change places, passing right shoulder to right *[4 bars]*, then Top men change places, also passing right shoulder to right *[4 bars]*. All turn in to face partners at the other side.

B. Dance In Place And Swing Partner

16 All dance opposite their partners *[8 bars]* and swing *[8 bars]*.

C. House

8 All couples house around in ordinary reel step.

D. Repeat

32 Side couples dance A and all repeat B and C.

E. Repeat

64 Starting in opposite positions, all repeat A–D.

St Patrick's Day

Bars **A. Lead Around**

16   Couples take inside hands, make a half turn to the right and with promenade step dance round anticlockwise. On the 8th bar of music the dancers release hands and reverse. Partners again take inside hands and dance back in the opposite direction, turning into original places on the last 2 bars.

B. Body

8   *(a) Sides:* Men side-step to the right behind their partners, while women side-step in front; all end with rising step. Side-step back to places, men now passing in front; finish as before.

6   *(b) Half right and left:* Partners take right hands and turn once in place. 1st Tops man changes place with the man of the couple on his left, passing right shoulder to right, while 2nd Tops and 2nd Sides men change places in like manner; women meanwhile dance two short threes. While the men dance two threes, 1st Tops and 2nd Tops women change places with 1st Sides and 2nd Sides women respectively, passing left shoulder to left.

8   *(c) Sides:* Repeat *(a)* in the new places.

6   *(d) Half right and left:* Repeat *(b)* to return to places.

16   *(e) Double quarter chain:* Men take their partner's right hand in their right and partners turn once in place; men chain with left hand to women on their left. Having turned in place, all chain back to their own partners with right hand and make a complete turn. Men continue the chain with left hand to women on the right; turn, and chain back to places as before, turning partners in place.

6   *(f) Extended sides:* Men side-step to the right, behind their partners, with women side-stepping to the left in front; finish with rising step. All again side-step in the same direction, finishing as before with rising step. Men take the right hands of women on their right and all make a full turn; chain back to original positions.

14   *(g) Full chain:* Partners face each other, give right hands and advance with promenade step, giving alternate hands to each dancer they meet, and so chaining back to original positions.

C. 1st Figure. Advance And Retire

16   Top couples advance towards each other and retire; repeat. They dance a complete circle anticlockwise around each other and back to places.

D. Body

64   Repeat *B*.

E. 1st Figure. Advance And Retire

16   Side couples dance *C*.

F. Body

64   Repeat *B*.

G. 2nd Figure. Women Chain

16   1st Top and 2nd Top women advance, give right hands in centre and continue to opposite man, giving left hand. Both turn in place and women return to their own partner, both making a full turn in place. Both couples then dance a complete circle around each other.

N. Body

64   Repeat *B*.

O. 2nd Figure. Women Chain

16   Side women dance *G*.

P. Lead Around

16   Lead around as at *A*, but on returning, couples swing to places during the last 4 bars.

Schottische

All couples adopt waltz hold. Music: Schottische.

Bars A. Twos

8   One three in to the centre and one three out; two threes around
     in place; one three in and one three out; two threes around as
     before.

B. Fours

8   (a) Four in, 1-2-3-4 to the centre, four out, 1-2-3-4, four threes
     around the house.

8   (b) Repeat (a).

C. Eights

8   Four in, 1-2-3-4 to the centre. Drop hands in front, turn out
     back-to-back and continue, four, 1-2-3-4, eight back in four, 1-2-
     3-4, back-to-back. Drop hands in front, turn out and face and
     continue for 4 bars, 1-2-3-4.

D. House Around

8   Around the house, doubling the last 2 bars.

E. Repeat

Repeat *A–D* as often as required.

Set Of Erin
Seit Éireann

1ST FIGURE. *SLIDE AND SWING BEHIND*   *(Jigs: 176 bars)*

Bars *A. Lead Around*

8   Lead around, men with right arm around women's waist and women with left hand on men's right shoulder.

B. 1st Tops House

8   1st Tops around the house.

C. Slide In And Out

32   All four couples slide in and out *[4 Bars]*; swing behind *[3 bars]* and batter *[1 bar]*. Repeat three times *[24 Bars]*.

D. 1st Sides House

8   1st Sides around the house.

E. Slide In And Out

32   Repeat *C*.

F. 2nd Tops House

8   2nd Tops around the house.

G. Slide In And Out

32   Repeat *C*.

H. 2nd Sides House

8   2nd Sides around the house.

I. Slide In And Out

32   Repeat *C*. All clap on the last beat of music to end the 1st Figure.

2ND FIGURE
(Jigs: 176 bars)

A. Lead Around

8   Lead around as at *1st Figure, A*.

B. 1st Tops House

8   1st Tops around the house.

C. Slide In And Out

32   All four couples slide in and out *[4 Bars]*; the four women dance past their own partner, left shoulder to left, and swing with the man to the left *[3 bars]* and batter *[1 bar]*. Repeat three times *[24 bars]*.

D. 1st Sides House

8   1st Sides around the house.

E. Slide In And Out

32   Repeat *C*.

F. 2nd Tops House

8   2nd Tops around the house.

G. Slide In And Out

32   Repeat *C*.

H. 2nd Sides House

8   2nd Sides around the house.

I. Slide In And Out

32   Repeat *C*. All clap on the last beat of music to end the 2nd Figure.

3RD FIGURE. *HALF SLIDE* *(Jigs: 176 bars)*

A. Lead Around

8 Lead around as at *1st Figure, A*.

B. 1st Tops House

8 1st Tops around the house.

C. Slide In And Out

8 *(a)* All four couples slide in and out *[4 Bars]*; Top men dance across and swing opposite woman *[3 bars]* and batter *[1 bar]*.

8 *(b)* All four couples slide in and out *[4 Bars]*; Top men dance to the left and swing their own partner *[3 bars]* and batter *[1 bar]*.

16 *(c)* Repeat *(a)* and *(b)*, dancing to the right at *(b)*.

D. 1st Sides House

8 1st Sides around the house.

E. Slide In And Out

32 Repeat *C*, with Side men leading.

F. 2nd Tops House

8 2nd Tops around the house.

G. Slide In And Out

32 Repeat *C*.

H. 2nd Sides House

8 2nd Sides around the house.

I. Slide In And Out

32 Repeat *C*, Side men leading. All clap on the last beat of music to end the 3rd Figure.

4TH FIGURE. *THE SKIP*   *(Jigs: 176 Bars)*

A. Lead Around

8 Lead around as at *1st Figure, A*.

B. 1st Tops House

8 1st Tops around the house.

C. Slide In And Out

16 *(a)* All four couples slide in and out *[4 Bars]*; Top Men cross over on 5th bar, Side men cross over on 6th bar, all swing on 7th bar, and batter on 8th bar *[4 Bars]*. Repeat *[8 bars]*.

8 *(b)* All four couples slide in and out *[4 Bars]*; the four men move to the right and swing original partners, battering the last bar.

D. 1st Sides House

8 1st Sides around the house.

E. Slide In And Out

32 Repeat *C*, with Side men leading.

F. 2nd Tops House

8 2nd Tops around the house.

G. Slide In And Out

32 Repeat *C*.

H. 2nd Sides House

8 2nd Sides around the house.

I. Slide In And Out

32 Repeat *C*, Side men leading. All clap on the last beat of music to end the 4th Figure.

Shanless Reel

A dance for four couples, danced in reel time.

Bars **A. Body**

24 *(a) Lead around:* Lead around to opposite places, take partner's two hands and turn full round; dance back to own place, taking both hands and turning into own positions. Slip sides with partner, Tops going to the right and Sides to the left, and dance sevens and two threes. Side-step past partner, dance sevens and two threes; taking partner's hand, side-step back to own side, then dance back into own place.

16 *(b) Round the ring:* All women dance to their left round the set: in front of their partner, behind the next man, in front of the next man and back to place *[8 bars]*. Men dance the movement, going to their right.

16 *(c) Back-to-back:* Taking partner's right hand in right, all make a back-to-back ring, men facing out, women facing in; continue on in the same direction, forming the ring, men now facing in, women out; on to next dancer, men facing out, women facing in; and then to partner. With right hand in right, dance back to place and turn partner in place.

16 *(d) Stamp and clap:* Stamp feet and clap once, then dance sevens (with no threes) past partner, stamp and clap again and dance sevens *[8 bars]*. Men continue to the right and women to the left. Stamp and clap, dance sevens only, back towards own side, men to the left, women right; stamp and clap and dance into original positions *[8 bars]*.

B. 1st Figure

16 *(a)* Top couples advance, men take hands of opposite women and face sides; dance round sides on the outside and dance in the inside to meet partner. Take partner's hand and dance sevens and two threes to place.

16 *(b)* Sides dance *(a)*.

C. Body

72   Repeat *A*.

D. 2nd Figure

16   *(a)* Top couples face each other, then Top women change places, dancing sevens only (no threes). Top men change places, dancing sevens only, then dance two sevens past partners *[8 bars]*. Repeat to get back to own places.

16   *(b)* Side couples dance *(a)*.

E. Body

72   Repeat *A*.

F. Lead Around

24   Repeat *A (a)*.

Shoo The Donkey

Music: Versa Vienna. *The man's right arm is around the woman's waist and her left arm is on his right shoulder.*

Bars *A. Advance*

8 (a) Advance hop 1-2, hop 1-2, hop 1-2, turn and stamp. At the same time as the turn, the man puts his left arm around the woman's waist and the woman puts her right arm on the man's left shoulder *[4 bars]*. Repeat these movements *[4 bars]*.

8 (b) Repeat (a).

B. Hop 1-2

8 Hop, 1-2, turn and stamp. Hop, 1-2, turn and stamp. Repeat six more times.

C. Repeat

Repeat *A* and *B* as often as required.

Siamsa Beirte

A two-hand dance, danced to hornpipes. Men hold women's left hand in their right hand, and all face anticlockwise around in a circle.

Bars *A. Advance And Retire*

4   *(a)* Dance forward; hop 1-2-3, hop 1-2-3, hop 1, hop 2, hop 1-2-3.

4   *(b)* Repeat *(a)*.

B. Dance Around

4   (a) Man dances around his partner clockwise without releasing hands; step, hop 1-2-3, hop 1-2-3, hop 1, hop 2, hop 1-2-3, while the woman turns anticlockwise dancing the same step.

4   *(b)* Take hands uncrossed and dance around each other clockwise, while moving anticlockwise around the circle.

C. Repeat

Repeat *A* and *B* as often as desired.

Sixteen-Hand Reel

Positions of the dancers:

(a) at the start of the Four-Hand Reel:

```
        B A
        C D
```

(b) for the Eight-Hand Reel *two more couples are added:*

```
              1
            B A

    4 G           F 3
      H           E

            C D
             2
```

(c) for the Sixteen-Hand Reel *four more couples are added:*

```
                1
              B A
        5 L         R 7
          M         P
    4 G                 F 3
      H                 E
        8 S         O 6
          T         N
              C D
               2
```

A, C, E, G, L, N, P, S are men; B, D, F, H, M, 0, R, T are women.

Assuming that couple AB are nearest the music, they are leading Tops. CD are opposite Tops; EF are leading Sides, and GH opposite Sides. Couples on the right of Tops, i.e. LM and NO are 2nd Tops, and couples on the right of Sides, i.e., PR and ST, are 2nd Sides.

Bars *A. Lead Around*

16 Dancers half-right turn and lead around a complete circle; release hands and about turn inwards. Each man takes his partner's right hand in his left and both lead back to place.

B. Body

8 (a) *Sides:* Men side-step behind partner while women side-step in front of partner, ending with two short threes. Side-step back to place, men in front, ending with two short threes.

8 (b) *Hands round:* Leading and opposite Tops and leading and opposite Sides each form a ring with the couple on their right by joining hands, shoulder high; all dance side-step to the left, ending with two short threes; side-step back, ending with two short threes, and release hands.

8 (c) *Sides:* Repeat (a).

8 (d) *Hands round:* Repeat (b), but forming rings with the couples on the left.

16 (e) *Half-chain:* All take partner's right hand and half-right turn. The men give left hand to the woman on their right, and the women give left hand to the man on their left; all advance to meet the oncoming dancer with right hand; continue by giving left and right hands alternately until meeting own partner with right hand in the position opposite their starting position. Take partner's two hands and lead round to place in the direction in which the man was dancing.

16 (f) *Link arms:* Leading and opposite Tops men and leading and opposite Sides men (i.e. A, C, E and G) advance and take the right arm of the respective contrary men (i.e. of L, N, P and S), the inner sides of fore-arms touching; dance around each other and release arms. Advance to meet the contrary woman, give left hand and dance around her; return to place, men passing right arm to right; give right hand to partner and turn once in place. Partners take hands and dance a complete circle around the contrary couple, i.e. couples 1 and 5 dance around each other, as do couples 2 and 6, 3 and 7, and 4 and 8.

C. 1st Figure. Advance And Retire

16 *(a)* Leading and opposite Tops men take partner's left hand in their right, both advance to meet the opposite couple and retire to place *[4 bars]*. Repeat the movement. Both couples then dance a complete circle around each other.

48 *(b) Repeat:* Repeat, with leading and opposite Sides, 2nd Tops and finally 2nd Sides leading in turn.

D. Body

64 Repeat *B*.

E. 2nd Figure. Right Hand To Opposite Woman

24 *(a)* Men of leading and opposite Tops advance to woman opposite, give right hand and turn once in place; return to own partner, give left hand and turn once in place. Both men advance to the centre, take right hands and turn once. Advance to opposite woman, give left hand and turn once in place; return to own partner. Take partner's hands; both couples dance around each other and back to place.

72 *(b)* Repeat, with leading and opposite Sides, 2nd Tops and finally 2nd Sides leading in turn.

F. Body

64 Repeat *B*.

G. 3rd Figure. Arch Arms

16 *(a)* Leading and opposite Tops dance a complete turn into the centre; leading Tops release left hands and raise right hands to form an arch, allowing the opposite woman to pass through; half-turn and allow opposite man to pass through the arch. Partners take hands and dance a complete turn to the position opposite their starting position. Again dance into the centre; opposite Tops release left hands and raise right hands to allow leading woman to pass through; half-turn and allow leading man to pass through. Partners take hands and dance to place.

48 (b) Repeat, with leading and opposite Sides, 2nd Tops and finally 2nd Sides leading in turn.

H. Body

64 Repeat *B*.

I. Finish

40 All dancers join hands in a circle, forearms bent sharply upwards and elbows held in to the sides. Advance to centre, retire, advance again and retire. All side-step anticlockwise and finish with two short threes; side-step back ending with two short threes. Advance and retire twice as before. All side-step clockwise and back, then the couples take hands and swing around to the right to finish off.

Skibbereen Set
Seit Sciobairín

1ST FIGURE   *(Polkas: 136 bars)*

Bars *A. Body*

32   All couples dance to centre and back *[4 bars]* and two turns to next position *[4 bars]*. Repeat until back home.

B. Body

8   *(a)* Top couples advance and retire, twice.
8   *(b)* Top women chain: right hands in centre, left to opposite partner. Women pass back to own partner.
8   *(c)* Side couples dance *(a)*.
8   *(d)* Side women dance *(b)*.
8   *(e)* Top man and opposite Top woman advance to centre and swing.
8   *(f)* Top man and opposite Top woman reverse and pick up their partners, holding left hands in left in front, right hands in right over the woman's shoulder, and dance forward to opposite positions.
8   *(g)* Opposite Top man and Top woman dance *(e)*.
8   *(h)* Opposite Top man and Top woman dance *(f)*.
32   *(i)* Side couples dance *(e)–(h)*; all couples dance in the last 4 bars.

2ND FIGURE. *SHORT SLIDE*   *(Slides: 80 bars)*

A. Slide

8   (a) Top couples adopt waltz hold and slide to centre and back to home; house to opposite position.
8   (b) Top couples slide to centre and back and house to home.

B. Slide

16   Side couples dance *A*.

C. Slide

16   Top couples repeat *A*.

D. Slide

16   Side couples repeat *A*.

E. Swing

8   All couples swing in place.

3RD FIGURE. *THE BASKET*   (Polkas: 208 bars)

A. Women Chain

8   Top women chain: right hands in centre, left hand to opposite man. Women pass back to own partner.

B. Swing

8   Top couples swing in place.

C. Advance To Opposites

8   While Top couple are dancing to the centre and back to position, the opposite Top couple are standing with the man holding his partner's right hand with his right, over her shoulder. The Top couple dance forward with the Top man wheeling his partner around twice, and the woman takes the left hand of the opposite man in her left hand, over her left shoulder.

D. Three And One

8   Top man takes his partner's right hand and the left hand of the opposite woman, and all four dancers (with Top man reversing) dance to home position and back to centre.

E. Basket

8   All four dancers swing in basket.

F. Women Chain

8   Top couples reverse back to original positions and women repeat *A*.

G. Repeat

48   Repeat *A–F*, 1st Sides dancing with 2nd Sides.

H. Repeat

48   Repeat *A–F*, 2nd Tops dancing with 1st Tops.

I. Repeat

48   Repeat *A–F*, 2nd Sides dancing with 1st Sides.

J. Swing

8   All couples swing in place.

4TH FIGURE. *LONG SLIDE*   *(Slides: 120 Bars)*

A. Lead Around

16   All couples lead around, facing anticlockwise; dance two threes to the next position and two threes in place; repeat until back home. (The women's left hand is on the man's shoulder, the man's right arm around the woman's waist).

B. Part

8   *(a)* Top couples adopt waltz hold, slide side-step to the opposite position (14 steps) and slide back to original position (14 steps).

8   *(b)* Top couples house to the opposite position and slide (14 steps) back to home.

8   *(c)* Top couples slide to the opposite position (14 steps) and house to home.

8   *(d)* The four women chain round partners once, finishing with the women on the outside; dance in place, facing anticlockwise.

C. Lead Around

16   Repeat *A*.

D. Part

32   Side couples dance *B*.

E. Lead Around

16   Repeat *A*.

5TH FIGURE   (Polkas: 120 bars)

A. Circle

8   All couples join hands to form a circle, advance and retire twice.

B. Swing

8   All couples swing in place.

C. Part

8   (a) All women dance outside partners and continue clockwise inside the next two men, to the third man (on the right of their original position), while men dance in place.

8   (b) All couples swing (with new partner).

48   (c) Repeat (a) and (b) until back with own partner; swing.

D. Body

32   Dance the Body as at *1st Figure, A*.

Sliabh gCua Polka Set
Seit Sliabh gCua

A march is performed at the start and finish to line up the dancers in their proper places. Steps: Set threes, slide or 1-2 and 1-2-3.

1ST FIGURE. *INTRODUCTION* (Polkas: 72 bars)

Bars **A. Slide And Swing**

8   Top couples slide to centre and back *[4 bars]*; swing *[4 bars]*.

B. Women Chain

8   Top women give right hands in the centre and turn opposite men with left hands; return to own partners.

C. House

8   Top couples house around each other.

D. Swing

8   Top couple swing.

E. Repeat

32   Sides dance *A–D*.

2ND FIGURE. *INTRODUCTION ALL ROUND*
(Polkas: 128 bars)

A. Slide And Swing

8   All couples slide to centre and back *[4 bars]*; swing *[4 bars]*.

B. Slide And Change

8   Top couples, with hands crossed, slide to the centre and back. Couples cross to opposite sides, men turning their partners under their right hands, crossing anticlockwise.

C. Slide And Change

8   Repeat *B*, back to own positions.

D. Swing

8   Top couples swing.

E. Repeat

24   Side couples dance *B–D*.

F. Slide And Change

8   Top couples repeat *B* and stand in opposite positions holding right hands.

G. Slide And Change

8   Side couples repeat *B*.

H. Chain

8   All chain back to their own positions, men anticlockwise, women clockwise, giving right hand first, then left hands and so on, until back with their own partners.

I. Swing

8   All couples swing.

J. Slide And Change

8   Top couples repeat *B*.

K. Slide And Change

8   Side couples repeat *B*.

L. Chain

8   Repeat *H*.

M. Swing

8   All swing.

3RD FIGURE. *MEN MEET OPPOSITE WOMAN*
(Polkas or Jigs: 152 bars)

A. Circle And Swing

16   All circle and swing.

B. Swing And Change

8   Top man advances to the centre and swings opposite woman while opposite man and Top woman exchange places, crossing anticlockwise.

C. Opposites Dance Around

8   Opposite man and Top woman stand in opposite positions while Top man and opposite woman release hands and dance around each other, anticlockwise, in the centre, and bow on the way back to their own partners in opposite positions.

D. Advance And Retire

8   Advance and retire once; half house back.

E. Repeat

24   Top couples repeat *A–C* with opposite man and Top woman swinging in the centre and bowing.

F. Swing

8   Top couples swing.

G. Repeat

56   Side couples dance *A–E* with 1st Sides man leading.

H. Circle And Swing

16   All circle and swing.

4TH FIGURE. *BRING UP THE FIGURE*   (Polkas: 248 bars)

A. Women Chain

8   Top women chain as at *1st Figure, B*.

B. House

8   Top couples house around each other.

C. Bring Up The Figure

8   Opposite Tops stand while Top couples 'bring up the figure', i.e. slide to the centre and back *[4 bars]*; turn once in place with threes *[4 bars]*.

D. Bring Up The Figure

8   Repeat *C*.

E. House

8   Top couples repeat *B*.

F. Repeat

40   Top couples repeat *A–E*, opposite Tops bringing up the figure.

G. Swing

8   Top couples swing.

H. Repeat

88   Side couples dance *A–G*.

I. Circle

8   All form circle, advance and retire twice.

J. Swing

8   All swing.

K. Polka

32   All couples slide to the centre and back and dance to the next position on the right, turning twice *[8 bars]*. Repeat three more times until all couples are back in their own positions.

L. Repeat

16   Repeat *I* and *J*.

Note: In olden times the 4th Figure, above, was broken into two parts, and K and L danced to hornpipe; thus the set would have six parts.

5TH FIGURE. *ALL TOGETHER ROUND THE HOUSE*
(Polkas or Jigs: 88 bars)

A. Circle

8   All form a circle, advance and retire, twice.

B. Swing

8   All swing.

C. Circle And Swing

16   Repeat *A* and *B* but on this occasion, each man swings the woman on his left and places her on his right.

D. Circle And Swing

48   Repeat *A* and *B* three times until each man swings his own partner in their own position.

Sneem Set
Seit Snaidhme

1ST FIGURE. *TOPS WHEEL*   *(Polkas: 144 bars)*

Bars   *A. Body*

16   All couples dance together, 1 bar into the centre and 1 bar back to their positions. They then dance 2 bars around to the position of the couple to their right, turning clockwise as they go. The four couples repeat this movement three more times until they end up back in their original starting positions.

B. House

8   All four couples dance house around.

C. Figure

8   *(a) Star:* Top couples join hands in the centre and wheel around clockwise *[4 bars]*, then turn, join left hands in the centre and wheel anticlockwise back to their starting position *[4 bars]*.

8   *(b) Swing:* Top couples swing.

8   *(c) Women chain:* Top women dance to centre, chain with right hands and pass each other; give left hands to opposite men, turn clockwise under their left arms and dance around behind them, the men turning with the women. The women then dance back to their own partners.

8   *(d) House:* Top couples house around the house inside.

D. Body

16   Repeat *A*.

E. House

8   Repeat *B*.

F. Figure

32   Side couples dance *C*.

G. Body

16 Repeat *A*.

H. House

8 Repeat *B*.

2ND FIGURE. *SLIDE AND HOME*   (Polkas: 112 bars)

A. Body

16 All four couples dance the Body as at *1st Figure, A*.

B. House

8 All four couples dance house around.

C. Figure

8 *(a) Slide and home:* Top couples advance to centre and retire once
   [4 bars], then dance around at home *[4 bars]*.

8 *(b) Slide and home:* Top couples repeat *(a)*.

D. Body

16 Repeat *A*.

E. House

8 Repeat *B*.

F. Figure

16 Side couples dance *C*.

G. Body

16 Repeat *A*.

H. House

8 Repeat *B*.

3RD FIGURE. *WOMEN WHEEL* (Polkas: 104 bars)

A. Body

16 All four couples dance the Body as at *1st Figure*, *A*.

B. House

8 All four couples dance house around.

C. Figure

8 (a) *Women right hand in:* The four women join right hands in the centre and wheel clockwise half-way around to the opposite men. Each woman joins left hand with the opposite man's left hand and turns clockwise under his left arm, dances around behind him and comes back in again on his right side. The four women again join right hands in the centre and wheel clockwise back to their own partners.

8 (b) *Swing:* All four couples swing in place.

8 (c) *Slide and change:* In waltz position, all four couples advance to the centre and retire once *[4 bars]*, then dance half-way around the house *[4 bars]*.

8 (d) *Slide and change:* All four couples repeat (c) to home.

32 (e) *Repeat:* All four couples repeat (a)–(d).

D. House

8 Repeat *B*.

4TH FIGURE. *HIGH GATES* (Polkas: 112 bars)

A. Body

16 All four couples dance the Body as at *1st Figure*, *A*.

B. House

8 All four couples dance house around.

C. Figure

8   (a) *Circle:* All four couples join hands in a circle and advance and retire, twice. While advancing and retiring, dancers swing hands up and down in time with the music.

4   (b) *Dance to left:* Keeping hands joined in a circle, dancers dance four threes to the left (half-way around square).

8   (c) *Circle:* All four couples repeat (a).

4   (d) *Dance to left:* All four couples repeat (b) to home.

8   (e) *Lead around:* All four couples lead around anticlockwise to home with each man's right arm around his partner's waist and each woman's left arm resting on her partner's left shoulder.

D. House

8   Repeat *B*.

E. Figure

32   All four couples repeat *C*.

F. House

8   Repeat *B*.

5TH FIGURE. *WOMEN DOUBLE CHAIN*   (Slides: 168 bars)

A. Body

16   All four couples dance the Body as at *1st Figure, A*.

B. House

8   All four couples dance house around.

C. Figure

8   (a) *Slide and change:* In waltz position, Top couples advance to the centre and retire once *[4 bars]*, then dance half-way around the house *[4 bars]*.

8   *(b) Slide and home:* Top couples advance to the centre and retire once *[4 bars]*, then dance around at home *[4 bars]*.

8   *(c) Slide and women across:* Top couples advance and retire once *[4 bars]*, then Top women dance straight across to opposite man.

8   *(d) House:* Top couples dance around the house inside.

16 *(e) Slide and women home:* Top couples advance and retire once *[4 bars]*, then Top women dance straight across home, giving left hand to own partner; turn clockwise under their left arm and dance around behind them, the men turning with the women. Women give right hands in the centre, left hand to opposite men, turn clockwise under their left arms and dance around behind them, the men turning with the women; women give right hands in the centre and back home to their partner in waltz position.

8   *(f) House:* Top couples dance house around.

D. Figure

56 Side couples dance *C*.

E. Body

16 Repeat *A*.

F. House

8   Repeat *B*.

6TH FIGURE   *(Hornpipes: 160 bars)*

A. Body

16 All four couples dance the Body as at *1st Figure, A*.

B. House

8   All four couples dance house around.

C. Figure

8   Circle and women move on: All four couples join hands and advance and retire six times. Men advance and retire two more times while women move on behind men and then turn clockwise into position.

D. Body

16   Repeat A.

E. House

8   Repeat B.

F. Figure

8   Repeat C. Women move one more place.

G. Body

16   Repeat A.

H. House

8   Repeat B.

I. Figure

8   Repeat C. Women move one more place.

J. Body

16   Repeat A.

K. House

8   Repeat B.

L. Figure

8   Repeat C. Women move one more place.

M. Body

16   Repeat *A*.

N. House

8   Repeat *B*.

South Galway Set
Seit Gaillimn Cheas

Opening position for all figures: Couples adopt the standard position.

1ST FIGURE

(Reels: 56 bars)

Bars ***A. House***

8   All four couples dance house around.

B. Figure

4   *(a) Pass through and return:* 1st Tops and 1st Sides turn towards each other, and 2nd Tops and 2nd Sides turn towards each other. All four couples dance forward and pass through, women on the inside, passing left shoulder to left. After passing, each couple dances into the position just vacated by the couple with whom they are dancing, the woman passing in front of the man, and they turn again to face each other.

4   *(b) Repeat:* Repeat to come back to original positions.

C. Swing

8   All four couples swing in place.

D. House

8   Repeat *A*.

E. Figure

8   Repeat *B*.

F. Swing

8   Repeat *C*.

2ND FIGURE   *(Reels: 72 bars)*

A. *House*

8   All four couples dance house around.

B. *Figure*

4   *(a) Advance and retire:* 1st Tops and 1st Sides, 2nd Tops and 2nd
     Sides turn towards each other. They advance and retire once.

4   *(b) Pass through and turn:* The couples facing each other advance
     again and pass through, the women on the inside passing left
     shoulder to left; then, passing in front of their partners, dance
     into the position of the couple with whom they are dancing,
     and turn to face each other again.

8   *(c) Repeat:* Repeat *(a)* and *(b)*.

C. *Swing*

8   All four couples swing in place.

D. *House*

8   Repeat *A.*

E. *Figure*

16   Repeat *B.*

F. *Swing*

8   Repeat *C.*

3RD FIGURE   *(Reels: 88 bars)*

A. *House*

8   All four couples dance house around.

B. *Figure*

4   *(a) Advance and retire:* Four couples advance to centre and retire.

4   *(b) Change:* All four couples dance half-way around the house to each other's positions.
4   *(c) Advance and retire:* Repeat *(a)*.
4   *(d) Change:* Repeat *(b)* to return to own positions again.
8   *(e) House:* All four couples dance house around.

C. Swing

8   All four couples swing in place.

D. House

8   Repeat *A*.

E. Figure

24   Repeat *B*.

F. Swing

8   Repeat *C*.

4TH FIGURE   *(Jigs: 88 bars)*

A. House

8   All four couples dance house around.

B. Figure

8   *(a) House:* Top couples dance house at home.
8   *(b) Advance and retire:* All four couples advance to the centre and retire twice.
8   *(c) House:* All four couples dance house around.

C. Swing

8   All four couples swing in place.

D. House

8   Repeat *B*.

E. Figure

24   Repeat *B*; Side couples dance house at *(a)*.

F. Swing

8   Repeat *C*.

5TH FIGURE   *(Reels: 104 bars)*

A. House

8   All four couples dance house around.

B. Figure

4   *(a) Advance and retire:* 1st Tops and 1st Sides, and 2nd Tops and 2nd Sides turn towards each other; advance and retire once.

4   *(b) Women change:* The women in each pair of couples dance across to each other's place.

8   *(c) House:* Women pick up new partners; all four couples dance house around.

8   *(d) Repeat:* Repeat *(a)* and *(b)*, to bring women back to partners.

8   *(e) House:* All four couples dance house around.

C. Swing

8   All four couples swing in place.

D. House

8   Repeat *A*.

E. Figure

32   Repeat *B*.

F. Circle

8   All dancers link up together into a big circle, arms behind each other's backs and dance around clockwise.

South Sligo Set Of Lancers
Lannsuidhthe Shligigh Theas

1ST FIGURE. *SIDE SWINGS*   *(Reels: 136 bars)*

Bars *A. Swing*

8   Leading man and opposite woman dance in and swing.

B. Half Diamond

16   Top couples advance, retire and half-diamond to opposite position; then advance, retire and half-diamond to home position.

C. House

8   All men house around with woman their on left and return to home position.

D. Repeat

32   Repeat *A–C*; 2nd Tops man and opposite woman dance *A* and *B*.

E. Repeat

32   Repeat *A–C*; 1st Sides man and opposite woman dance *A* and *B*.

F. Repeat

32   Repeat *A–C*; 2nd Sides man and opposite woman dance *A* and *B*.

2ND FIGURE. *PASS THE WOMAN OUT*   *(Reels: 168 bars)*

A. Advance And Retire

8   Top couples advance and retire twice.

B. Pass The Woman Out

16   Pass the woman out twice, holding left hands only *[8 bars]*. Top couples house around each other while Sides dance in place *[4 bars]*; Sides split to join Top couples *[4 bars]*, all catching hands in a line of four.

C. Advance And Retire

8   All couples advance, retire and advance again; Top couples retire again and Sides dance in place.

D. House

8   All dance around the house with partners.

E. Repeat

40   Repeat A–D.

F. Advance And Retire

8   Side couples advance and retire, twice.

G. Pass The Woman Out

16   Pass the woman out, holding left hands only [8 bars]. Side couples house around each other while Tops dance in place [4 bars]; Tops split to join Side couples [4 bars], all catching hands in a line of four.

H. Advance And Retire

8   Repeat C; Side couples retire again and Tops dance in place.

I. House

8   All dance around the house with partners.

J. Repeat

40   Repeat F–I.

3RD FIGURE. GATHERING IN   (Jigs: 88 bars)

A. Circle

8   All couples take hands in a circle, advance and retire twice.

B. House

8   All couples house around.

C. Circle

8   Repeat *A*.

D. House

8   Each man houses with first woman on his left. On completing the movement he leaves first woman on his right-hand side.

E. Circle

8   Repeat *A*.

F. House

8   Each man repeats *D* with second woman on his left.

G. Circle

8   Repeat *A*.

H. House

8   Each man repeats *D* with third woman on his left.

I. Circle

8   Repeat *A*.

J. House

8   Men house with their own partner.

4TH FIGURE. *WOMEN IN*   (Reels: 232 bars)

A. Wheel

8   The four women give right hands in and wheel clockwise, then

left hands anticlockwise back to place. Men dance anticlockwise half-way and clockwise back to place.

B. Lead Around

16 Top couples lead around and drop women in Tops position; men dance back to opposite position. Side couples lead around and drop women beside Tops position; men dance back to opposite position.

C. Advance And Retire

8 Women facing men advance and retire twice.

D. Dance To Home

8 Women dance back to own partner [2 bars]; dance at home.

E. Christmas

16 Top couples lead around to the couple on their left. Women shake hands, men shake hands then in a four-hand swing all couples dance back to place.

F. Wheel

8 Women give left hands in and wheel anticlockwise, then right hands clockwise back to place. Men dance clockwise half-way and anticlockwise back to place.

G. Lead Around

16 Top couples repeat B, but drop woman in opposite Tops position; men dance back to opposite position.

H. Advance And Retire

8 Repeat C.

I. Dance To Home

8 Repeat D.

J. Christmas

8   Top couples repeat *E*, but lead around the opposite way to the couple on their right.

K. Wheel

8   Repeat *A*.

L. Repeat

104   Repeat *A–K*, Side couples leading.

M. Wheel

8   Repeat *F*.

N. Repeat

112   Repeat *A–M*.

5TH FIGURE. *GRAND CHAIN*   *(Hornpipes or March: 112 bars)*

A. Chain

16   Each man faces his partner; right hand in right, chain around, turning the woman as she passes by, men going anticlockwise, women going clockwise.

B. House

8   All house with partner.

C. Chain

64   Repeat *A* four times.

D. House

24   Repeat *B* three times.

Sweets Of May

Bars **A. Rings**

16 All dancers join hands in a ring of eight and side-step clockwise, finishing with two short threes; return anticlockwise, finishing as before. The side-step movement is then repeated, this time moving anticlockwise and returning clockwise. While doing the last two threes, all couples break the ring and fall back to their original places, partners retaining inside hands.

B. Body

8 *(a) Cross-over and back:* Couples 1 and 2, with partners holding inside hands, exchange places with promenade step, passing across, men left shoulder to left. (While the Top couples are exchanging places couples 3 and 4 dance two threes in place.) Side couples then exchange places in the same way while the Top couples dance two threes in place. Repeat these movements to leave all couples back in their original positions.

8 *(b) Advance and retire:* Top couples, still holding inside hands, advance to meet in the centre while Side couples mark time with two threes; then Sides advance to the centre while Tops retire; Tops then advance while Sides retire; and Tops retire while Sides mark time.

16 *(c) Ringing the bells:* All dancers bend and beat left hand on left knee and right hand on right knee four times; then clap hands in front of forehead twice; repeat the whole movement. Partners side-step past each other, the man passing behind, and all dance two threes in new places. Repeat the movement but with partners side-stepping back to place, the men now passing in front.

C. 1st Figure. Lead Around

16 Partners hold inside hands and lead around anticlockwise a complete circle; release hands, about turn inwards and take inside hands. Return, clockwise, back to original positions.

D. Body

32   Repeat *B*.

E. 2nd Figure. See-Saw

16   All couples take uncrossed hands and swing around clockwise, moving in an anticlockwise direction. Couples reverse their swing and return, moving in a clockwise direction to place. (The arms are not moved up and down in this movement.)

F. Body

32   Repeat *B*.

G. 3rd Figure. Sides Under Arms

16   Partners take inside hands. Top couples, holding up hands to form an arch and with promenade step, change places with Sides, 2nd Sides passing under the arch of 1st Tops and 1st Sides passsing under 2nd Tops' arch; release hands and face about. All take inside hands again and dance back to places, this time with Sides making arches and Tops passing underneath. Repeat on opposite side: i.e. 1st Sides passing under arch of 1st Tops, and 2nd Sides passing under that of 2nd Tops; return to places with Sides forming the arches.

H. Body

32   Repeat *B*.

I. Rings

16   Repeat *A*.

Televara Set
Seit Theileabhara

Opening position for all figures, except where stated: All four couples face anticlockwise around the circle, men on the inside. Each woman and man have an arm around each other's waist, and each man places his left hand on the left shoulder of the man in front of him. This position is called the 'lock'.

1ST FIGURE. *DOUBLE CHAIN* (*Jigs: 248 bars*)

Bars *A. Body*

8   *(a) Lock:* In the lock position the dancers wheel around until all couples are back in their own places.

8   *(b) House:* All four couples dance around the house.

B. Figure

16   *(a) House and square:* 1st Tops dance around the house inside *[8 bars]*. When they return to their own place they dance 2 bars towards the couple to their right (women step R-L-RLR; men step L-R-LRL), dance backwards using the opposite steps towards their opposite couple *[2 bars]*, and finally dance around the house back to their own position *[4 bars]*.

16   *(b) Women chain:* Top women chain right hands in middle, left hands to opposite men; turn under and dance around them, right hands in middle, left to own partners; turn under and dance around them. Man turns with woman each time. Repeat.

8   *(c) Swing:* Top couples swing in place.

C. Body

16   Repeat *A*.

D. Figure

40   Side couples dance *B*, with 1st Sides dancing *(a)*.

E. Body

16   Repeat *A*.

F. Figure

40   Top couples dance *B* with 2nd Tops dancing *(a)*.

G. Body

16   Repeat *A*.

H. Figure

40   Side couples dance *B* with 2nd Sides dancing *(a)*.

I. Body

16   Repeat *A*.

2ND FIGURE. *SIDES*   *(Jigs: 312 bars)*

A. Body

8   *(a) Lock:* In the lock position the dancers wheel around until all couples are back in their own places.

8   *(b) House:* All four couples dance around the house.

B. Figure

16   *(a) House and square:* 1st Tops dance around the house inside *[8 bars]*. When they return to their own place they dance 2 bars towards the couple to their right (women step R-L-RLR; men step L-R-LRL), dance backwards using the opposite steps towards their opposite couple *[2 bars]*, and finally dance around the house back to their own position *[4 bars]*.

32   *(b) Slide and change:* 1st Tops and 1st Sides turn to each other, and 2nd Tops and 2nd Sides turn to each other. Facing couples slide in and out *[4 bars]* and dance around into each other's places *[4 bars]*. Each couple repeats this movement with the next couple they meet *[8 bars]* and so on, two more times until they return to their own places again *[16 bars]*.

8   *(c) Swing:* All four couples swing in place.

C. Body

16 Repeat *A*.

D. Figure

56 Repeat *B* with 1st Sides dancing *(a)*; Side couples face the couples to their left to begin.

E. Body

16 Repeat *A*.

F. Figure

56 Repeat *B* with 2nd Tops dancing *(a)*; Top couples face the couples to their left to begin.

G. Body

16 Repeat *A*.

H. Figure

56 Repeat *B* with 2nd Sides dancing *(a)*; Side couples face the couples to their left to begin.

I. Body

16 Repeat *A*.

3RD FIGURE. *FROG IN THE MIDDLE*   *(Jigs: 192 bars)*

A. Body

8 *(a) Lock:* In the lock position the dancers wheel around until all couples are back in their own places.

8 *(b) House:* All four couples dance around the house.

B. Figure

16 *(a) House and square:* 1st Tops dance around the house inside *[8 bars]*. When they return to their own place they dance 2 bars

towards the couple to their right (women step R-L-RLR; men step L-R-LRL), dance backwards using the opposite steps towards their opposite couple *[2 bars]*, and finally dance around the house back to their own position *[4 bars]*.

8 (b) *Swing in the circle:* 1st Tops man leaves his partner back and takes out the opposite woman. They swing in the middle of the set while the other six dancers join hands in a circle and dance in a clockwise direction around the outside.

C. Body

16 Repeat *A*.

D. Figure

24 Side couples dance *B* with 1st Side couples dancing *(a)*.

E. Body

16 Repeat *A*.

F. Figure

24 Top couples dance *B* with 2nd Tops dancing *(a)*.

G. Body

16 Repeat *A*.

H. Figure

24 Side couples dance *B* with 2nd Sides dancing *(a)*.

I. Body

16 Repeat *A*.

4TH FIGURE. *STOOK OF OATS* (Jigs: 192 bars)

A. Body

8 (a) *Lock:* In the lock position the dancers wheel around until all

couples are back in their own places.

8   *(b) House:* All four couples dance around the house.

B. Figure

16   *(a) House and square:* 1st Tops dance around the house inside *[8 bars]*. When they return to their own place they dance 2 bars towards the couple to their right (women step R-L-RLR; men step L-R-LRL), dance backwards using the opposite steps towards their opposite couple *[2 bars]*, and finally dance around the house back to their own position *[4 bars]*.

8   *(b) Swing behind:* Each woman and man turns away from their partner to the man or woman nearest them and swings with them, in the man's position.

C. Body

16   The new couples repeat *A*.

D. Figure

24   Repeat *B* with 1st Sides man and his new partner dancing *(a)*.

E. Body

16   The new couples repeat *A*.

F. Figure

24   Repeat *B* with 2nd Tops man and his new partner dancing *(a)*.

G. Body

16   The new couples repeat *A*.

H. Figure

24   Repeat *B* with 2nd Sides man and his new partner dancing *(a)*.

I. Body

16   The original couples repeat *A*.

5TH FIGURE. *FACE THE HOB*   *(Jigs: 408 bars)*

A. Body

8   *(a) Lock:* In the lock position the dancers wheel around until all couples are back in their own places.

8   *(b) House:* All four couples dance around the house.

B. Figure

16   *(a) House and square:* 1st Tops dance around the house inside *[8 bars]*. When they return to their own place they dance 2 bars towards the couple to their right (women step R-L-RLR; men step L-R-LRL), dance backwards using the opposite steps towards their opposite couple *[2 bars]*, and finally dance around the house back to their own position *[4 bars]*.

16   *(b) Repeat:* 1st Sides dance *(a)* and line up behind 1st Tops.

16   *(c) Repeat:* 2nd Tops repeat and line up behind 1st Sides.

16   *(d) Repeat:* 2nd Sides repeat and line up behind 2nd Tops.

8   *(e) Dance around:* The men lead off to the left and women to the right. They dance through their starting positions and around again. As they lead around the second time the women place their hands on their hips and the men their right hands on the shoulder of the man in front.

8   *(f) Lead around:* As each couple rejoins they lead off to the left and around the circle, arms around each other's waists.

C. Body

16   Repeat *A*.

D. Figure

80   Repeat *B* with 1st Sides dancing *(a)* first, and the other couples repeating it in order around the set.

E. Body

16   Repeat *A*.

F. Figure

80   Repeat *B* with 2nd Tops dancing *(a)* first, and the other couples repeating it in order around the set.

G. Body

16   Repeat *A*.

H. Figure

80   Repeat *B* with 2nd Sides dancing *(a)* first, and the other couples repeating it in order around the set.

I. Body

16   Repeat *A*.

6TH FIGURE   (Slides: 232 bars)

Opening position: Couples adopt the standard position.

A. Figure

8   *(a) House:* Top couples dance around the house.

8   *(b) Square:* Top couples dance straight over to the next position to their right, men passing back-to-back, and turn slightly clock-wise so they are ready to step off with the 'wrong' feet to reach the next position (women dance R-L-RLR; men dance L-R-LRL) *[2 bars]*. Repeat with opposite steps to bring each couple to the position opposite their own, women passing back-to-back *[2 bars]*; dance a half house to get back to own places *[4 bars]*.

8   *(c) Square:* Repeat *(b)*.

8   *(d) House:* Top couples dance around the house.

16   *(e) Square and house:* Top couples repeat *(b)* and *(c)*.

8   *(f) House:* Top couples dance around the house.

B. Figure

56   Side couples dance *A*.

C. Figure

56 Top couples repeat *A*.

D. Figure

56 Side couples repeat *A*.

7TH FIGURE   (Reels: 272 bars)

Opening position: All four couples join hands in front and face anticlockwise around the circle, men on the inside.

A. Lead Around

8 All four couples dance anticlockwise around until back in their original places.

B. Turn The Lady

8 The four men, their backs towards the centre of the set, turn their partners clockwise four times, left hand to left while dancing on the spot themselves.

C. Swing

8 All four couples swing in place.

D. Figure

8 *(a) Square:* The two Top couples square all the way around.
8 *(b) House:* The two Top couples dance around the house inside.
8 *(c) Swing opposites:* The two Top men leave their partners, cross over to the opposite women and swing with them.
8 *(d) Link arms:* The two Top men return to the centre, link left arms and dance around each other, doubling the last 2 bars.

E. Repeat

24 Repeat *A–C*.

F. Figure

32   Side couples dance *D*.

G. Repeat

24   Repeat *A–C*.

H. Figure

32   Top couples repeat *D*.

I. Repeat

24   Repeat *A–C*.

J. Figure

32   Side couples repeat *D*.

K. Repeat

24   Repeat *A–C*.

L. Finish

8   *(a) Square:* All four couples square all the way around.
8   *(b) House:* All four couples dance around the house.

Three Tunes

Danced to the tune, **The Three Tunes**.

Bars **A. Sides**

16   All dance side-step to the left, finishing with two short threes, and return to right, finishing as before; repeat this side-step movement to the right, and back to places. While doing the last two threes, all couples fall back to places as shown:

1
B A

4 G   F **3**
   H   E

C D
2

1st Tops are couple 1, 2nd Tops are couple 2, 1st Sides are couple 3 and 2nd Sides are couple 4.
A, C, E, G are men; B, D, F and H are women.

B. Rings

16   Women advance to the centre, take hands and, with promenade step, dance round clockwise to places; all clap hands twice. Partners dance a half side-step past each other, men passing behind (count 1-2-3) then side-step back to places, women now passing behind *[8 bars]*. Repeat the movement, the men dancing round in the centre this time instead of the women.

C. Lead Around

16   Partners hold inside hands and lead around anticlockwise a complete circle; release hands, reverse and again taking inside hands, lead back to places.

D. Stamp And Clap

16 All dancers stamp first the right foot, then the left, then the right again, to 1 bar of music and clap hands three times on the second bar; then side-step past each other, the man passing behind, and back to places, the man this time passing in front. Clap alternate hands five times quickly on legs above knees, beginning with right hand on right knee; clap hands together three times [8 bars]. Repeat this movement.

E. See-Saw

16 Dancers take partners' hands uncrossed and swing around in couples anticlockwise. Return clockwise, swinging in reverse direction.

F. Roly-Poly

24 All dancers hold fists at chest level and roll them round each other in a forward direction, and then roll them in the opposite direction; pivot once clockwise on the right heel, clap hands together once; men shake right fist forward in air once (in a threatening manner), band about shoulder level, at the same time placing right foot forward on ground, bringing it back as hand is returned to side. Shake left fist in similar manner, placing the left foot forward, stamp feet three times and clap hands together three times towards partner. Partners sidestep past each other and back to places [12 bars]. Repeat this movement.

G. Hook And Chain

16 Each man hooks the left arm of the woman on the left in his left, turning her once in place and chains back to his partner, taking her right hand in his right. He continues the chain movement, giving alternate hands to each woman in turn until all return to places.

H. Rings

16 Repeat B.

I. Sides Under Arms

16 Partners take inside hands, Top couples holding up hands to form an arch, and with promenade step, Tops and Sides change places, 1st Sides passing under arch of 1st Tops, while 2nd Sides pass under that of 2nd Tops; release hands and face about. All take inside hands again and dance back to places, this time Sides making the arches and Tops passing underneath *[8 bars]*. Repeat on the opposite side, i.e. 2nd Sides passing under the arch of 1st Tops, and 1st Sides passing under that of 2nd Tops, returning to places as before.

J. Stamp And Clap

16 Repeat D.

K. Thread The Needle

16 All take hands in a ring, except 1st Tops man and 1st Sides woman; she passes under the raised hands of the couple on her right and takes all the other dancers of the line after her, and so back to places *[8 bars]*. Repeat this movement, 1st Tops man now passing under the arch of the couple on his left, and the others following.

L. Roly-Poly

24 Repeat F.

Tipperary Lancers Set
Lannsuidhthe Thiobraid Arainn

All dance the lancer batter during the last 2 bars of each introduction.

1ST FIGURE   *(Polkas: 104 bars)*

Bars *A. Swing*

8   Top man and opposite woman swing in waltz hold in the cen-
     tre *[6 bars]* and dance from the swing to face their own corner
     [2 bars]; men face left from their own position to their corner
     and women face right from their position.

     B. Swing

8   All swing the person facing them in the corner *[6 bars]*, danc-
     ing the batter from the swing to face their own partner *[2 bars]*.

     C. Swing

8   All swing their own partners, dancing out the last 2 bars.

     D. Repeat

24   Repeat *A–C* with Top woman and opposite man leading.

     E. Repeat

48   Repeat *A–D* with Side couples leading. (1st Side couple are on
     the left of 1st Top couple.)

2ND FIGURE   *(Polkas: 104 bars)*

     A. Line Up

8   During the last 2 bars of the introduction, Side couples dance
     away from their partners to line up in Top positions, Side men
     to their left, Side women to their right. 1st Top couple house
     inside.

B. Advance And Retire

8 With arms around each other's backs, the two lines advance and retire twice. They advance to the centre dancing the batter and retire dancing 1-2-3-4 or 1-2, 1-2-3.

C. Swing

8 All couples swing in place.

D. Repeat

24 Repeat A–C with 2nd Top couple dancing A.

E. Repeat

48 Repeat A–D, Side couples leading. Line up at Side positions at A.

3RD FIGURE   (Polkas: 136 bars)

A. House

16 Top couples house around each other twice.

B. Lead Around

16 All couples lead around anticlockwise with arms around their partners' backs. Women are on the inside, holding left hands in the centre [8 bars]. During the last 2 bars all dance the batter as women pass in front of their partners to the outside and all couples lead around with men inside. The men do not hold hands in the centre.

C. Repeat

32 Repeat A and B, with Side couples dancing A.

D. Repeat

64 Repeat A–C.

4TH FIGURE (Polkas: 152 bars)

A. Chain

16   All face their partners, taking right hands and chain all round, men anticlockwise and women clockwise. When partners meet in opposite positions, they dance the batter; then continue the chain until back to place.

B. House

8   1st Top couple house inside.

C. House

8   Both Top couples house around each other.

D. Repeat

32   Repeat A–C, with 2nd Top couple dancing B.

E. Repeat

64   Repeat A–D, with Side couples leading.

F. Chain

16   Repeat A, the chain finishing in a huddle (a circle, with arms around each other's backs).

5TH FIGURE (Jigs: 168 bars)

A. Advance And Retire

8   Holding hands in a circle, all advance and retire twice, dancing a batter as they advance and dancing 1-2-3-4, or 1-2, 1-2-3, as they retire each time.

B. Swing

8   All couples swing in place.

C. Advance And Retire

8   Facing into the centre in waltz hold, without holding hands and sometimes on their own, away from their partners, Top couples advance, dancing the batter and retire dancing 1-2-3-4 or 1-2, 1-2-3; then house across to opposite positions.

D. Advance And Retire

8   Top couples repeat C, starting in opposite positions and crossing back to their own side.

E. House

8   Top couples house around each other.

F. Repeat

40   Repeat A–E with Side couples dancing C–E.

G. Repeat

80   Repeat A–F.

Cory Lancers Set
Lannsuidhthe Choraidh

Note: 1st Sides are on the left of Tops.

1ST FIGURE   *(Single Jigs: 152 bars)*

Bars *A. Lead Around*

8   All lead around; men turn their partners under arm.

B. Swing

8   All swing in hug swing.

C. Opposites Swing

8   *(a)* 1st Tops man and opposite woman swing, finishing up with the man's back to opposite Side couple and woman's back to 1st Sides. Man takes his partner's right hand in his left; dance 2 bars to opposite Tops position, man changing the woman to his right-hand side on 2nd bar. Opposite Tops woman also takes her partner across to the other position (her left hand in his right hand) in 2 bars. Throughout this movement, i.e. with each couple, swinging man always changes his partner to his right.

8   *(b)* Both Top couples advance and retire, holding near hands. On the 7th and 8th bars the women cross, passing right shoulder to right, slightly in front of the men, who cross right to right, and all go to corners.

D. Swing

8   All swing in corners, i.e. Tops with sides.

E. Swing

8   Swing partners.

F. Repeat

32   Repeat C–E with opposite Top man and 1st Top woman leading.

G. Repeat

32 Repeat *C–E* with 1st Side man (on left) and 2nd Side woman leading.

H. Repeat

32 Repeat *C–E* with 2nd Side man and 1st Side woman leading.

2ND FIGURE   *(Single Jigs: 184 bars)*

A. Lead Around

8 All lead around.

B. Swing

8 All swing.

C. Turn The Lady And Swing

16 Top couple advance, right hand in right *[2 bars]*. The man turns the woman anticlockwise under his right arm, dancing clockwise at the same time into the woman's position *[2 bars]*. They then swing for 12 bars. Side couples move away from each other on the last 2 bars to form two lines in Tops' position, Side men to the left and women to the right.

D. Advance And Retire

16 All advance and retire four times. Side couples do not retire the last time.

E. Swing

8 Swing own partners.

F. Repeat

40 Repeat *C–E*, opposite Tops leading.

G. Repeat

40   Repeat *C–E*, 1st Sides leading.

H. Repeat

40   Repeat *C–E*, 2nd sides leading.

3RD FIGURE   (Polkas: 72 bars)

A. Lead Around

8   All lead around.

B. Swing

8   All swing.

C. Wheel

8   All four women put right hands in the centre and dance around *[4 bars]* then left hands in and back *[4 bars]*, while the men go around on the outside anticlockwise, half-way and back.

D. Swing

8   All swing.

E. Repeat

32   Repeat *C* and *D* twice.

4TH FIGURE   (Polkas: 120 bars)

A. Lead Around

8   All lead around.

B. Swing

8   All swing.

C. Dance To The Left

16   1st Tops and 2nd Tops dance to the left, holding their partner's right hand in their right hand *[2 bars]* and in to opposite position *[2 bars]*. Repeat this movement back to place *[4 bars]*; then repeat again *[8 bars]*.

D. Swing

8   Both Tops swing.

E. Repeat

24   Tops repeat *C* and *D*.

F. Repeat

48   Sides dance *C–E*, all swinging the last 8 bars.

5TH FIGURE   (Single Jigs: 160 bars)

A. Lead Around

8   All lead around.

B. Swing

8   All swing.

C. Dance In Place

8   All dance eight steps in place facing partners.

D. Half-Way Around Dance In Place

24   All dance around half-way (like a chain, not holding hands) *[8 bars]*. Dance 8 bars facing partners and continue back to place, passing right shoulder to right, left to left, etc. for 8 bars.

E. Arches

16   1st Top couple make an arch, the man taking the woman's left

hand in his right; dance to opposite position, 2nd Tops passing under the arch *[8 bars]*. Repeat the movement on the way back; opposite Tops make an arch this time and 1st Tops pass under.

F. Repeat

32   Repeat *C* and *D*.

G. Arches

16   1st Sides forming the arch, dance *E*.

H. Repeat

32   Repeat *C* and *D*.

I. Swing

8   All swing.

Trip To The Cottage
Turas 'Un Toighe

This is an eight-hand figure dance from Co. Armagh, in double jig time, done to the tune of the same name.

Position of the dancers:

```
                    1
                  B A

       4 G                    F 3
         H                    E

                  C D
                   2
```

1st Tops are couple 1, 2nd Tops are couple 2, 1st Sides are couple 3 and 2nd Sides are couple 4.

Bars **A. Cross-Over And Lead Around**

8   *(a) Cross over:* Top couples advance to each other's places with promenade step, men passing left shoulder to shoulder, and turn into places without releasing hands *[2 bars]*; Sides change places in similar manner *[2 bars]*. Tops dance back to places *[2 bars]*; all dance two threes in these positions *[2 bars]*.

8   *(b) Lead around:* All couples lead around anticlockwise to opposite places with promenade step *[4 bars]*; Tops cross to change places as before with promenade step (back to original positions) *[2 bars]*. All dance two short threes in place *[2 bars]*.

16   *(c) Repeat:* Repeat *(a)* and *(b)*, Sides crossing over first.

B. Body

8   *(a)* Each Top man holds his partner's left hand and the right hand of the woman on his left, at shoulder height. The trios advance towads each other with promenade step diagonally across the set, twice, retiring each time.

8   *(b)* Each trio then hold hands in a ring and side-steps to the left,

finishing with two short threes *[4 bars]*; on the second three they take the other man into the ring between the two women and each four now side-steps to the right, finishing as before *[4 bars]*.

8   *(c)* Each ring breaks into couples who swing round each other anticlockwise and back to places.

24   *(d)* Side men dance *(a)*–*(c)*, advancing with their partner and woman on their left.

C. 1st Figure

8   *(a)* 2nd Tops woman advances to meet 1st Tops couple, and taking the left hand of the man in her right hand, passes under the arched arms of 1st Tops, the man turning under in place; 1st Tops woman now passes under the arch on her partner's left, the man turning again; 2nd Tops woman passes under the arch as before.

16   *(b)* The three then take 2nd Tops man into the ring between the women, and all side-step to the right, finishing with two short threes *[4 bars]*. Then the following movement is performed to 4 bars of music without releasing hands:

2nd Tops pass together under the arch made by the raised arms of 1st Tops and then turn outwards under their own arch; 1st Tops pass under the arch made by their own arms, and so backwards under the arch made by 2nd Tops, all falling into the ring again *[4 bars]*. The four then side-step to the left, finishing with two short threes *[4 bars]*, and the couples swing back to places *[4 bars]*.

24   *(c) Repeat:* Repeat *(a)* and *(b)*, 1st Tops woman advancing to meet 2nd Tops.

24   *(d) Repeat:* Repeat *(a)* and *(b)*, 2nd Sides woman advancing to meet 1st Sides.

24   *(e) Repeat:* Repeat *(a)* and *(b)*, 1st Sides woman advancing to meet 2nd Sides.

D. Body

48   Repeat *B*.

E. 2nd Figure

16 *(a)* Tops advance towards each other twice, retiring each time *[8 bars]*. Top women pass with promenade step between the Side couple on their left, dance around the man, cross over to pass between opposite Sides, and so back to places. At the same time, Tops men pass between the couple on their right, around the woman, cross over to pass between opposite Sides, and so back to places (the women pass in advance of the men in each movement). *[8 bars]*.

16 *(b)* Sides dance *(a)*.

F. Body

48 Repeat *B*.

G. Finish

32 Repeat *A*.

Tubbercurry Lancers
Lannsuidhthe Thobar a' Choire

1ST FIGURE   *(Reels: 168 bars)*

Bars *A. Opposites Swing*

8   Top man and opposite woman dance in (1-2-3) to the centre and
     swing in céilí hold; retire to place on last 2 bars.

B. Advance And Retire And Change Places

8   Top couples advance (1-2-3, kick), retire (1-2, 1-2-3), dance to
     face the couple on their left, and reverse to the opposite side.

C. Advance And Retire And Change Places

8   Top couples advance, retire and cross back.

D. House

16   All men house with the woman on their left, using the jazzing
     step. Men start on the right foot, women on the left and all dou-
     ble on the last two bars, breaking away to their own positions.

E. Repeat

24   Repeat *A–C* with Top woman and opposite man swinging at *A*.

F. House

16   Repeat *D*.

G. Repeat

80   Repeat *A–F* with Side couples leading; 1st Side couple are to the
     left of 1st Top couple.

2ND FIGURE   *(Reels: 168 bars)*

A. Advance And Retire

8   Top couples advance and retire holding right hands *[4 bars]*; ad-

vance again with women dancing anticlockwise round partner to finish in a circle of four; women put hands on men's shoulders.

B. Christmas

8   Top couples swing in four [6 bars] and break back to form lines of four in Side positions.

C. Advance And Retire

8   Advance and retire twice. Top couples stay in, facing their partners the second time.

D. House

16   All house, jazzing with their own partners.

E. Repeat

40   Repeat A–D with Side couples leading.

F. Repeat

80   Repeat A–E.

3RD FIGURE   (Jigs: 128 bars)

A. Circle

8   All take hands in a circle, advance and retire twice, dancing hop 1, hop 2, hop 1-2-3-4.

B. House

16   All house, jazzing with their own partners.

C. Circle

8   Circle; women move on to the man on their right.

D. House

16   All house, jazzing with their new partners.

E. Circle

8   Circle, women moving on to opposite man.

F. House

16   All house, jazzing with their new partners.

G. Circle

8   Circle; women move on to the man left of their own position.

H. House

16   All house, jazzing with their new partners.

I. Circle

8   Circle; women move back to their own partners.

J. House

16   All house, jazzing with their own partners.

4TH FIGURE   (Hornpipes: 136 bars)

A. Chain

16   All face their partners, take right hands and chain all round. The chain is continuous: each dancer takes the next person's hand before releasing the last one. When partners meet in opposite position, all dance 2 bars on the spot, men facing in and women facing out; then continue the chain back to place.

B. House

16   All house, jazzing with their own partners.

C. Repeat

96   Repeat *A* and *B* three times.

Two-Hand Country Dance

A two-hand country dance, danced to reels. Position: Couples form a big ring, men with backs to the centre and women facing them; men take women's hands.

Bars **A. Sevens**

8 Couples take seven side-steps to the man's right, followed by two threes *[4 bars]*; then they take seven side-steps back to their original position, followed by two threes *[4 bars]*.

B. Clap

16 Couples face each other and clap as follows:
(*a*) clap own hands together twice;
(*b*) clap right hand to partner's right hand twice;
(*c*) clap own hands together twice;
(*d*) clap left hand to partner's left hand twice;
(*e*) clap own hands together once;
(*f*) clap right hand to partner's right hand once;
(*g*) clap own hands together once;
(*h*) clap left hand to partner's left hand once;
(*i*) clap own hands together once;
(*j*) clap own hands together behind back once;
(*k*) clap own hands together once;
(*l*) clap both hands with both hands of partner once.

C. Swing

8 Couples swing in place.

D. Sevens And Change

8 All dancers take seven side-steps to their right, then two threes *[4 bars]*, then seven side-steps back to the left. Women join with a new man on original partner's left, and men with a new woman on original partner's left; then two threes *[4 bars]*.

E. Repeat

Begin the dance again with a new partner.

Two-Hand Hornpipe

A two-hand dance, danced to hornpipes. Formation: Two circles, men forming the inner circle and women the outer, each facing partners and holding right hand in right.

Bars **A. Hop 1-2-3**

1   (a) Couples dance anticlockwise; hop 1-2-3.
1   (b) Return clockwise; hop 1-2-3.
2   (c) Dance on the hop 1, hop 2, hop 1-2-3.
4   (d) Repeat (a)–(c), dancing clockwise first.

B. Change Places And Lead

4   (a) Partners change places, dancing hop 1-2-3, with the woman turning anticlockwise under the man's right arm. Dance hop 1-2-3 in place. Repeat to return to original position.
4   (b) Cross hands and lead around.

C. Repeat

Repeat *A* and *B* as often as required.

Two-Hand Jig

*A two-hand dance, danced to jigs. Formation: Partners face anticlockwise,
women with left hand in the men's right, in a circle.*

Bars **A. Advance And Retire**

2   *(a)* Couples dance two threes forward.

2   *(b)* Couples retire two threes.

4   *(c)* Repeat *(a)* and *(b)*.

B. Side-Step To The Left

4   *(a)* Side-step to the left and jig step: hop lightly on the left foot,
at the same time kick the right foot forward, hop again on the
left foot and at the same time bring the right behind the left
foot. Hop on the right foot and bring the left foot behind the
right, lifting the right foot off the ground, right down and lift
left, right foot down followed by left foot.

4   *(b)* Side-step to the right and jig step. On the last bar of jig step
men turn clockwise and women anticlockwise to face the opposite direction. Men take the women's right hand in their left.

C. Advance And Retire

8   Repeat *A*.

D. Side-Step To The Right

4   *(a)* Side-step to the right and jig step.

4   *(b)* Side-step to the left and jig step. On last bar men turn anticlockwise and women clockwise to face their original position.

E. Lead Around

8   Men hold women's left hand in their right and lead around
anticlockwise.

F. Repeat

Repeat *A–E* as often as required.

Two-Hand Reel

A two-hand dance, danced to reels.

Bars

A. Side-Step And Threes

8 Men face their partners, right hand in right. Side-step to the men's left, two threes; then side-step and two threes back to original positions.

B. Change Places

8 Still holding right hand in right, both partners jump slightly in the air, landing on both feet; kick right foot out in front, bring right foot behind left and dance one three *[2 bars]*. Swap places, turning the woman anticlockwise under the man's right arm *[2 bars]*. Repeat these movements, returning to original position *[4 bars]*.

C. Lead Around

8 Cross hands and lead around anticlockwise. On the seventh bar of the music partners face each other, right hand in right, ready to start again.

D. Repeat

Repeat *A–C* as often as required.

Uibh Rathach Set

Opening position, except where stated: All four couples adopt the standard hold.

1ST FIGURE   **(Polkas: 88 bars)**

Bars   **A. Figure**

16   *(a) Men chain and swing:* Top men dance to the centre and chain, right hand in right, then dance back to place *[6 bars]* and swing *[10 bars]*. While the men chain the women move into the men's positions.

8   *(b) Women chain:* Top women dance straight across to the opposite men, chain left hand in left with them, the men turning with the women, then dance back to face their own partners.

8   *(c) House:* Top couples dance house around, the men reversing the women for the first 2 bars.

8   *(d) Slide and home:* Top couples slide into the centre and back to place *[4 bars]* then dance around at home *[4 bars]*, turning once.

B. Figure

40   Side couples dance *A*.

2ND FIGURE   **(Jigs: 152 bars)**

A. House And Square To Home

16   All four men reverse the women into the corners of the set *[2 bars]*, then dance three-quarters' way around the house, turning three times, the men ending with their backs to the centre, facing out of the set *[6 bars]*. All four couples slide to the corners (men L-R- and swivel on left foot to face into the set; women R-L- and swivel on right foot to face out of the set), then slide into home positions (men dance R-L, R-L-R and women L-R L-R-L) *[4 bars]* and dance in place, turning once *[4 bars]*.

B. Figure

8   *(a) Slide and home:* Top couples slide into the centre and back to

place *[4 bars]*, then dance around at home *[4 bars]*.

8   *(b) Repeat:* Top couples repeat *(a)*.

C. House And Square To Home

16   All four couples repeat *A*.

D. Figure

16   Top couples repeat *B*.

E. House And Square To Home

16   All four couples repeat *A*.

F. Figure

16   Side couples dance *B*.

G. House And Square To Home

16   All four couples repeat *A*.

H. Figure

16   Side couples repeat *B*.

I. House And Square To Home

16   All four couples repeat *A*.

3RD FIGURE   *(Polkas: 104 bars)*

A. House And Square To Home

16   All four men reverse the women into the corners of the set *[2
     bars]*, then dance three-quarters' way around the house, turn-
     ing three times, the men ending with their backs to the centre,
     facing out of the set *[6 bars]*. All four couples slide to the cor-
     ners (men L-R- and swivel on left foot to face into the set;
     women R-L- and swivel on right foot to face out of the set), then

slide into home positions (men dance R-L, R-L-R and women L-R, L-R-L) *[4 bars]* and dance in place, turning once *[4 bars]*.

B. Figure

16   Chain and swing: Top women dance straight across to the opposite men, chain left hand in left with them, the men turning with the women, and then dance back to place *[6 bars]* and swing with their own partners *[10 bars]*.

C. Body

8   *(a) Lead around:* All four couples dance anticlockwise around until back in their original places, men with their right arms around the women's waists and women with their left hands on the men's shoulders.

16   *(b) House and square to home:* All four couples repeat *A*, turning immediately for first 2 bars and not reversing into the corners.

D. Figure

16   Side couples repeat *B*.

E. Body

24   All four couples repeat *C*.

4TH FIGURE   *(Polkas: 144 bars)*

A. House And Square To Home

16   All four men reverse the women into the corners of the set *[2 bars]*, then dance three-quarters' way around the house, turning three times, the men ending with their backs to the centre, facing out of the set *[6 bars]*. All four couples slide to the corners (men L-R- and swivel on left foot to face into the set; women R-L- and swivel on right foot to face out of the set), then slide into home positions (men dance R-L, R-L-R and women L-R, L-R-L) *[4 bars]* and dance in place, turning once *[4 bars]*.

B. Figure

4   (a) Advance and retire: Top couples advance and retire once with right hand in right.

4   *(b) Change:* Top couples dance clockwise to opposite positions, men leading on the left in front of the women.

4   *(c) Advance and retire:* Top couples repeat *(a)*.

4   *(d) Change:* Top couples repeat *(b)*.

8   *(e) Swing:* Top couples swing in place.

24   *(f) Repeat:* Top couples repeat *(a)–(e)*.

C. Figure

48   Side couples repeat *B*.

D. Body

8   *(a) Lead around:* All four couples dance anticlockwise around until back in their original places, men with their right arms around the women's waists and women with their left hands on the men's shoulders.

16   *(b) House and square to home:* All four couples repeat *A*, turning immediately for first 2 bars and not reversing into the corners.

5TH FIGURE   *(Polkas: 136 bars)*

A. House And Square To Home

16   All four men reverse the women into the corners of the set *[2 bars]*, then dance three-quarters' way around the house, turning three times, the men ending with their backs to the centre, facing out of the set *[6 bars]*. All four couples slide to the corners (men L-R- and swivel on left foot to face into the set; women R-L- and swivel on right foot to face out of the set), then slide into home positions (men dance R-L, R-L-R and women L-R, L-R-L) *[4 bars]* and dance in place, turning once *[4 bars]*.

B. Figure

8   *(a) Slide to change:* Top couples slide into the centre and back to

place *[4 bars]*, then dance half-way round the house to opposite places *[4 bars]*.

8   *(b) Slide to change:* Top couples repeat *(a)* to bring them back to place.

8   *(c) Slide and cross over:* Top couples slide into the centre and back to place *[4 bars]*. Top women change places, passing right shoulder to right in the centre *[4 bars]*.

8   *(d) House:* Top men dance house around with new women, reversing the woman for the first 2 bars.

16   *(e) Slide to change:* Top couples slide into the centre and back to place *[4 bars]*. Top women dance across to the opposite men (their original partners), chain left hand in left with them, the men turning with the women, then dance to the centre, chaining right hand in right. They then dance to the opposite man and chain left hand in left, finally dancing back to their original partners *[12 bars]*.

8   *(f) House:* Top couples dance house around, the men reversing the woman for the first 2 bars.

C. Figure

56   Side couples repeat *B*.

6TH FIGURE   *(Polkas: 224 bars)*

Opening position: All four face to centre joining hands in a circle.

A. Circle

8   All four couples advance and retire twice.

B. Swing

8   All four couples swing in place.

C. Figure

16   *(a) Wheel and swing:* The four men join right hands in the centre and dance clockwise around until back in their original positions *[8 bars]* and swing own partners *[8 bars]*. (While the men

wheel, the women move into the men's positions.)

8   *(b) Lead around:* All four couples dance anticlockwise around until back in their original places.

16   *(c) House and square to home:* All four couples dance house and square to home, turning immediately for the first 2 bars, and not reversing into the corners.

D. Figure

40   Repeat C with the women moving one position anticlockwise into the men's places while the men wheel at *(a)*.

E. Figure

40   Repeat C with the women moving one more position anticlockwise into the men's places while the men wheel at *(a)*.

F. Figure

40   Repeat C with the women moving one more position anticlockwise into the men's places while the men wheel at *(a)*.

G. Figure

40   Repeat C with the women moving into their original partners' positions while the men wheel at *(a)*.

Valentia Right And Left Set
Seit An Rinn Aird (Deas Agus Clé)

1ST FIGURE *(Polkas: 96 bars)*

Bars **A. Lead Across**

8   Top couples lead across on left, holding right hands; the women turn anticlockwise under the men's arms in opposite position. Repeat back to place; women turn again.

B. Swing

8   Top couples swing.

C. Chain

8   Top women pass in the centre, right shoulder to right; chain left hands with opposite man and return to partner.

D. Lead Across

8   Top couples lead across on the left, holding both hands. The woman turns anticlockwise under her partner's right arm in opposite position. Repeat back to place.

E. Repeat

32   Side couples dance *A–D*.

F. Lead Around And Double House

24   All couples lead around, with men on the inside holding their partners' right hand; house around twice, reversing the woman for the first 2 bars of each house.

2ND FIGURE *(Polkas: 96 bars)*

A. Arch

8   Top couples take right hands, advance, retire with the woman

turning anticlockwise under her partner's arm, then cross to other side with the opposite woman passing under an arch formed by the Top couple. The opposite man crosses on the left and dances into place outside his partner; she turns anticlockwise into place. 1st Top couple lower hands after the woman has passed under and turn clockwise into place, side-by-side.

B. Arch

8 Repeat *A*; this time, Top woman passes under the arch made by opposite Top couple.

C. Repeat

16 Side couples dance *A* and *B*. (1st Side couple are on the right.)

D. Repeat

32 Top couples and Side couples repeat *A* and *B*, with opposite couples making the arch first.

E. Lead Around And Double House

24 All couples lead around and house around twice.

3RD FIGURE   *(Polkas: 160 bars)*

A. Swing

8 Top man swings opposite woman in the centre.

B. Advance And Retire And Lead Across

8 Top couples advance and retire once, then lead across on the left. Each woman turns under the man's arm in the opposite position.

C. Advance And Retire

8 Swinging couple advance and retire twice.

D. Advance And Retire

8   Top couples advance and retire once, then lead back to their own side.

E. Repeat

32   Top couples repeat *A–D* with the other man and woman dancing *A* and *C*.

F. Repeat

64   Side couples dance *A–E*.

G. Lead Around And Double House

24   All couples lead around and house around twice.

4TH FIGURE   (Polkas: 192 bars)

A. Women Chain

8   Top women pass in the centre, right shoulder to right; chain left hands with opposite man and return to place.

B. Swing

8   While 1st Top couple swing in place, 2nd couple advance and retire once, then house across, turning twice. The woman stays on the left side of Top man.

C. Advance In Three

8   As the opposite man reverses to place, Top man takes the women's outside hands in front and the three advance, retire and advance; the man turns the women outwards to leave them beside the other man in opposite position.

D. Advance In Three

8   Opposite man and the two women now advance, retire and

advance; the women turn again to form a circle of four.

E. Swing

8   The two couples swing in four.

F. Repeat

40   Top couples repeat *A–E* with 2nd couple leading; break back to place after 6 bars the second time (at *E*).

G. Repeat

80   Side couples dance *A–F*.

H. Lead Around And Double House

24   All lead around and house around twice.

5TH FIGURE   (Polkas: 96 bars)

A. House

8   Top couples house around each other.

B. Slide And Change

8   Top couples slide in, back and house to opposite position.

C. Slide And Change

8   Top couples slide in, back and house back to own side.

D. Women Chain

8   Top women pass right shoulder to right in the centre, chain left hands with opposite man and dance back to place.

E. Repeat

32   Side couples dance *A–D*.

F. Lead Around And Double House

24 All lead around and house around twice.

6TH FIGURE   *(Polkas: 288 bars)*

A. Circle

8 Circle, advance and retire twice.

B. Swing

8 All swing.

C. Women Wheel

8 The four women join right hands in the centre. dance 4 bars clockwise, turn, put left hands in and dance back to place.

D. Men Wheel

8 The four men dance C.

E. Lead Around And Double House

24 All lead around and house around twice.

F. Circle

8 Circle again; all women move on to the man on their right.

G. Swing

8 All swing new partner.

H. Repeat

168 Repeat C–G until swinging own partner again.

I. Repeat

40 Dance C–E again to finish.

Waltz Cotillon
Seit Chiarrai Chair

(Waltzes: 320 bars)

During the 8-bar introduction, dancers turn to their left or right and bow to that person, then turn and bow to their own partner.

Bars **A. Figure**

8 1st Tops couple, after the usual salutations (above), waltz around the house inside.

B. Body

16 *(a) Change places:* Top women change places, turning twice clockwise *[4 bars]*, followed by Top men *[4 bars]*. Side women change places *[4 bars]*, followed by Side men *[4 bars]*.

8 *(b) Change places:* Top couples dance anticlockwise to their original positions *[4 bars]*, followed by Side couples *[4 bars]*.

16 *(c) Waltz chain:* All dancers chain around, the women dancing clockwise and the men anticlockwise; the men begin by presenting their right hands to their partners' right hands and turning them anticlockwise under their arms, then left hands to the next dancer, turning her clockwise and so on, until back to their original positions. The man does not turn his partner under.

8 *(d) Promenade:* All four couples promenade anticlockwise around with hands joined in front, until back in their original positions; the men turn the women clockwise under both arms during the last 2 bars.

8 *(e) House:* All four couples waltz around the house.

C. Figure

8 1st Sides couple waltz around the house inside.

D. Body

56 All four couples repeat *B*, with Side women and men changing first at *(a)*, and Side couples changing first at *(b)*.

E. Figure

8   2nd Tops couple waltz around the house inside.

F. Body

56   All four couples repeat *B*.

G. Figure

8   2nd Sides couple waltz around the house inside.

H. Body

56   All four couples repeat *B*, with Side women and men changing first at *(a)*, and Side couples changing first at *(b)*.

I. General Waltz

56   All couples complete the dance with a short general waltz, breaking away from their set after the last house at *H*.

Wexford Half Set
Leathsheit Loch Garman

In some areas the 1st Figure of this set is danced as two figures.
Formation: Couples face each other, hands crossed. Steps: Reel trebles, threes
and jig trebles. Dancers stamp the last beat of the introduction in each figure.
In the set all chains are danced and all crossings of partners are walked.

1ST FIGURE.   (Reels: 72 bars)

Bars **A. Dance On The Spot**

8   Couples dance on the spot.

B. Change Places

8   Couples change positions by walking, the women turning
       under the men's arms, and dance facing each other.

C. Change Places

8   Repeat *B*.

D. Swing

8   All swing.

E. Women Chain

16   Women chain with right hands in the centre and meet opposite
       man with the left, turning to meet their own partners with the
       right, bringing them to the opposite side; and dance out bars.

F. Back To Places

8   Couples return to own positions, women turning under men's
       arms; dance on the spot, holding partners' hands while facing
       each other.

G. Swing

8   Swing and end the 1st Figure facing partner.

2ND FIGURE   *(Jigs: 104 bars)*

A. Cross

8   Top woman and opposite man walk around each other to form a cross (left to left); the couple then dance facing each other.

B. Swing

8   The couple swing, then the man returns to his original position.

C. Repeat

32   Repeat as at *1st Figure, E–G*.

D. Repeat

48   Opposite woman and Top man dance *A–C*.

3RD FIGURE   *(Jigs or Reels: 136 bars)*

A. Repeat

32   Repeat as at *1st Figure, E–G*. After *G*, Top woman is swung over to the opposite couple; the man is in centre of the trio.

B. Three And One

8   All dance, with the trio facing the solo dancer (Top man).

C. Little Christmas

8   All dancers join to form a ring of four and swing.

D. Repeat

48   Repeat *A–C*, with opposite woman swinging over to the Top couple after *A*.

E. Repeat

32   Repeat as at *1st Figure, E–G*.

4TH FIGURE
(Reels: 56 bars)

A. Sevens Pass

8   Partners side-step past each other, women in front, and catch the opposite dancers' hands; dance on the spot.

B. Swing

8   Swing with new partners.

C. Sevens Pass

8   Side-step back to original positions, men in front; dance on spot.

D. Repeat

24   Repeat *A–C*.

5TH FIGURE
(Jigs: 72 bars)

A. Dance On The Spot

8   Both couples dance on the spot.

B. Pass Through

8   All pass through, women in the centre; turn and pass back to own positions.

C. Dance On The Spot

8   Partners face each other, holding hands, and dance on the spot.

D. Swing

8   All swing.

E. Repeat

32   Repeat *A–D*.